COMPLETE HOCKEY INSTRUCTION

Skills and Strategies for Coaches and Players

DAVE CHAMBERS

KEY PORTER BOOKS

The author wishes to express his thanks to Noroc Sport Services, Inc and the *Hockey Coaching Journal* for their guidance in the preparation and typing of this manuscript. A special word of thanks to Robert Thom, Production Manager of the *Hockey Coaching Journal*, for the preparation of the diagrams and overall layout of the book.

Special appreciation is extended to the many coaches I have played for and been associated with who contributed greatly to my knowledge of ice hockey.

Canadian Cataloguing in Publication Data

Chambers, Dave, 1940-
Complete hockey instruction

ISBN 1-55013-154-0

1. Hockey.   I. Title.

GV847.C48 1989   796.96'2   C89-094096-7

Key Porter Books Limited
70 The Esplanade
Toronto, Ontario
Canada M5E 1R2

Photographs by Doug MacLellan/Hockey Hall of Fame

Printed and bound in Canada

89 90 91 92 93 5 4 3 2 1

CONTENTS

This book is dedicated to the memory of my
father, Lee Chambers, to my wife, Irene,
and my two daughters, Lori and Linda.

PREFACE

Hockey is one of the most exciting and fast moving sports in the world. The game is comprised of many intricate skills which, when blended together, produce a very highly skilled athlete. Hockey coaching has changed greatly in recent years. The influence of the Europeans is being felt in the areas of conditioning and tactics. North Americans are thinking more about how the game should be taught to the players. Coaching clinics and coaching certification programs are quite common in North America now and the overall result is better coaching for hockey players of all ages.

This book is an accumulation of materials from my twenty years of coaching hockey at the university, junior and international levels. I have accumulated the drills from my work in hockey schools, from observing other coaches' practices, from my former coaches, and from my own innovations and experiences.

I have attempted to include all aspects of the technical areas of coaching hockey so that this book will be useful for both coaches and players. Other ideas and experiences in hockey should help you to become more proficient as a coach or a player. I hope this book will add to your knowledge of the great game of ice hockey.

LEGEND

PUCK(S)		TIGHT/180° TURN		PASS	
PYLON(S)		360° TURN		DROP PASS	
FORWARD SKATING		PIVOT		SHOT	
FORWARD STICKHANDLE		STOP	= OR ‖	KNEE DROP	— OR ‖
BACKWARD SKATING		KERIOAKAS		SCREEN/PIC	
BACKWARD STICKHANDLE		CROSSOVERS		BODYCHECK	
RIGHT WINGER	RW	OPPOSITION R W	RW	PLAYER	X
LEFT WINGER	LW	OPPOSITION L W	LW	OPPOSITION PLAYER	X
CENTRE	C	OPPOSITION C	C	DEFENSEMAN	D
RIGHT DEFENSEMAN	RD	OPPOSITION RD	RD	OPPOSITION D	D
LEFT DEFENSEMAN	LD	OPPOSITION LD	LD	GOALTENDER	G

1. PHILOSOPHY OF COACHING

Coaching is a very complex and demanding job. It requires many technical and personal skills and a sound coaching philosophy. Rewards of coaching include competition, and the development of athletes' physical, mental, emotional, and social skills.

The philosopher Will Durant once said, "Science gives us knowledge, but only philosophy can give us wisdom." It is therefore very important for every coach to have a well-thought-out philosophy of coaching, that will guide the coach in decision making and in the direction he and his team will take. The coach must develop a philosophy of competition, winning and losing, the value of athletics, criticism, and interacting with and motovating athletes. A sound philosophy determines aims and objectives and is the basis of all decision making.

Coaching is a great challenge and not for the faint of heart. It requires long hours and intense interaction with people who are in competition with themselves and others. It runs the gamut of emotions involving success and failure, joy and despair. It involves wanting and trying to win and learning how to accept defeat. It also involves the opportunity of participating, having fun, and learning to work together for a common goal.

Walter Gillet probably summarized the job of a coach best in "What is a Coach."

> A Coach is a politician, a judge, a public speaker, a teacher, a trainer, a financier, a laborer, a psychologist, psychiatrist, and a chaplain. He must be an optimist, and yet at times appear a pessimist, seem humble and yet be very proud, strong but at times weak, confident yet not overconfident, enthusiastic but not too enthusiastic.

> He must have the hide of an elephant, the fierceness of a lion, the pep of a young pup, the guts of an ox, the stamina of an antelope, the wisdom of an owl, the cunning of a fox and the heart of a kitten.

> He must be willing to give freely of his time, his money, his energy, his youth, his family life, and his health. In return he must expect little if any financial reward, little comfort on earth, little praise but plenty of criticism.

> However, a good coach is respected and is a leader in his community, is loved by his team, and makes lasting friends wherever he goes.

> He has the satisfaction of seeing young people develop and improve in ability. He learns the thrill of victory and how to accept defeat with grace. His associations with athletes help keep him young in mind and spirit, and he too must grow and improve in ability with his team.

> In his heart he knows that, in spite of the inconvenience, the criticism and the demands on his time, he loves his work, for his is The Coach.

QUALITIES OF A GOOD COACH

Successful coaches do not seem to have any specific type of personality. They are as individual as the general population but they do have specific leadership qualities. Many good coaches are outgoing and extroverted while others are quiet and somewhat withdrawn. Some coaches are autocratic and hard nosed while others are democratic and accommodating. Here are some common characteristics of good coaches:

1. Knowledge of the Sport

To be effective, the coach must have a sound knowledge of the sport. An athlete can learn a great deal from various coaches. However, in most cases, participation alone does not ensure a complete knowledge of the sport. A good coach will continually read, observe and use any other methods to further his knowledge of the sport. Most good coaches attend at least one coaching clinic per year and take any coaching certification that is available.

2. Organization Skills

One common characteristic of all good coaches is that they are highly organized in all areas of the team operation. A well organized team both on and off the ice gives the athletes confidence and pride in the team and the coach. An organized coach will generally be respected by the athletes for the time and effort spent to achieve a highly efficient organization. Today's coach should have a yearly, monthly, weekly, and daily plan for the organization of his team. The physical, technical, tactical, and psychological preparation of the athletes should be organized and directed in a year-round training plan.

3. Knowledge of Training and Conditioning Methods

A coach should have an up-to-date knowledge of various training and conditioning methods. This knowledge can be applied in the day-to-day training of a team or individuals and the coach should also be able to advise athletes regarding off-season training programs. The coach should have the ability to develop a plan for improving and/or maintaining his athletes' conditioning levels throughout the year.

4. Effectively Run Practices

One of the most important aspects of coaching is the ability to run effective, well organized practice sessions. Most coaches believe the key to the success of teams and/or individual athletes is in the training or practice sessions. If the coach has the ability to run organized, active practices stressing the techniques used in competition, he has accomplished a great deal.

5. Evaluation of Athletes

A good coach should be able to evaluate the ability of the athletes. This is an ongoing process for the coach, but it is most important in the initial selection of a team. Good coaches have an ability to subjectively evaluate athletes based on previous observations of athletes and techniques in their sport. However, most good coaches also rely on other factors such as specific drills, reports by other observers, skill tests, potential, physical attributes, personality traits, etc., to make their final selection of athletes.

6. Strategy

The ability to prepare a team for an opponent is an important attribute of a coach. The skill is developed through experience, learning, and the ability to analyze an opponent's strengths and weaknesses. As well as preparing a team for a contest, the coach should be able to improvise and adjust strategy during games.

7. Effective Use of Personnel

In team sports a good coach has the ability to effectively use certain athletes at certain times. The coach must have a good understanding of what athletes can do in certain situations and must be able to react quickly and effectively in games to select the right players for critical situations such as late in a game, face-offs, behind by a goal, ahead by a goal, etc.

8. Communication

A good coach is an effective communicator with the athletes. Good communication leads to mutual understanding. Problem areas should be dealt with before they become further polarized. Effective communication between coach and athlete is essential for a good coach-athlete relationship, and an athlete should feel that the coach is approachable.

9. Ability to Understand and Handle the Athlete

The ability to communicate is also related to the ability to handle and understand people. For the coach to be an effective communicator, he must understand the athlete and be able to relate to him. A lack of understanding of the athlete's motives and problems is one of the major reasons for the breakdown in the coach-athlete relationship.

10. Fairness

It is important that the coach give fair treatment to the athletes on a team. Athletes can turn quickly on a coach if they feel he has been unfair in his treatment of the team or favours certain individuals over others.

11. Motivation

Athletes should be self-motivated. A coach must also be able to motivate them in order to be effective. Not all coaches have this ability, but it appears to be a common quality of all outstanding coaches.

12. Dedication, Enthusiasm, Maturity, Rectitude

Good coaches are dedicated to coaching and this has a positive effect on the athletes. A lack of dedication can seriously affect the athletes' view of the coach and can be extremely detrimental as the coach may even be viewed as lazy.

Enthusiasm is an important quality in a coach. As most training seasons are long, it is important that the coach show enthusiasm throughout the year to help motivate the athletes.

The coach should act in a mature manner. Immature behaviour such as harassing officials can affect the athletes. They could imitate this behaviour or lose respect for the coach.

The ethical conduct of the coach on and off the ice is important. The coach is a role model whom the athletes may or may not admire. The coach should realize the importance of this position and be aware of the effect that he has on the more impressionable, younger athletes.

13. Knowledge of How the Body Works (Exercise Physiology)

The coach should have a basic knowledge of exercise physiology in order to understand how the body works. This basic knowledge will allow the coach to understand the science behind various training techniques, such as work-rest ratios during training and games. A coach should also be able to interpret scientific articles on various training methods and conduct or interpret various fitness testing items.

14. Knowledge of Growth and Development Principles

In many cases, coaches are working with growing and developing younger players. It is important that the coach have a knowledge of both the physical and emotional stages that younger players go through. In some cases, the growth spurt may have an effect on the athletes' coordination and create certain emotional problems for younger players. This, in turn, may affect their athletic performance.

15. Ability to Teach

The coach is in many ways a teacher and as such he must have an understanding of basic learning principles and teaching techniques. The ability to teach requires teaching a progression of fundamental skills as well as team play. Voice, appearance, teaching formation, planning, and progression are equally important to the coach as they are to the classroom teacher.

16. Concern for the Athlete

An individual concern for each athlete is very important for a coach. The athlete must feel that the coach cares about him and that he is important to the team. On a team, the athlete who is not playing as much as the others may need more attention from the coach than the ones who play more often. Athletes do not like to feel that they're pawns and that the coach has no concern for them other than as athletes. The coach should also show concern for the athletes after they have moved on, and some coaches receive a great deal of satisfaction by keeping in touch with athletes after they have stopped participating for their team or organization.

17. Knowledge of the Rules

An effective coach should have a thorough knowledge of the playing rules. This knowledge should be passed on to the players and is important in both practice and game situations.

18. Discipline

Most good teams have a basic discipline code in which guidelines for behaviour are set. Team rules are best set up when the athletes have input and agree with the coach on rules such as punctuality for practices and games, general conduct on and off the playing surface, etc. It is usually up to the coach to enforce team rules, but in general, rules should not be too numerous nor should they be so inflexible as not to allow for extenuating circumstances.

19. Media

A coach should have a good relationship with the media as publicity can greatly affect the support the team receives. It is important to be available and cordial no matter what the circumstances when dealing with the media. Regular reporting of game results and informing the media of team information can help the coach develop a good relationship with them.

20. Humour

Not all situations in sports are serious. A good coach should have a sense of humour. Athletes will feel more relaxed if the coach is able to see humour in some situations. A coach who is serious on all occasions may put added pressure on the athletes and may not be able to relate to them. It is also important that the coach not take himself too seriously and start to believe that he is the only reason for the success of an athlete or a team.

21. Ability to Recruit and Build a Program

Most good coaches have the ability to relate and sell both themselves and their program to a prospective athlete. If recruiting athletes is part of a successful program, the coach should have a recruiting plan in which he is able to identify, and relate information about himself and the program to the potential athlete.

It is important to realize that each coach has his or her own personality. Coaches should attempt to study and adapt the good coaching techniques of successful coaches rather than attempting to emulate the personality of the individual. Be yourself, but do attempt to make yourself better by working hard at improving your coaching techniques.

2. EVALUATION OF TALENT

Evaluating talent and selecting the team is one of the more difficult tasks in coaching. The better and poorer players are usually quite evident, but the selecting from the middle group of talent is where evaluation criteria are extremely important.

Evaluation of hockey players can be categorized in four areas: physical, technical, tactical and mental.

The physical attributes include size, strength, cardiovascular endurance, quickness, and agility. Size is an important aspect in hockey but quickness and agility are also extremely important. Don't rule out a small player if that player has strength and quickness.

The technical skills include skating, passing, puck handling, shooting, and checking. All these skills are important. The checking skill can be taught to all players, provided they have the basic skating skills.

The tactical skills lie in the player's ability to read the play and react; to understand team systems; and to adjust to different situations. Hockey sense and intelligence are important factors which some players seem to have more of than others. The great hockey players have hockey sense and that great ability to read and react to different situations.

The mental attributes include motivation, intensity, work habits, general attitude and character, leadership, coachability, mental toughness, self-confidence, and team orientation. A brief description of these attributes is outlined as follows:

Motivation

A highly motivated player wants to make the team, to improve, and to be a success.

Intensity

A player with intensity plays hard on the ice and in practice.

Work Habits

The player works hard during practices and games.

General Attitude and Character

Does the player mix well with his teammates and is enthusiastic? Can he handle adversity with a positive attitude? Character signs to watch for are moodiness and negativity.

Leadership

Not every player can be a leader but leadership skills are evident in successful players in varying degrees. Some players are quiet and lead by example, while other players are more vocal. Good teams have more than one leader and the leaders cooperate with each other and the coach.

Coachability

Does the player accept the coach's direction and is he willing to learn and improve? Most top players are very coachable as they wish to improve their skills and need the feedback and direction of the coach.

Mental Toughness

Does the player react well under pressure and adversity? Is the player able to be positive and be under control when situations are not going well?

Self-Confidence

Does the player have confidence in his own ability? Can the player keep his confidence when he is not playing or does he loose confidence when things are not going well?

Team Orientation

Does the player put the team first and himself second? Will he sacrifice for the team or is he selfish? Can the player accept his role on a team especially if does not get as much ice time as other players?

The mental attributes are sometimes more difficult to determine in a short period of time and it is probably wise to get as much background information on a player as possible before the selection process begins.

The psychological Test of Attentional and Interpersonal Style (TAIS) can assist in assessing talent but should not be used to select players. A sport psychologist could be consulted on the use of this test. The test measures the following factors: leadership capabilities, impulsive behaviour, extroversion, performance anxiety, desire to win, and ability to organize and plan. This test and the coaches' observations of the athletes are used by some teams to help develop mental preparation and team-building skills.

Figure 1

BACKGROUND INFORMATION SHEET

Name: _____   Position: _____

_____

_____   Telephone: _____

_____

Hospitalization No: _____   Doctor's Telephone No: _____

Next Year's School: _____   Grade: _____

Age: _____ Height: _____ Weight: _____   Date of Birth: _____

Skate Preference: _____   Skate Size: _____

PLAYING EXPERIENCE (List teams and stats for last four years)

Year	Team	League	Goals	Assists	Points

Have you ever been on a championship team? If so, complete the section below:

Year	Team	League	Championship

Have you won an academic (e.g., scholarship) or athletic (e.g., MVP) award in the past three years? If so, complete the section below:

Year	Award

Have you played on a state, provincial or national (e.g., under 18) team? If so, complete the section below:

Year	Team

During training camps it is important to have a standard evaluation form. The coach should meet with the evaluators before the training camp to discuss what he is looking for in players and then the evaluators should meet after each practice or scrimmage to discuss and compare their observations. Evaluation at training camp usually comes from observing scrimmage games, regular practice drills and special evaluation drills.

In the regular practice drills and scrimmage games the evaluators should be looking for a subjective evaluation of the physical, technical, tactical and mental skills previously mentioned. Subjective evaluation forms (Figure 2 and Figure 3) can aid in the evaluation process.

Figure 2

SUBJECTIVE EVALUATION FORM

SKATING (agility, speed. acceleration, pivots) Can the player skate at this level? Does he have a definite liability in his skating?	
PUCK CONTROL SKILLS (passing, receiving, stickhandling) Can he handle the puck in a crowd? Can he handle the puck under pressure? Are his hands good or bad? Can he handle the puck at top speed?	
DEFENSIVE PLAY Does he show a desire to check? Is he active away from the puck? Does he show defensive anticipation, taking away options from the puck carrier? Would you use him as penalty killer? Would you use him in critical situations (one goal lead late in the game)?	
OFFENSIVE PLAY Does he display imagination and variation in moves? Can he beat the defender with speed and/or finesse? Would you consider him a "threat" man you as an opposition coach would worry about? Would you give him special attention?	
OVERALL COMMENTS Would you want him on your team? Do you rate him in top ten percent or top one percent? Do you consider him dependable? Does he have the skills and intelligence to play at a more competitive level in a few years?	

Figure 3

SUBJECTIVE EVALUATION FORM

The following criteria have been identified as parameters by which players may be evaluated at the camp. Each player is to be ranked on these criteria on a scale of 1 to 5.

1	2	3	4	5
Very Poor	Poor	Good	Very Good	Excellent

The five criteria and some specific indications for each are as follows:

1. Hockey Sense

- Does he play with a sense of anticipation?
- Does he make the high percentage play both offensively and defensively?
- Does he display an understanding of important concepts, i.e., headmanning, support, angling, etc.?
- Does he understand the concept of picking or blocking-out players?
- Does he play well away from the puck?

2. Positional Play

- Does he play with discipline in his own end?
- Is he capable of moving to open ice at the right time when attacking?
- Can he adjust his positioning to the movement of others?

3. Determination

- Does he show second effort when required or does he quit?
- Does he work hard both offensively and defensively (is he "tough" on the puck and is he persistent when checking)?

4. Maturity

- Is he coachable (will he accept suggestions)?
- What is his attitude toward referees (can he accept a bad call)?
- What is his attitude toward opponents (does he retaliate or is he cool)?

5. Techniques

- Does he have any weak skill area?
- Does he have skating agility (speed is a prime concern)?
- Identify the strongest skill areas.

An overall ranking form may be helpful in evaluation when observing game scrimmages and practice drills.

Figure 4

SCRIMMAGE EVALUATION FORM

To aid in the analysis and selection process, we are asking you as an evaluator to observe the ice sessions and assist us in the evaluation process.

These are the rosters for both the red and white teams for our scrimmages. Please indicate in the boxes your evaluation of the player based upon *this* observation:

> 2 for outstanding, exceptional performance
> 1 for good, average performance
> 0 for below average performance

Red Team

1.
2.
3.
4.
5.
6.
7.
8.
9.
10.
11.
12.
13.
14.
15.
16.
17.
18.
19.
20.
21.
22.
23.
24.
25.

White Team

1.
2.
3.
4.
5.
6.
7.
8.
9.
10.
11.
12.
13.
14.
15.
16.
17.
18.
19.
20.
21.
22.
23.
24.
25.

Goal - Rank all players from the best to the poorest

1.
2.
3.
4.

Defense

1.
2.
3.
4.
5.
6.
7.
8.
9.
10.

Centre

1.
2.
3.
4.
5.

Left Wing

1.
2.
3.
4.
5.

Right Wing

1.
2.
3.
4.
5.

From the performance that you observed, who were the six most impressive players, regardless of position?

_____   _____   _____

_____   _____   _____

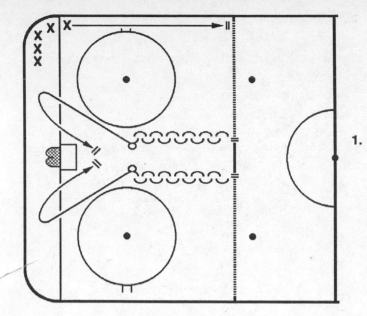

EVALUATION DRILLS

Evaluation drills can be of assistance when the coaches have the final decisions to make. The following are some sample drills which can be used to assess defensemen, forwards, and goaltenders.

1. **EVALUATION DRILLS FOR DEFENSEMEN**

Agility

Front player in each line skates from the goal line to the blueline, chop-steps halfway across the blueline, skates backward to the middle of the circle, pivots to the outside and skates to the corner. There, he makes a sharp turn and returns to the front of the net.

2. Backward skating

F starts from the corner and skates behind the net where he picks up the puck. He then skates down the boards outside the face-off marker. As soon as F touches the puck, D starts skating backward without turning until he reaches the centreline. He then turns and tries to ride F out to the boards; F attempts to cut in and score.

NOTE: D starts this drill halfway between the top of the goal crease and an imaginary line drawn between the face-off markers.

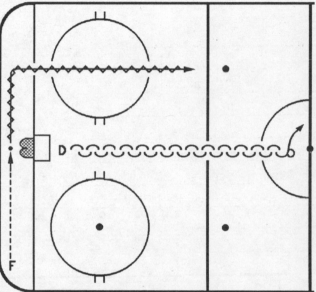

3. Agility, skating, and shooting

The coach dumps the puck into the corner. D1 skates backward, turns at the face-off marker, and skates to the corner to pick up the puck, executing a head-and-shoulder fake. He skates behind the net and toward the face-off circle where he does a tight turn and returns behind the net. He stops, then starts again and passes to D2 near the boards. D1 skates out in front for the return pass from D2, does another tight turn and shoots on goal. D1 then skates to D2's place on the boards, and D2 goes to the blueline to repeat the drill.

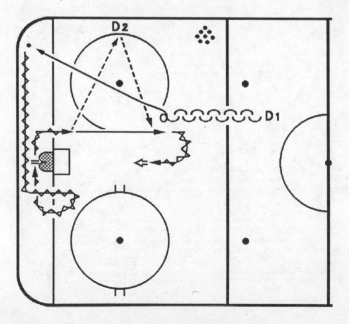

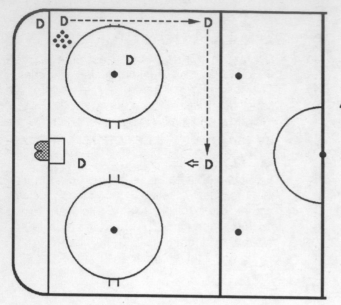

4. Shooting

The defenseman passes the puck from the corner to the near blueline, to the middle of the ice for a low shot on goal. The defenseman in front deflects the puck at the goalie or acts as a screen. The defensemen rotate clockwise in this drill.

EVALUATION DRILLS FOR FORWARDS

1. Skating Speed

The players skate for speed at four distances: centreline and back; far blueline and back; far boards (one length); down and back (two lengths); and down and back, twice (four lengths).

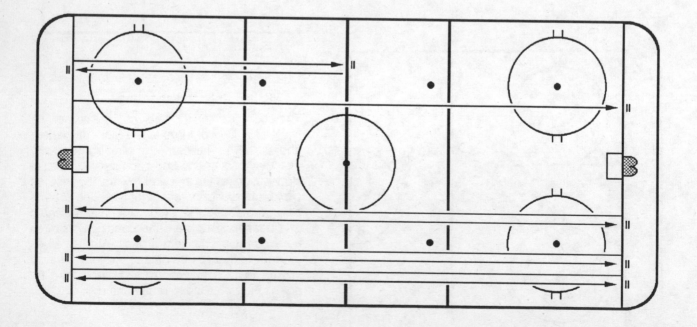

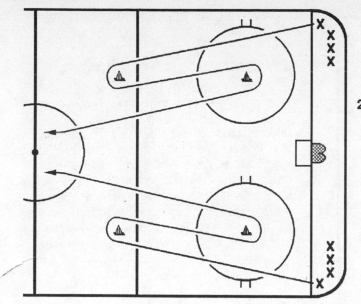

2. Race for the puck

The forwards start in opposite corners, skate around the pylons, race for the puck and shoot on the goaltender at the far end. The coach at the far blueline places a puck at the centre of that blueline for which the players have to race.

3. One-on-One

The coach shoots the puck into the corner and the two players race for the puck and attempt to score. Play continues until the coach blows the whistle, a goal is scored, or the goalie freezes the puck.

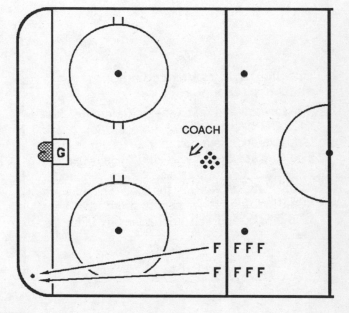

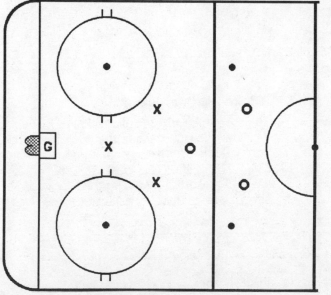

4. Three-on-Three

The forwards play three-on-three on the entire ice surface or in the two halves. Rotate the players and change every minute. The players change on the fly with a whistle and the team with the puck on the change passes back to their own goalie.

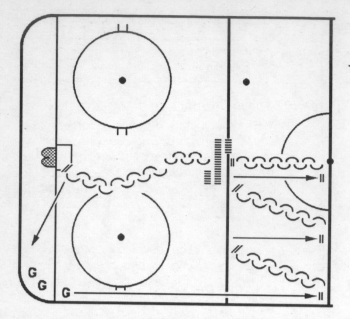

1. EVALUATION DRILLS FOR GOALIES

Start from the goal line, skate in the goaltender's stance to the blueline, skate full stride to the red line and stop, skate sideways and backward to the blueline, skate forward in the goaltender's stance to the red line, sideways and backward to the blueline, full stride to the red line, backward to the blue line, shuffle three steps left, six steps right, three steps, back to the middle, backward to the top of the circles, backward and sideways to the right and then to the left, and end up in the crease.

2. Reaction, agility and stopping, shots and rebounds

The forward and rebounder start from the first line. The shooter shoots from the top of the far circle and the rebounder drives for the net. The forward from the second line skates in and shoots from in close. The rebounder follows and drives for the net. The forward from the third line shoots from the near face-off dot and the rebounder drives for the net.

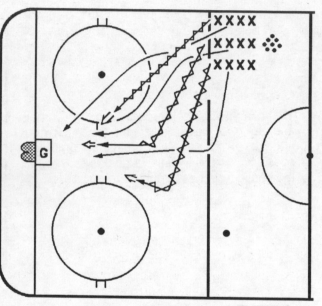

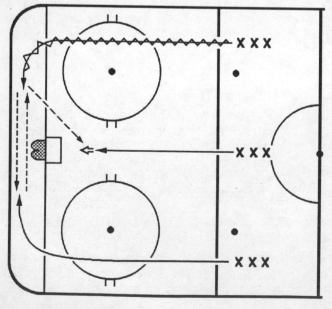

3. Side-to-Side Movement

The forward from one side skates in behind the goal line and passes the puck behind the net to the other forward coming from the other side of the ice. The pass is returned and passed out to the incoming third forward who shoots a quick shot from the slot.

3. ORGANIZATION AND IMPLEMENTATION OF TEAM PRACTICE

One of the most important aspects of coaching is the organization and running of effective practices. Practices should be developed with the following points in mind:

Organization

Practices should be organized down to the last detail. Drills should show a natural progression through the practice from individual skills to team skills. The practice should have a smooth transition from drill to drill with constant movement and very little standing around.

Drills

Drills should be meaningful and related to the game of hockey. They should be used to develop individual and team skills and in most cases be at game intensity. New drills can be explained, diagrammed and demonstrated before commencing. Drills should be repeated a number of times during the season for improvement, and it is the coach's responsibility to give the athletes feedback on errors.

The coach should make sure the drills are done correctly. Repetition and patience are important in the perfection of skills. Drills should also be competitive and at the intensity and duration used in a game wherever possible. The coach should also make sure the length of time spent on a drill is neither too short nor too long. It is important that the drills be interesting and that the coach have a number of drills to accomplish such skills as one-on-one, two-on-one. Using the same drills over and over can become monotonous so the coach should attempt to keep drills and practices interesting. The coach should also guard against giving the athletes too many drills, especially if they are not meaningful.

Warm up and cool down

It is important that the athletes be fully stretched and warmed up before the intense part of the practice begins. Stretching exercises should be performed in the dressing room or in an exercise room in the arena if possible.

At the end of each practice the few remaining minutes should consist of stretching and slowing the intensity of work. The practice can end as it began with basically the same stretching and flexing.

Other details

It is important that water be available to the athletes during practice. Individual plastic squirt bottles are best. The coach should schedule two or three water-breaks during the practice.

The number of pucks available should be checked before each practice. The standard number for a team of 20 players is usually 40 pucks.

It is important that the practices are interesting and fun, there should be good discipline and order. The coach should talk to the players in a semicircle formation so that no player is behind the coach when he is speaking. Signals such as a short double whistle could be the signal to assemble in front of the coach for practice directions.

It is sometimes a good idea to have a light short skate between drills, especially if the drill was not of high intensity.

Use of assistant coaches

It is important that the assistant coaches are used effectively during practices. The assistant coaches should be active in giving feedback to the players and should have specific duties to support the coach. There are many occasions when the ice can be divided for specific defense and forward drills. A good practice has constant activity and high intensity with drills at both ends of the ice. The assistant coach should be constantly evaluating talent and should meet with the head coach after each practice to evaluate and plan the next practice.

Often assistant coaches direct the warm-up and conditioning part of the practices and in some situations the head coach may have the assistant coach run certain drills.

It is important that the assistant coach feel part of the practice's organization and implementation and that all coaches have agreed on systems of play and teaching techniques. The designing and implementation of conditioning programs is also another area in which assistant coaches play an active role.

On ice stretching drills

If time permits the PNF stretching drills can be used for flexibility training (see Chapter 20).

The regular skating warm up can consist of leg and groin stretches, leg slow kick to outstretched hands knee to chest, trunk twisting with the stick on the shoulders, toe touching by raising the arms with the stick in both hands over the shoulders and then touching the toes, wrist rotation holding the stick in one hand and then the other.

This type of stretching is usually followed by fast and slow skating, either on the whistle or sprinting between the bluelines. Agility can be added to this skating by turning backward between the bluelines, turning 360 degrees, or going down on one or both knees at the blue and red lines.

Carrying a puck can be added to this warm-up with the players starting by kicking the puck in the skates. Here is an example of a skating warm-up that can be used with or without pucks. Players form two lines. Pairs of players skate together forward and backward down the ice. Turning at lines can be added. The players then skate down the ice and back, passing the puck.

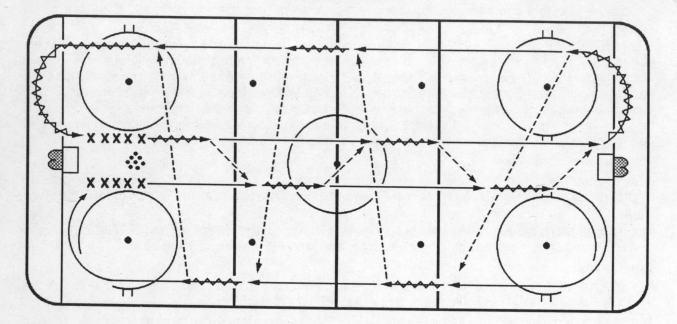

CONTENT OF A TYPICAL PRACTICE (90 MINUTES)

Dressing room stretch 45 minutes before practice
Pre-practice drill explanation 10 minutes before on-ice practice is to begin

On Ice

1) Stretching exercises 5 minutes
2) Skating warm up 5 minutes
3) Goalie warm up 5 minutes

It is important that all hockey players be able to take a body check, to recover quickly and get back into the play.

1 Three lines shoot one drill from the following:

(a) A player from each line skates in and shoots from the top of the circles starting at the right, centre, then left. Players should alternate lines and use wrist shots only **OR**

(b) One player from each line skates toward the goalie simultaneously. The player on one side shoots from just inside the blueline, the player in the middle shoots from the high slot and the player on the far side pulls the goalie. The three players can start skating in on the goalie on the command of the coach. The players can change lines and the order can be switched for shooting or pulling the goalie.

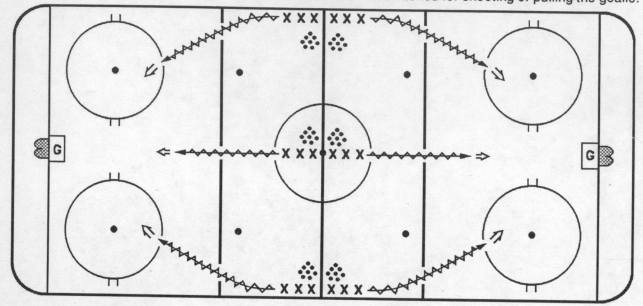

(c) Rapid shoot

The players skate in one line coming in from the right, the centre, and then the left. The players are a few feet apart and shoot wrist shots in rapid succession.

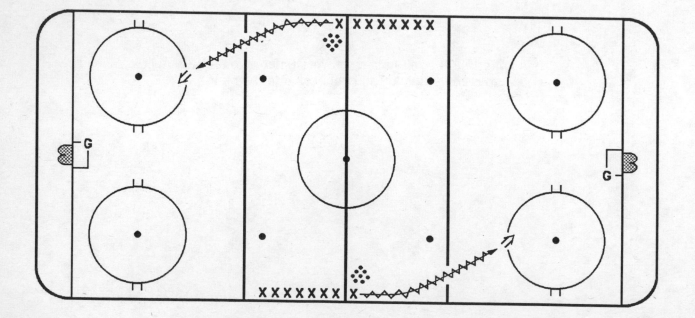

2 One drill from the following:

One-on-none

(a) Carousel and variation

Players loop inside the blueline and receive a pass from the opposite line. The player passing the puck then goes over the far blueline, skates in and shoots on the goalie from the end he started.

A variation of this drill has the player receiving a pass, turning backward between the red and the blueline, and then turning forward, skating and shooting on the net.

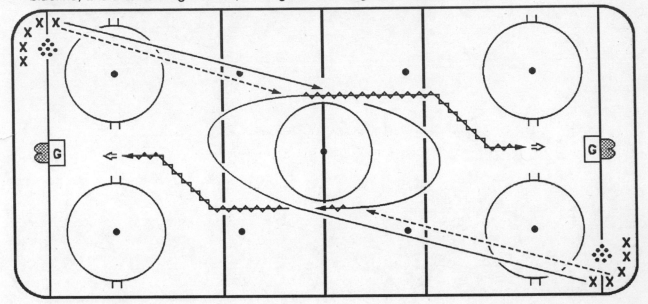

(b) Neutral zone one-on-none

The player skates from the corner to the centre red line and passes the puck to the near defenseman. The near defenseman passes the puck to his defense partner who then passes the puck back to the forward who has skated in front of the defensemen. The forward skates back to the end he came out of, shoots on the goalie, and then returns to the same line he started from.

A variation of this drill is for the forward to skate behind the defenseman, skate up the middle of the ice, and receive a pass from the other defense partner.

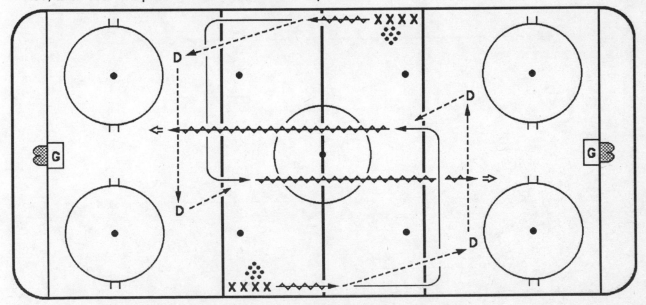

(c) Rebound drill

Two players start the drill. The first player goes in on the net and shoots. The second player trails the first and goes for the rebound (if there is one), turns off, and receives a pass from the first player in the other line. He then skates the length of the ice and shoots. The player passing the puck then follows the shooter down the ice going to net for a rebound, takes a pass from the other line, and returns and shoots at the same end he started at.

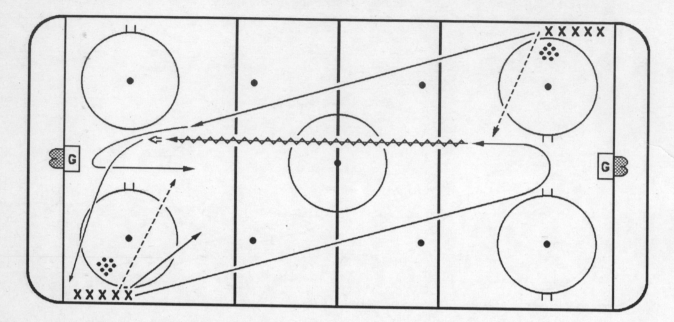

(d) Half-ice two-on-none: 5 minutes

Two players skate down the ice passing the puck between them. Moving over the far blueline, the player on the board side shoots from just inside the blueline.

Moving in the opposite direction and after passing the far blueline, the player on the board side skates wide and passes the puck back to the trailing player in the high slot. The player who is shooting attempts to shoot the puck in one motion.

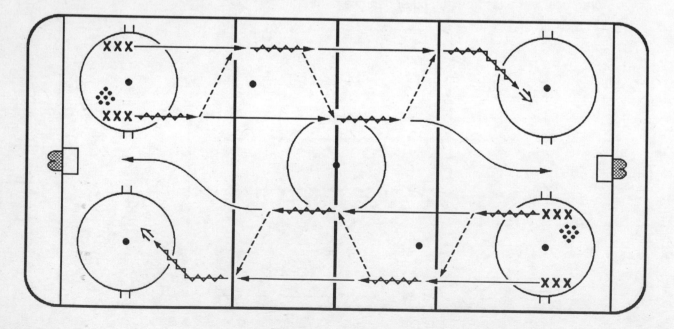

(e) One-on-none, two-on-none, pucks in the middle drill

The player skates to the middle of the ice, gets a puck, skates back to the same end, shoots and returns to the same line he started in.

A variation of this drill is to have two players skate from opposite corners of the same end with one player picking up a puck at centre and then returning to the same end two-on-none.

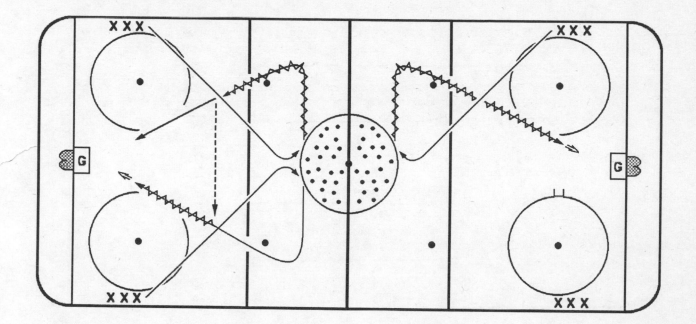

(f) Variation:

Add a defensemen on each blueline. The player, after picking the puck up at centre ice, passes to the defenseman at the far blueline, receives a return pass, skates in and shoots on the goalie at the end he started from.

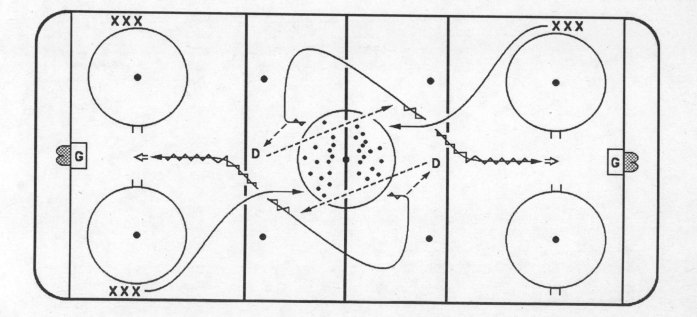

(g) Variation:

This drill can be done as a two-on-none as well having two players skate from opposite corners, one picking up a puck at centre, passing to the defenseman and returning two-on-none to the end they started from.

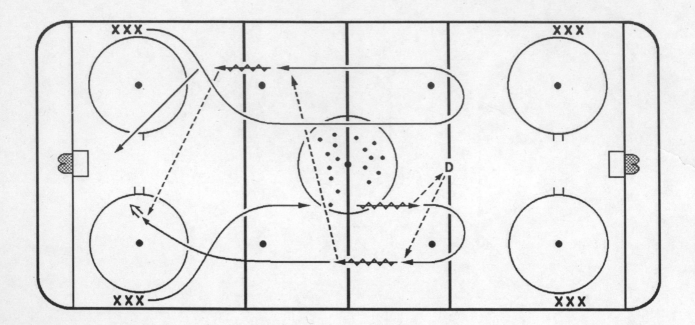

3 Select one drill from the following: 5 minutes

(a) One-on-one drills

Pucks are at the blueline.

The defenseman skates two strides in from the blueline, passes the puck to the forward, and skates backward to take the forward on a one-on-one. The defenseman returns to the same side of the rink while the forward moves to the opposite corner after attempting to shoot the puck on net.

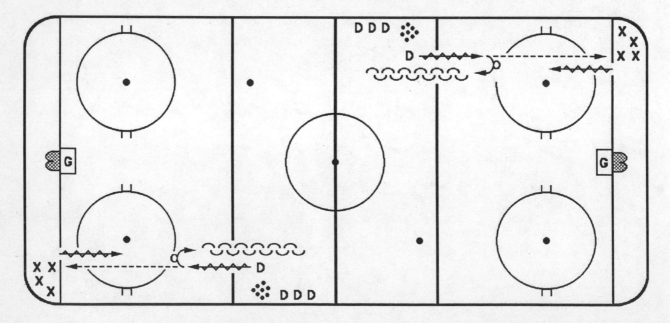

(b) One-on-one flow

The defenseman skates around the centre circle and turns backward. The forward skates inside the blueline and receives a pass from the defenseman standing at the far end. After the defenseman passes the puck, he and the forward beside him start another one-on-one by skating down the ice and taking a pass from the defenseman at the far end.

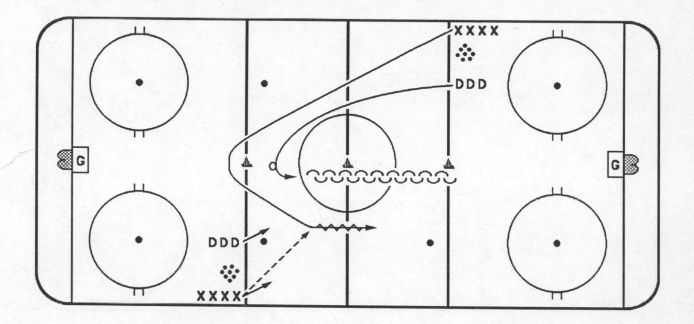

(c) One-on-one from the middle of the ice

The defenseman passes the puck to the forward at the face-off dot. The defenseman skates forward around a pylon, turns, skates backward, and takes the forward on a one-on-one. The defenseman returns to the same starting position while the forward moves to the opposite corner after completing the one-on-one.

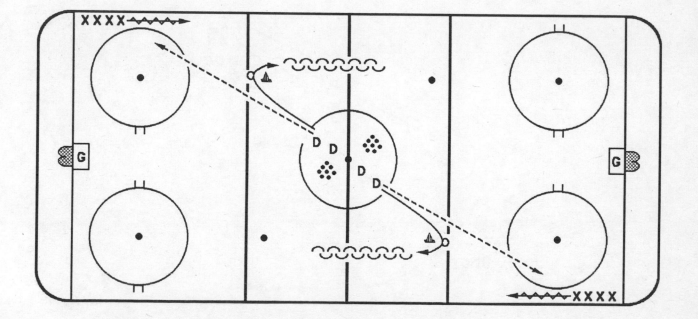

27

4 Two-on-one

(a) One drill from the following: 5 minutes

The defenseman starts the play by coming from behind the net, passing the puck to the forwards, continuing up ice to take part in the play, and then taking a two-on-one defensively from the opposite end.

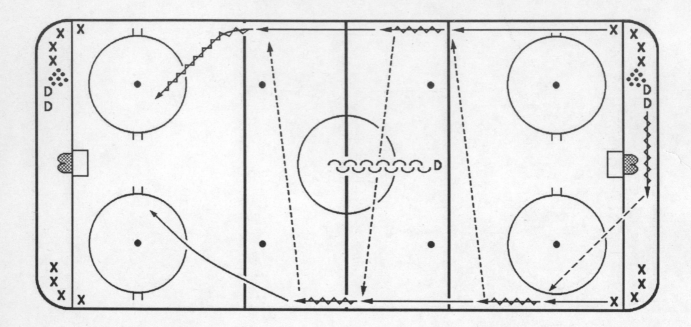

(b) Two-on-one flow drill

The two forwards skate inside the far blueline and take a pass from the defenseman at the far net. The defenseman skates forward around the centre circle, and takes the forwards on a two-on-one situation.

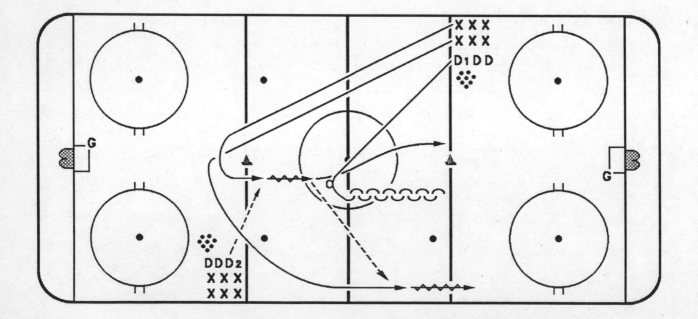

(c) Two-on-one half-ice:

The defenseman passes to the forward. The forwards pass the puck between them, move outside the blueline, and swing back to the same end. The defenseman skates forward to the blueline and skates backward taking the forwards on a two-on-one.

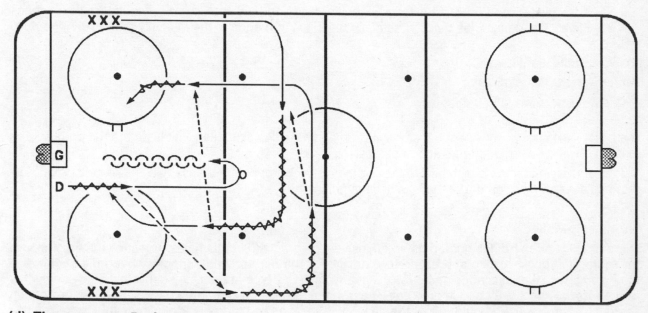

(d) Three-on-one: 5 minutes

The defenseman starts the play and follows it up the ice to take a three-on-one in the opposite direction. Variation: Five-on-two breakouts in both directions (20 minutes).

The centre shoots the puck in, the three forwards and two defensemen breakout against two defensemen using various breakout plays. If there is no direct play on the net in the offensive zone, have the forward with the puck pass it back to the defenseman at the blueline, who will pass across to the other defenseman, who then shoots a low shot at the net. The forwards then drive to the net to deflect the puck or screen the goaltender. If the offensive play is broken up at the offensive blueline, the five attacking players can regroup in the neutral zone and attack again.

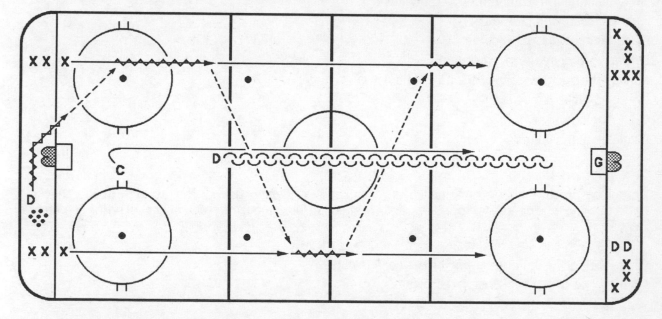

Short conditioning skate: 5 minutes

Three groups over and back across the ice. Work 10 seconds, rest 30 seconds, five repetitions.

Resurface the Ice: 15 minutes

Use this time for a dressing room talk and/or rest.

Controlled scrimmage: 20 minutes

The coach should stop the scrimmage for major errors and, along with the assistant coaches, give feedback to the players. Changing lines quickly (as in a game situation) adds to the intensity of the scrimmage.

Shooting Drills: 5 minutes

Conditioning Drills: 8 minutes

Cool-down and short talk: 3 minutes

The cool-down should consist of the same skating and flexibility exercises which started the practice and could end with bent knee sit-ups and push-ups.

A short discussion by the coach before leaving the ice is appropriate here. Details for the next practice or game plus a comment on the practice is usual at this time.

Offensive practice

Some practices can be designated as an offensive-type practice. In this type of practice the emphasis is on moving the puck quickly and accurately, driving for the net and scoring goals. Even the scrimmage should emphasize goal scoring and offensive team play. This type of practice seems to be very enjoyable for the players and it is a good idea to have it early in the week or two or three days before the next game. The defensive practice should follow the offensive practice, and the power play/penalty killing practice should take place the day before the next game.

Offensive practice: 90 minutes

Stretching and warm up: 5 minutes

Drive-for-the-net-drill: 6 minutes

Neutral zone lead-up drills: 8 minutes

Flow drills one-on-one, two-on-one: 8 minutes

Breakouts, neutral zone regroup: 15 minutes

Emphasize driving for the net

Resurface the ice: 15 minutes

Offensive scrimmage: 15 minutes

Moving the puck, shooting, driving for the net

Shooting drills: 5 minutes

Conditioning drills: 10 minutes

Cool down: 3 minutes

Defensive practice

Defensive practice should emphasise checking and preventing goals. The aspects of forechecking, backchecking, and defensive zone coverage are stressed throughout the practice, including the scrimmage.

Defensive Practice: 90 minutes

Cross-ice agility and one-on-one cross-ice: 5 minutes

Give and go with a backchecker: 5 minutes

Two groups: 15 minutes

Defense taking the man in front of the net

Taking the man coming from the corner
Forechecking drill
Backchecking drill: 15 minutes
Breakouts five-on-two with one and two checkers
One forechecker, one backchecker

Defensive zone coverage: 5 minutes
Five-on-none defensive zone
Five-on-five defensive zone

Resurface the ice: 15 minutes

Defensive scrimmage: 10 minutes
Emphasis on defensive zone
Coverage and preventing goals

Conditioning: 8 minutes

Cool down: 3 minutes

POWER PLAY PRACTICE: 90 minutes

The power play and penalty killing practices are usually not as fatiguing as the other types of practices and are ideal as the day before the game practices. The emphasis is on execution and quick shooting in the power play and positioning in penalty killing.

Warm-up and stretching: 8 minutes

Power play shooting: 8 minutes

POWER PLAY SHOOTING DRILLS
FORWARDS

Playing the offside (right shots on left side, left shots on right side), the forward skates out of the corner and passes the puck across to the stationary forward who one times the puck (shoots in one motion). The passer of the puck then receives a pass from the opposite side and shoots.

DEFENSE

The defenseman passes the puck from the corner to the near point. The defenseman moves across the blueline to the middle and shoots low. Another defenseman deflects the puck in front of the net. Rotate clockwise, work on one side of the ice and then move to the other side.

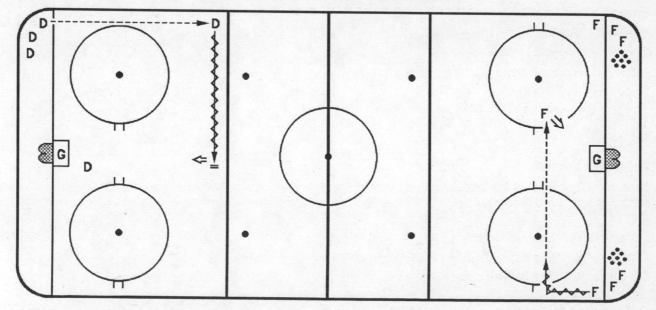

Offensive zone: 20 minutes

Defense coming across the blueline

The defenseman moves across the blueline and passes to the forward who comes off the boards. Work right-handed defensemen and forwards at one end and left handed defensemen and forwards at the other end. The forwards shoot in one motion. A guide to this drill is to have the forwards skate on the face-off circle line before receiving the pass.

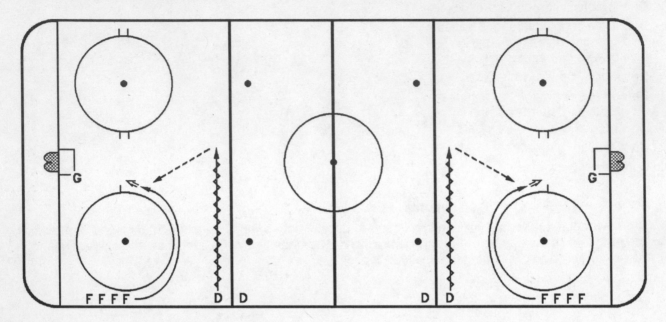

Offensive zone power play at the blueline 5 on 0

Use numbers to work the various plays

1. The defenseman moves across the middle of the blueline and shoots.
2. The defenseman passes to the forward coming off the boards. The forward shoots.
3. The defenseman passes to the forward on the boards and then passes to the offside forward who shoots.
4. The defenseman moves across the blueline and passes to the defense partner who has moved to the top of the circle. The defenseman shoots the puck in one motion, if possible.

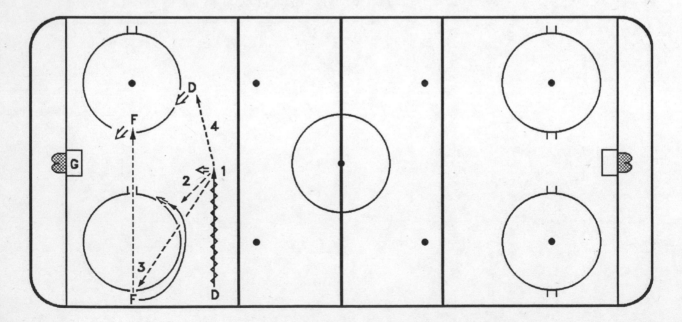

Offensive Zone Power Play from the Corners

Give and go for the net.
Going around the net, the offside forward picks (blocks out) the defenseman.
The forward moves to the near side and the other near side forward picks the defenseman. The forward moving out passes the puck across to the offside forward who then shoots.

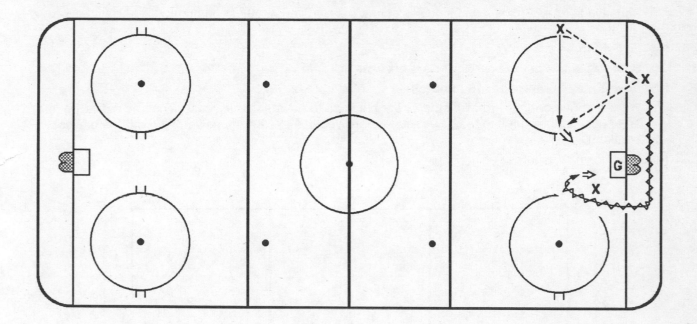

The forward (right-hand shot) moves out in front of the net and shoots or passes across to the offside forward who then shoots.

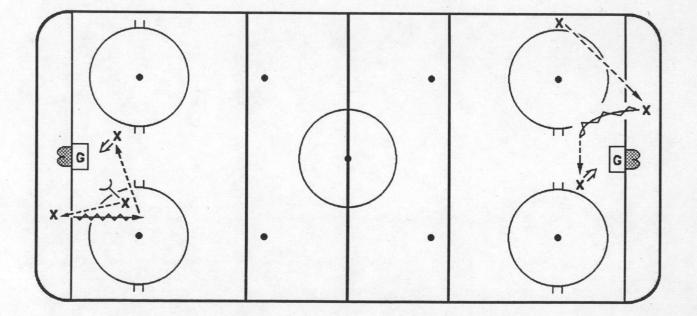

Power Play Breakouts: 10 minutes

(a) Five-on-none then five-on-two

Work the full length of the ice. This drill can be worked from one end at a time or can be worked from the normal both directions break out drill.

One man short, two men short

(b) Five-on-four

Penalty killers work first without sticks, then with sticks turned blade end up, then with the sticks as usual.

(c) Five-on-three

Same as above but the penalty killers are working three versus five. Work at both ends of the rink.

(d) Power play scrimmage: 15 minutes

Work first five-on-three to allow the power play unit to have some success. Then work five-on-four. The puck can be shot into the power play defensive zone to start the power play with the power play breakout.

(e) Cool down: 3 minutes

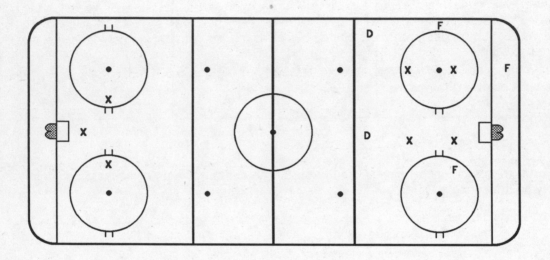

4. BASIC HOCKEY GUIDELINES

There are some basic rules which both the coach and the player must follow in order to become successful. The coach will teach his players these rules both on and off the ice in a manner so that they are clearly understood.

DEFENSIVE ZONE

1. Think defense first and offense only when in full control of the puck.
2. Keep your head up and take the man first and then the puck. Take the offensive man out after he has passed the puck to eliminate a return pass.
3. Only one man moves to cover the point. If two men move to the point, the second man should drop back on the board side. Keep the head up when moving to the point and don't let the defenseman move around you.
4. Cover the slot at all times. Move to a man coming from behind the net only when he is a direct threat to score.
5. One defenseman should always be in front of the net and control any player in the low slot area. The defenseman should face up ice and be aware of players in front of the net. To watch the play in the corner, the defenseman should turn his head but keep the body squared up ice. The defenseman should not turn his back from the slot area unless a player is coming from behind the net and is a direct threat to score.
6. When the defenseman has the puck just inside the blueline and is being pressured, he should dump the puck out over the blueline on the board side.
7. When experiencing difficulty in moving the puck out under pressure, freeze or ice the puck to get a face-off.
8. Never pass the puck rink wide or through the centre in your own end.
9. Never pass the puck up the middle in your own zone unless you are 100 percent sure. Pass to the winger on the boards or a defenseman in the corner if in doubt.
10. Never pass the puck without looking in your own zone. The man must be there.
11. Don't shoot the puck around the boards unless a man is in position or the puck has been shot in directly and the far side offensive defenseman is not in a position to pinch in.
12. Never go backward in your own zone unless on a power play.
13. Never allow your team to be out-numbered in the defensive zone, i.e., forwards up too high.

NEUTRAL ZONE

Offense

1. If men are covered, dump the puck in or turn back and pass to the defense, regroup and attack again.
2. Never try to stickhandle past the opposition when teammates are with you.
3. The forwards without the puck should move to open ice with the stick on the ice preparing to take a pass.
4. Never go offside; straddle the blueline or cut in front or behind the puck carrier.

Defense

1. Back check by picking up the offside forward. Take the man to the net if he stays outside the defenseman. If the player cuts to the middle in front of the defense stay in the lane. The back checker should be on the inside of the offensive man and should be slightly ahead of the man. Make contact with the man.
2. If two forwards are back, pick up the wings and the defense can force the play at the defensive blueline.
3. If the back checker is trailing the play, pick up the high slot area.
4. Some teams have the first back checker chase the puck carrier in the neutral zone.

OFFENSIVE ZONE

1. One man always drives for the net.
2. Drive for the rebounds. You must want to score. Release the puck quickly.
3. One man should always be in the slot with the stick on the ice ready to score or in a position to screen the goalie.
4. Shoot the puck when in the scoring area (slot). Extra passes can end up in missed opportunities.
5. The defenseman must shoot the puck quickly from the point. If the puck is mishandled or too much time is taken, the puck should be passed or shot back into the corner.
6. Never pass the puck blindly from behind the net. If you do not see a man and have to release the puck, shoot the puck at the goaltender's skates.

PENALTY SITUATIONS

1. Force the play in opponent's zone but keep skating.
2. Pick up the lane in the neutral zone whether an offensive player is there or not.
3. Never go by the opponent's point man in the defensive zone.
4. Cover the slot for cross passes.
5. Force the play in the defensive zone until the offensive team sets up. Some teams continue to force the play.
6. The man in the penalty box replaces the missing forward position, i.e. right winger, centre, or left winger no matter what position he usually plays.

POWER PLAY

1. On a delayed penalty, the centre on the next line replaces the goaltender. Some coaches designate a certain player to replace the goalie. If the puck is in your zone, the player goes to the centreline, in the offensive zone the player goes to the front of the net.
2. Have designated methods of moving the puck out of your own end.
3. Use four men in the neutral zone to move the puck over the offensive blueline.
4. Move the puck to the point in the offensive zone.
5. Move the puck quickly. If there is no man to pass to, the player should move. Don't stand still with the puck. Moving the puck quickly allows a man to move to the opening.

5. SKATING

Skates

It is very important to have a good pair of well fitting skates. Growing children should not wear a skate more than one-half size larger than necessary. Most hockey shops now have specialists who will fit skates properly.

Tying the skates

The middle eyelets should be pulled tightly together around the ankle. The top eyelets do not need to be pulled too closely together. The laces should not be tied around the skate (leg) as this could cause a lack of blood circulation to the feet. Hockey experts in the Soviet Union believe that the top eyelets in the skates should not be used in order to facilitate better flexion and extension at the ankle joint.

Sharpening the skates

Skates should be sharpened regularly to allow quick stops and turns. The sharpness of the skates can be tested by executing quick stops or tight turns. Off the ice, scraping a fingernail on the edge of the skate blade or placing a coin on the bottom of the blade to see how much hollow there is in the blade will give you an indication if the skate blade is still sharp.

Starting

A Front Start
- The back foot turns to nearly a right angle to the direction of motion, (this permits a larger contact area of the blade on the ice and puts the drive leg in optimum position). The knee of the back leg is flexed.
- The feet are shoulder-width apart.
- The body leans well forward over the front of the feet.
- The front foot is lifted slightly off the ice for a short stride.
- The player moves to a full stride as quickly as possible by short quick strides which lengthen with each stride.

B Side Start
- The back leg flexes at the knee and the toe of the skate digs into the ice.
- The back leg crosses over the front in a long pushing stride.
- The body turns forward and leans forward over the feet.
- Short quick strides are used to gain full skating stride.

Forward skating

A solid, well-balanced stance is important in skating.

The feet should be shoulder-width apart.

The foot of the drive leg, (back leg) is turned outward for maximum surface thrust.

The drive leg is fully extended at the hip, knee, and ankle joint.

The body is leaned forward to place the weight over the glide leg (front leg).

The trunk and glide leg should form an approximate 90° angle.

The drive leg should be recovered close to the ice.

DRIVE LEG

GLIDE LEG

Allow for a natural arm swing, but do not over swing the arms to cause over shift which will interfere with the forward motion.

Try to develop a smooth action stride with maximum thrust from the drive leg.

Excess motions are a waste of energy and may cause a reduction in the forward speed.

Stopping

A Two foot stop
- The knees are bent when moving into a stop.
- The shoulders and hips rotate, and the legs turn sideways.
- The body leans back.
- The weight is put on the front skate which digs in and is mainly responsible for the stopping action.

B One foot stop
- **Back foot**: The action is the same as the two-foot stop except the front skate does not touch the ice.
- The front leg can be crossed over the back leg and motion in the opposite direction can be initiated immediately.
- **Front foot**: This is the same motion as the back-foot stop except the back leg does not touch the ice.

Forward crossover

The forward crossover is used for turning while continuing or accelerating.
Push sideways with the drive leg and lean in toward the inside leg or glide leg.
In the recovery, cross the drive leg over in front of the glide leg.
Push out with the inside leg over the crossover leg.
Keep the inside shoulder up.
Repeat this action and keep the legs moving.

Backward starting

The feet are shoulder-width apart.
The knees are bent.
The drive leg turns inward and forcefully extends in a semi-circular motion.
The weight is shifted to the other leg and the motion is repeated.
The legs do not cross over in this form of backward skating.

Stopping backward

A One-foot stop
- The back foot turns outward.
- The blade of the skate digs into the ice.
- The knee flexes and the body leans forward over the front leg.
- The leg extends to start the move in the opposite direction.

B Two-foot stop
- Both skates turn outward simultaneously.
- Flex at the knees.
- Both legs flex and push forward.

Turning

A Two-skate quick turn
- Both skates turn in the direction desired.
- The body leans to the inside.
- The weight is on the inside edge of both skates.

B Forward to backward
- Turn the inside skate in and pivot with the blade on the ice.
- Push with the outside leg.
- Rotate the body and swing the outside leg in a 180° angle motion, (the skate may stay on the ice or can be lifted).

C Backward to forward
- Push off the outside leg.
- Turn the inside skate outward at 135° angle.
- Rotate the upper body in the direction of the turn.
- Bring the outside leg across and over the inside leg.
- Push off the inside leg in a forward skating motion.

A solid, balanced stance is important in skating. The foot of the drive leg is turned outward for maximum thrust, and the body is leaned forward to place the weight over the glide leg.

SKATING AND TURNING DRILLS

1. Note: These drills can be done skating backward or forward.
2. Skate around the rink going behind the nets. Move in both directions.

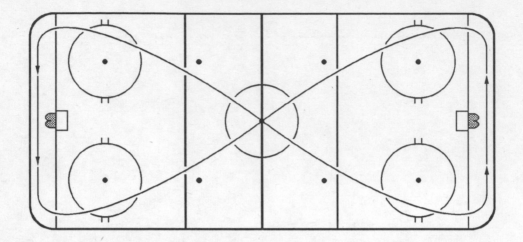

3. Small figure "8"

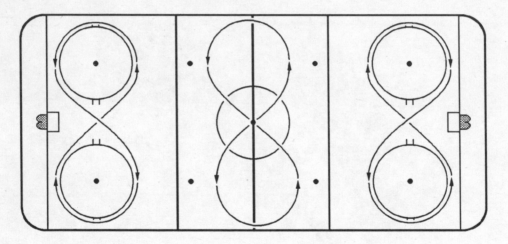

4. Skate in circles. Five groups. Change direction forward and backward.

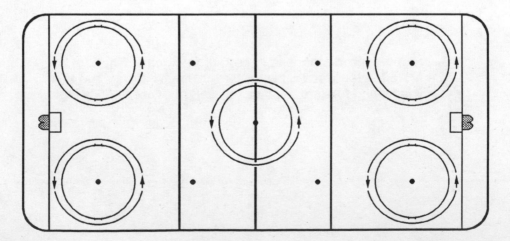

5. Skate the circles: two groups

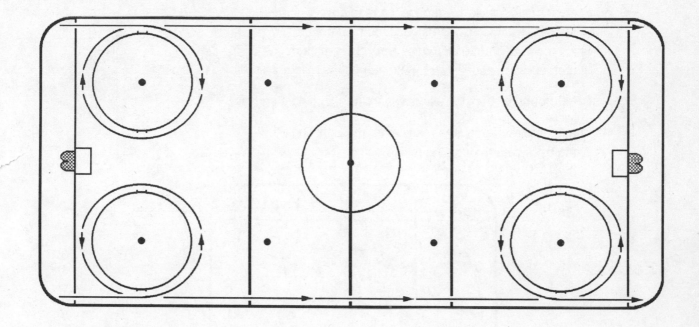

6. Skate the circles: one group

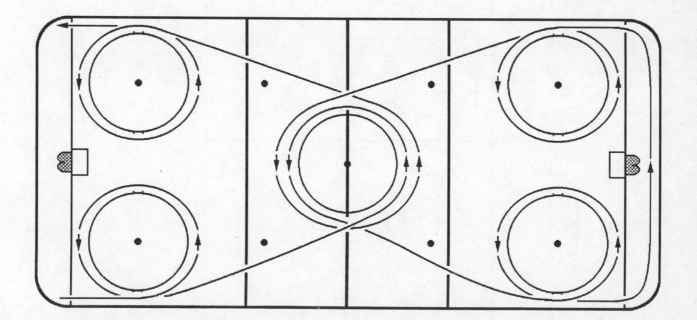

41

7. Weaving through markers

A • Move the pylons in a zig zag position
- Skate forward through the markers
- Skate backward through the markers

B • Skate forward, clockwise around the markers
- Skate backward, clockwise around the markers
- Skate forward, counterclockwise around the markers
- Skate backward counter clockwise around the markers

C • Deke around each pylon using a sharp turn both right and left

D • Skate forward through the markers in a straight line
- Skate backward through the markers in a straight line

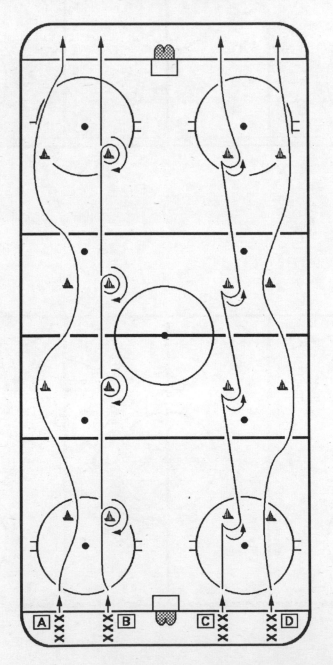

8. Zig Zag Drill: All players skate forward stopping at each point (1 through 7) up the ice. The second player leaves when the first reaches the blueline. All players stay at one end when they complete the drill, then reverse directions.

   Variation: All players skate forward to points 1, 3, 5 and 7 and backward to points 2, 4, and 6

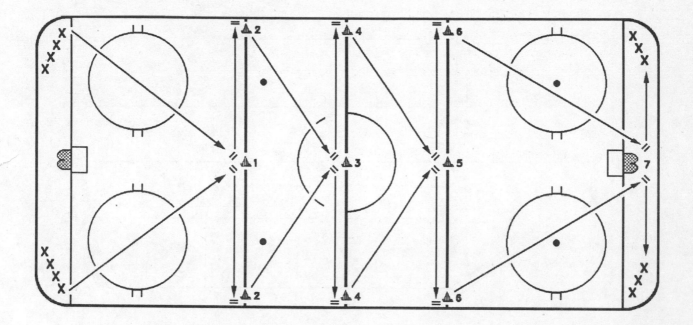

9. Overback Drill: Skate forward across the blueline, stop, skate backward to the top of the face-off circle, pivot toward your group and skate to the corner, stop, then move into the back of the line.

   Note: You must have groups 1 and 4 and 2 and 3 switch sides halfway through the drill to be sure the players work on stopping and turning both ways.

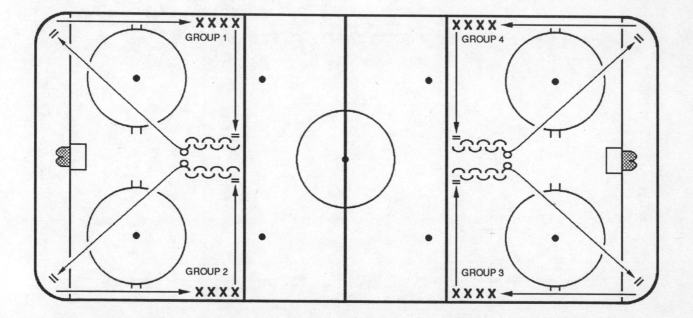

10. Three forwards and two defensemen skate down the ice.
    - The wingers cut at the far blueline and skate directly to the net and back to the blueline twice
    - The centre skates to the crease and moves laterally side to side twice
    - The defensemen skate to the far blueline and cross step to the pylons three times
   After this skate, the players skate the length of the ice to the starting position.

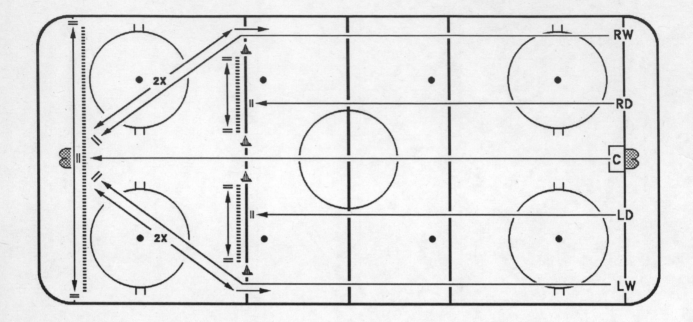

11. Skate forward. On the whistle, skate backward. Repeat.
   Turn the opposite way each time in order to practise the movement in both directions.

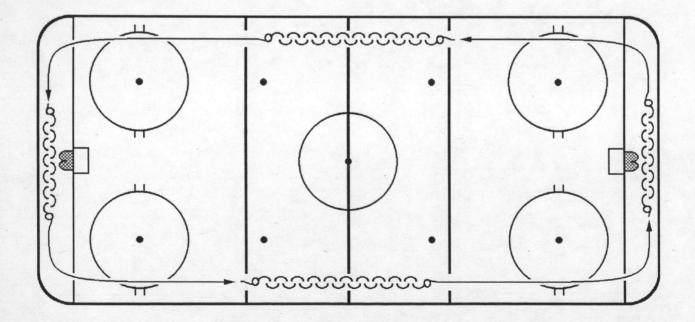

12. Same drill as 11 except the players skate around the outside of the rink and change directions at the bluelines.

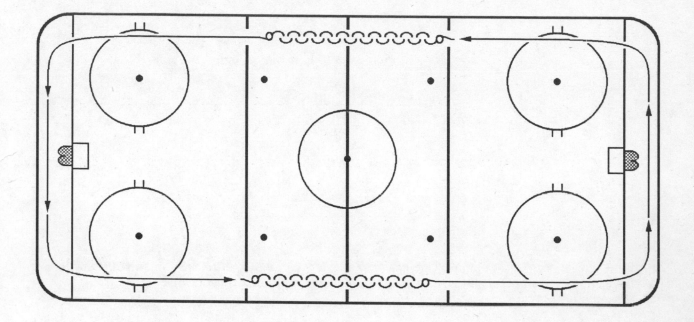

13. Skate backward around the circles and forward between the circles.

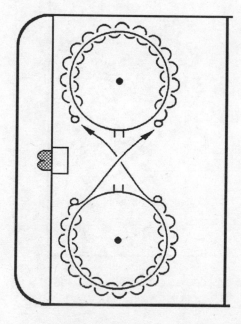

14. Skate forwards straight up and down the rink, skating backwards between the bluelines. (Not Shown)

15. Skate around the rink doing 360 degree turns, as many as you can, between the bluelines. (Not Shown)

AGILITY DRILLS

1. Wave Drill: On the instructor's hand signals, move forward, backward, and sideways. Keep your head up and stay up on toes.

2. Shadow Drill: Work with partner. One player skates forward, the other backward. The offensive player moves and the defensive player must react to the offensive player. (Not shown)

3. Skate backward moving laterally side to side across the ice.

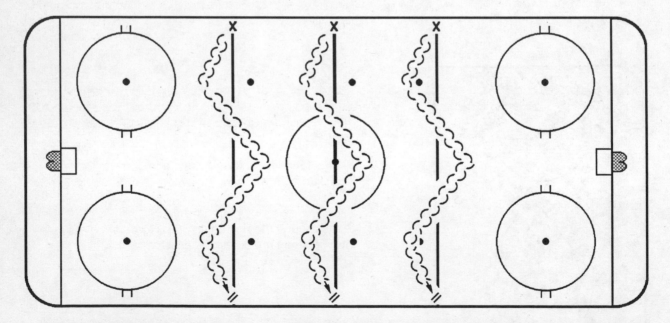

4. Knee Drops: Skate around the rink and at the red and bluelines, drop down on both knees and quickly recover. Skate around the rink and at the red and bluelines, drop down on one knee and recover (alternate knee each time). (Not shown)

6. PASSING AND RECEIVING

STICKHANDLING AND PUCK CONTROL

Choosing a stick

It is very important that you choose a stick that feels right and is correct for your skating and puckhandling styles. The thickness of the shaft varies from manufacturer to manufacturer. Be sure to pick one that allows you to close your hands completely around it.

Length of stick

The length of the stick varies with the individual. In general, the stick should reach the player's chin in shoes and the player's collarbone on skates. The style of skating is also a very important consideration in choosing a stick, as some players skate with the upper body in a more upright position than others.

Lie of stick

Lies of sticks normally range from four to seven with five and six being the most common. The skating style is important. More upper body lean means a lower lie stick and less upper body lean dictates a higher lie stick. A test for the proper lie of a stick is to have players stand at a normal stance with the stick on the ice in front of them. If the heel of the blade is off the ice, a higher lie should be used. If the toe of the blade is off the ice a lower lie should be used. When a player is skating, check if the heel or toe of the stick is off the ice. If so, you have the wrong lie of stick.

Weight of the stick

It is important that the stick feel comfortable as each individual has a different preference. As a general rule, the stick should be stiff but not whippy. Bigger, stronger players often need longer, heavier sticks.

Curved stick

It is generally recommended that young boys should not use a curved stick. Some stick manufacturers have reintroduced the straight blade stick. When all passing, stickhandling, and shooting fundamentals have been mastered, older boys should be allowed to experiment with a curved blade. The curve is measured by the distance of a perpendicular line measured from a straight line drawn from any point of the heel to the end of the blade.

The rules state that the curve should be no greater than half an inch. All instructors and coaches should be alert to pick out boys who are having difficulty with passing, stickhandling or shooting. A curved stick may be one of the reasons for these problems. Backhand passing and shooting are the skills most affected by the curved stick.

Taping the stick: the knob

Taping the knob depends on the grip and feel desired by the player. If the upper hand is on or over the end of the stick, the knob is usually smaller. If the upper hand does not reach the end but rests against the knob, larger amounts of tape are usually used. White tape (as opposed to black friction tape) should be used on the knob to prevent the glove palm from deteriorating.

Taping the stick: the blade

Taping the blade is usually a matter of choice. Some players now use little or no tape on the blade. Generally, tape the stick from heel to toe, and don't use large amounts of overlap. The use of talcum powder or rubbing the blade of the stick on the bottom of a shoe is sometimes used to take the stickiness off the tape. White tape is easier to apply, adheres better, and is now preferred by many players.

PASSING AND RECEIVING

Passing

The puck is cradled with the blade of the stick slightly over the puck. The puck should be in the centre of the blade or slightly to the heel of it. The weight shift moves from the back foot to the front foot with a sweeping motion of the stick blade on the ice. Push with the lower hand and pull with the upper one. The puck should be released with the blade at 90° angle to the direction the puck is travelling. **Remember: lead the man and make your passes quickly.**

Receiving

To be in position to receive a pass, keep the stick blade on the ice or just slightly off. The hands are tight on the stick but arms remain loose. Give with the blade of the stick and tilt it toward the puck. Turn the blade of the stick to the direction the puck should go.

TYPES OF PASSING

Forehand sweep

The stick blade is on the ice and the puck remains in contact with it until it is released. Body weight transfers from back to front leg and the follow through is low.

Backhand sweep

The same fundamentals are used as in the forehand sweep only the puck is moved on the backhand side. The puck begins well on the backhand side and the weight shifts from the back foot to the front foot. The backhand sweep is a more difficult pass and requires an accurate and low follow through.

Snap pass

The snap pass is similar to the forehand sweep. The stick is brought back slightly from contact with the puck in a sweeping motion and snapped. It is a quick, hard pass.

Flip pass (saucer pass)

The flip pass is used to pass over an opponent's stick. The puck spins off the stick from the heel to the toe. The puck should be approximately four to six inches off the ice and lands flat in a spinning motion. The puck must land before the receiver's stick. Lead the receiver more than usual as the pass is usually slower.

Drop pass

The offensive player skates in front of the defensive player and drops the puck to his trailing teammate. The puck is dropped from the forehand or backhand position but is not passed back as this allows the trailer to skate into the puck.

Back pass

This pass differs from the drop pass because the puck is passed back to a teammate. The puck can be passed back from the forehand or backhand side. The trailing teammate is usually ten to 15 feet behind.

Board pass

The board pass is used by defensemen behind the net or by any player attempting to pass by a defensive man with a teammate slipping behind. The pass should be low and not too hard so the rebound will be easy to handle. The puck rebounds in such a way that the angle of incidence equals the angle of reflection.

Bank pass

This is used by a forward driving down the boards in the offensive zone and bouncing the puck back off the boards to a trailing player or a pass off the boards to another defenseman behind the net (sometimes called a defense reverse). The pass is executed by bouncing the puck off the boards backward where it is picked up by a trailing player. The puck is kept on the ice and is at a sharp angle without being passed too hard. It is a form of a drop pass off the boards.

TYPES OF RECEIVING

Receiving passes off skates

Put the weight on the non receiving skate. Turn the blade of the receiving skate with the toe pointing slightly in. Deflect the puck up to the blade of the stick.

Receiving pass in air

Attempt to knock down a low pass in the air with the blade of the stick in a downward slapping motion. Attempt to bunt down a pass high in the air with the glove or body.

Receiving pass too far ahead

Completely extend the arms and extend the stick in one hand. A player may go down on one knee and extend the stick flat on the ice if the puck is coming from behind at an angle.

Receiving pass off boards

A. If no defensive man is in the area, start skating and pick up the puck while moving.
B. Stop and/or deflect the puck with the back skate onto the blade of the stick.

PASSING DRILLS

1. In a stationary position, pass a puck with a partner across the ice. Lengthen the distance of the passes in stages. Pass over a stick for flip passes.

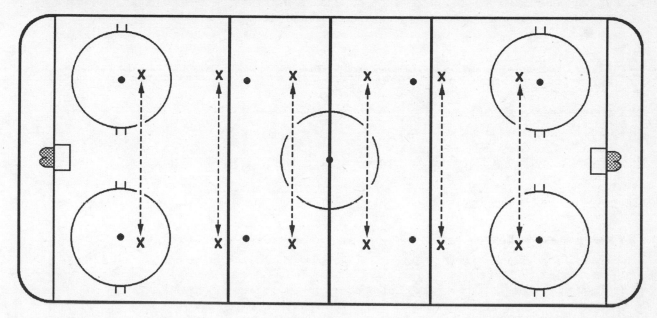

2. Pass in circles, across and around. (Not shown).
   Same drill except the passing player follows the pass and replaces the receiver in his

3. Pass in circle with one man in centre attempting to intercept the passes.
   (Not shown)

4. Pepper passing: Players keep the puck moving as quickly as possible.

5. Pass in pairs around the ice. Forehand and backhand passes.

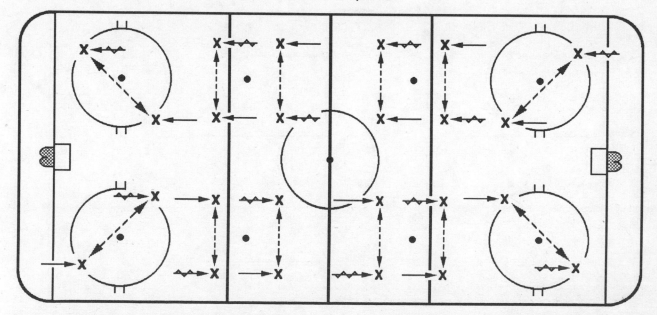

6. Pass in pairs around the ice with passes deliberately aimed at the skates.

7. Pass in pairs down the ice. Stop at the far end, return in the opposite direction when the drill is completed. Forehand passes then progress to backhand passes.

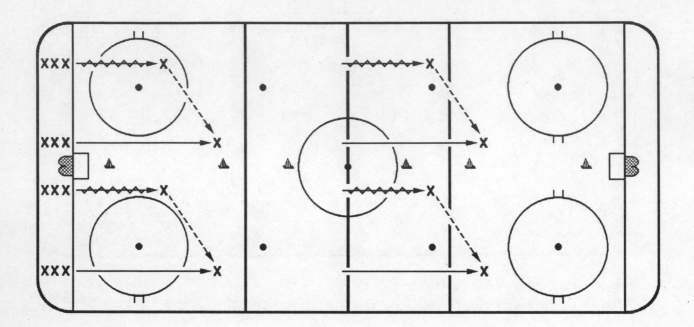

8. Same drill as 7, only the pylons are put in a line between the two passing players.

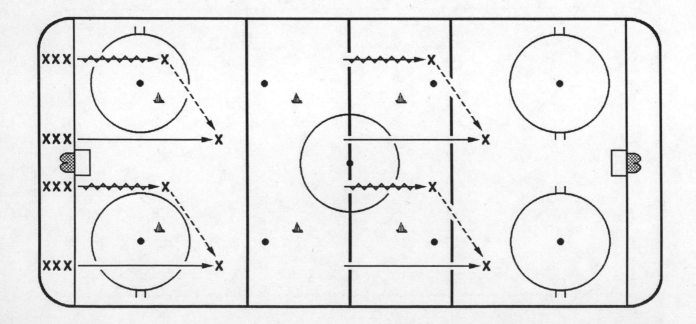

9. Give-and-Go. The player with the puck passes to a stationary man who returns the pass.

Variation: Two players start at the X2 position. After X2 returns the pass to X1, he joins the back of the X1 line. X2 who shot on goal, returns to the X2 position.

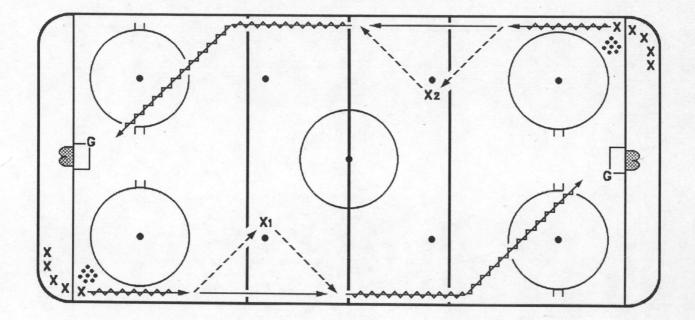

10. Two-on-none in both directions.

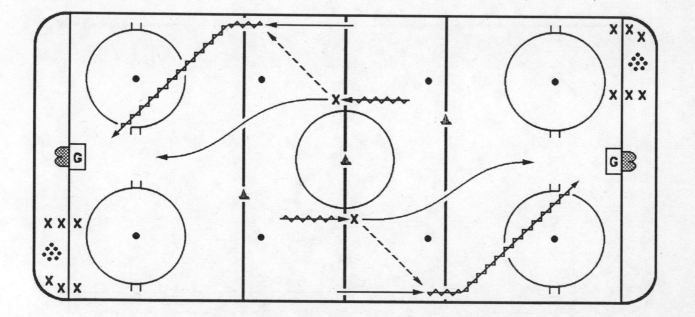

11. Two-on-none in both directions. This is a variation of drill 9, only one group must wait until the two-on-none is finished from the other direction. Passes are longer and more accuracy is required than in drill 9.

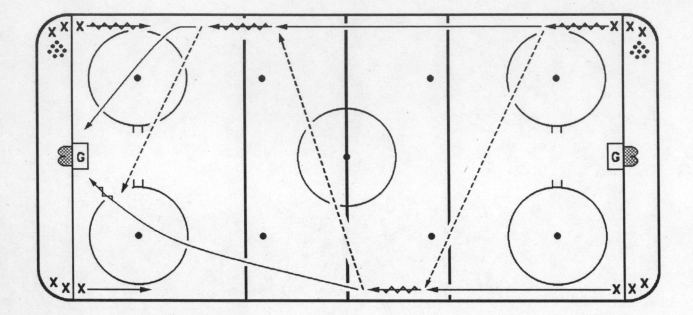

12. Same as drill 11 except a defenseman starts the two-on-one from behind the net and passes to the forward. The defensemen operate out of both ends. The defenseman who starts the play goes to the blueline, stops, and skates backward to the goal line.

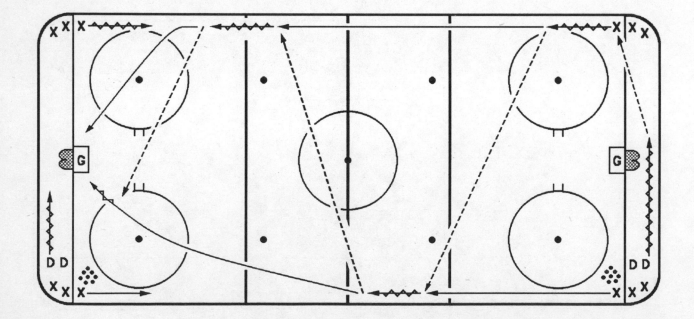

13. Three-on-none in both directions. Groups of three, passing one puck between them, spread out after passing centre ice.

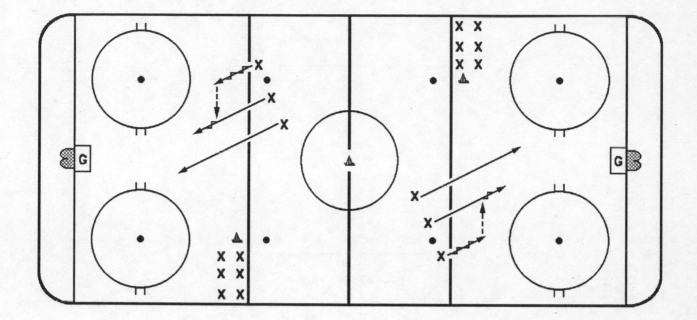

14. Passing off the boards: The player skates the length of the ice passing off the boards and receiving his own pass back.

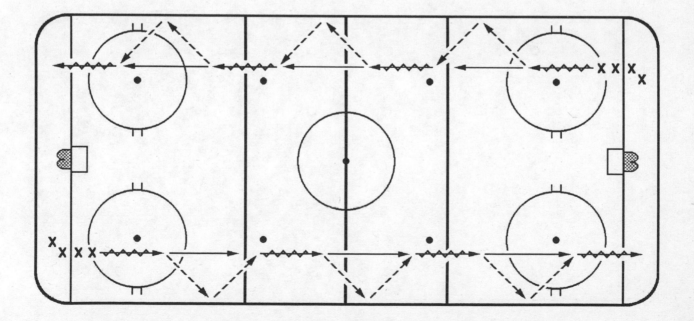

15. Passing off the boards - working in pairs. Alternate passing off boards and receiving it.

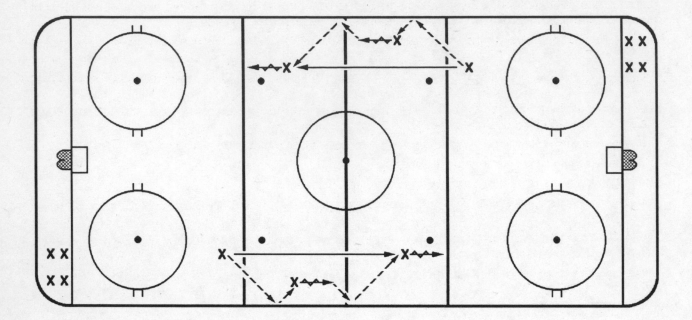

16. Keep away. Using the three zones of the rink and three to four players on a team, play a game of keep away.

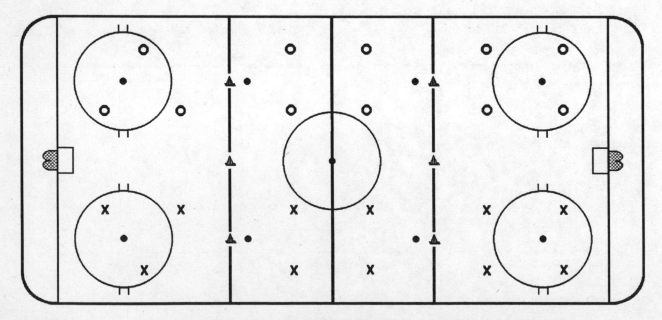

17. All two-on-one, three-on-one, three-on-two team play drills involve passing and receiving.

7. SHOOTING

Accuracy and getting the shot away quickly are key factors in goal scoring. Speed and power of the shot depend on strength, mechanics, and the co-ordination of the shooting movement.

The puck should be placed in the middle of the blade. Any deviation from this position will result in a loss of power and accuracy.

The base of support (i.e., the relationship of the puck and the skates) is very important for obtaining maximum velocity in shooting.

Shooting should be performed at the base of support between the two skates. The puck should be released at a 90° angle to the intended direction.

The lower arm provides the pushing action while the upper arm provides the pulling motion.

Upper body rotation is also important in shooting.

Strength in the arms, shoulders, and wrists is essential in shooting.

Getting the shot away quickly is important and therefore a player should be able to shoot the puck off either foot.

The follow-through should be toward the net and the shooter should be ready for any rebound and maintain balance to receive a possible body check.

In shooting, the force exerted on the stick is downward and forward, throwing the puck forward.

TYPES OF SHOOTING

Forehand

The lower hand is a comfortable distance from the upper hand (usually 12 to 18 inches apart).

The puck is brought back to the side and opposite or slightly behind the rear skate.

The body is at a 45° angle to the direction of the puck.

The puck is in the middle of the blade of the stick which is slightly cupped.

The lower wrist is extended.

The puck comes forward in a sweeping motion.

The weight shifts from the rear foot to the front foot and the puck is released from the front skate at a 90 degree angle to its intended direction.

The arms extend, the body rotates quickly, and the lower wrist flexes.

The turning of the stick blade follow-through determines the height of the shot.

If the blade is turned over the puck, the shot is low.

If the blade is turned under the puck, the shot is high.

Balance should also be maintained at all times to receive a possible body check.

Backhand

The backhand shot is often neglected because players tend to use the curved stick.

The shot is valuable coming off a shift to the backhand side and cutting towards the net.

The shooting principles are similar to the forehand shot and the follow through is important.

The puck is drawn to the backhand side and the lower wrist is in a reversed or flexed position.

The weight shift is from back to front foot.

The upper body rotates quickly.

Snap

The snap shot is a valuable shot as it is quick and accurate from 30 feet away.

The stick blade is at a 90 degree angle to the desired direction of the puck and is cupped in the middle of the stick blade.

The stick is drawn back six to eight inches from the puck.

The wrists are extended and flexed when the stick blade hits the puck. The follow-through is short.

Slap

The slap shot should be developed after the forehand and snap shots have been mastered.

The slap shot is valuable because the puck can be shot at a greater speed from a greater distance.

Accuracy and quickness of release are sacrificed for velocity.

The body is parallel to the desired direction of the puck and the puck is close to the heel of the skate.

The lower hand is shifted down the shaft of the stick until fully extended.

The stick is drawn backward to shoulder height with lower arm rigid with the eyes focussed on the puck.

On the downswing, the weight shifts from the back leg to the front leg.

The stick contacts the ice just before it hits the puck, usually one to two 2 inches from the puck. The puck is struck at the middle of the blade.

The wrist moves from extension to flexion and pressure is exerted downward on the ice as contact is made with the puck.

Flip

The flip shot is used to get the puck up in the air quickly when clearing the puck from the defensive zone, lifting the puck over a fallen goaltender, or flipping the puck into the offensive end.

The lower hand is moved further down the blade than usual.

The blade of the stick is open, and the puck is lifted, and the follow-through is high.

The flip shot can be executed with a forehand or backhand motion.

Tip-ins

Many goals are scored by a player changing the direction of a shot using the blade of the stick.

It is important to get in a good scoring position for a tip-in, in order to prevent the opposition defenseman from tying the player up.

The forward should attempt to block the goaltender's vision by moving in front of the goal crease.

Keep the feet in an open stance to avoid being knocked down by opponents. Angle the blade of the stick down to deflect the puck downward and angle the blade of the stick upward to deflect the puck upward.

Keep a tight grip on the stick for all deflections. Maintain a low balance stance.

Shooting off the wrong foot

Players should be able to shoot the puck off either foot in order to get the shot off quickly.

The weight is on the foot nearest the puck.

The shot is used to execute a quick shot and the speed of the shot comes from the arm, wrist, and shoulder action with little or no body rotation.

The follow-through is short as the player is not in a stable position and is vulnerable to a body check.

All good goal scorers are able to shoot the puck off either foot as in many cases there is no time to relocate the footing when receiving the puck in a shooting position.

Accuracy and getting the **shot** away quickly **are key factors** in goal scoring. All good goal scorers are able to shoot the puck off either foot in order to shoot as quickly as possible.

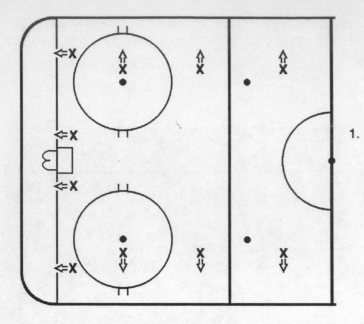

SHOOTING DRILLS

1. Shoot against the boards in a stationary position. Shoot ten high shots, ten low shots, then alternate high and low shots. Mark the spots on the boards low and high and have the players shoot for the marks. Use half or full ice.

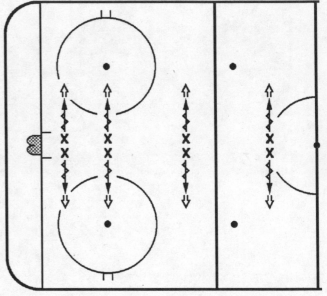

2. Shoot against the boards from a moving position with the players working from the centre of the ice. Use half or full-ice.

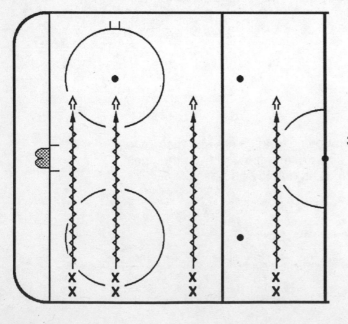

3. Shoot against boards starting from one side to the other side. For large numbers, divide into two groups. Use half or full-ice.

4. Divide the players into two groups. Players skate the length of the ice and shoot on the goaltender from the slot area. The shot area can be marked by pylons on the ice. Switch sides halfway through the drill. The drill can be varied with the give-and-go drill.

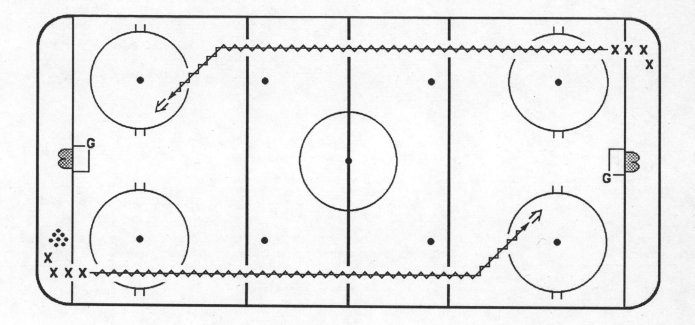

5. Same drill as 4 except players cut around pylons and shoot. This drill can be varied with the give-and-go drill.

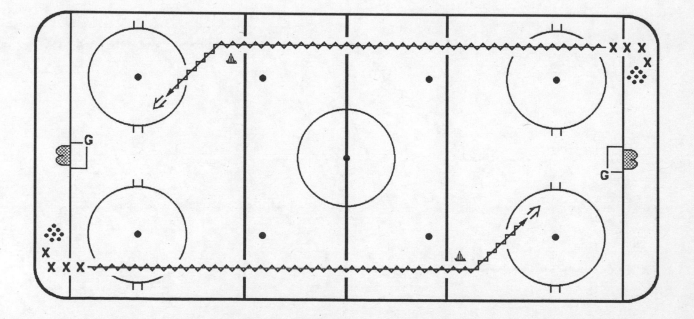

6. Divide the players in half in two corners at the same end of the rink. Alternate shooting from right and left side. This drill can be useful if only one goaltenders available for practice. Players should shoot from both sides. The drill can be varied using pylons and the give-and-go drill.

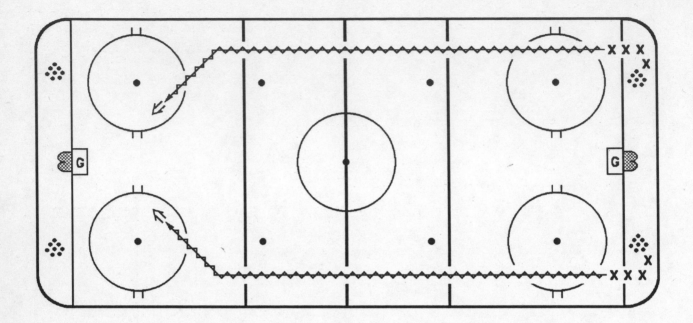

7. Players start at the same time from opposite corners, each carrying pucks. Between the bluelines, each player passes the puck to the other player and then continues on and shoots after receiving the pass. The players move to the opposite corners after shooting.

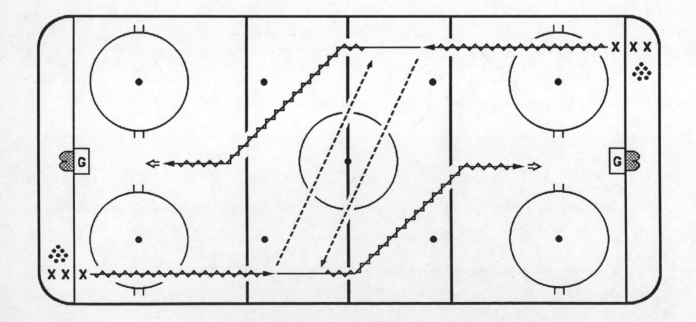

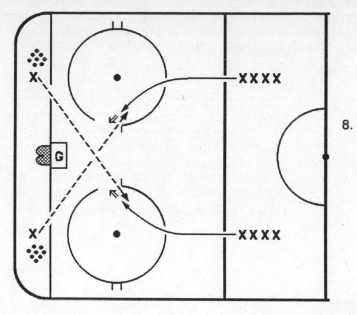

8. Pass Out: A player in each corner passes the puck alternately to the players skating in on goal. Players should follow the puck after shooting and go for a second shot if a rebound comes out.

9. After shooting the puck, the player goes to the corner where the pass came from. The player passing the puck then goes to the end of the line on the same side of the rink.

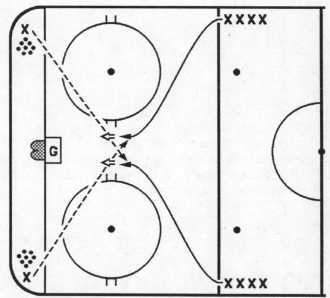

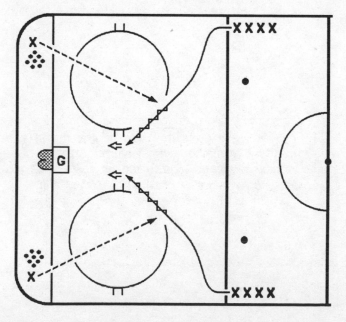

10. This is a variation of the previous drill, only the pass comes from the same side. The player goes to the corner from which he received the pass.

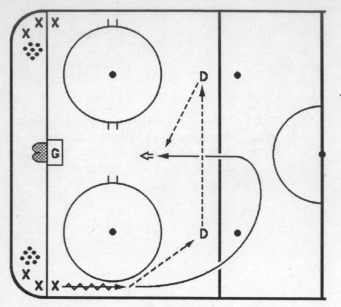

11. The player skates from the corner and passes to the nearest defenseman. The defenseman passes to the other defenseman and then back to the forward. The forward then goes in and shoots to the goaltender and moves to the other corner. The next forward up moves from the other corner. The defensemen stay in the same positions for this drill.

12. The pass goes from X1 to X2, then to X3, who goes to the line in the corner after a shot on goal while X2 goes to the position of X1. X1 goes to the shooting line. This drill differs from the previous one because all players rotate, playing all positions.

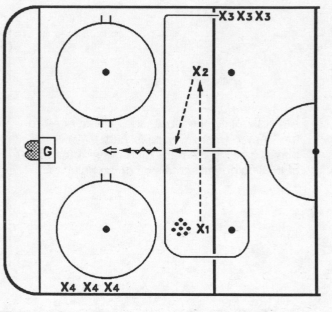

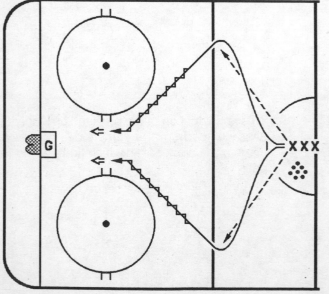

13. Receive a pass from the centre, cut in and shoot from the wing. Return to centre. The next player swings to the opposite side and receives a pass from the next player in line.

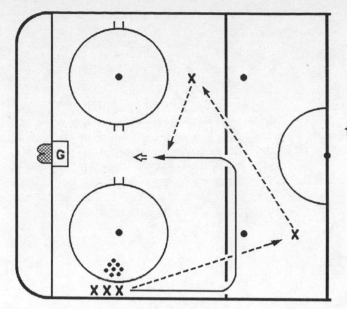

14. The player skates from the corner, passes the puck to one man who passes to the other stationary man, and then a return pass is made to the forward.

15. Race for the puck and shoot: Players must start at the same time, round the pylons, and the first player then shoots on net while the other player tries to check him.

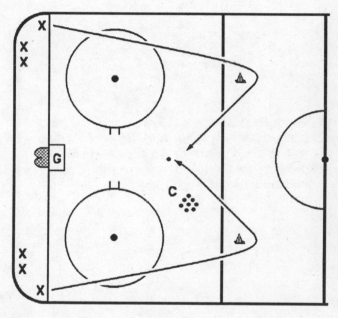

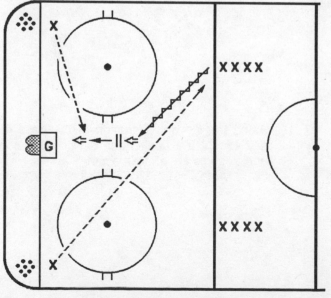

16. A. Variation of the pass out drill: After the player has taken the first shot, he stops in the high slot, receives a second pass out from the opposite corner, and then shoots again.
   B. Same drill as above but X is now moving while trying to take a second shot.

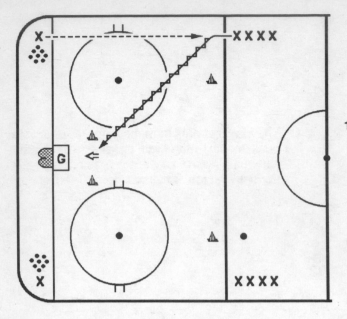

17. Backhand drill: Same drill as the pass out except the pass comes early from the corner and the player cuts around a pylon and shoots from his backhand side from the slot area.

18. Rebound drill: This is a variation of the pass out drill with a player from the opposite line trailing the shooter, and picking-up and shooting any rebound. Alternate the shooter and the rebounder each time,

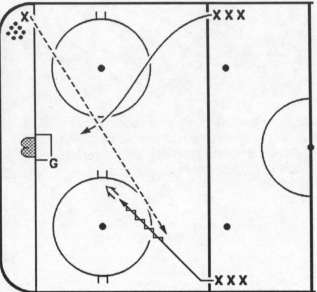

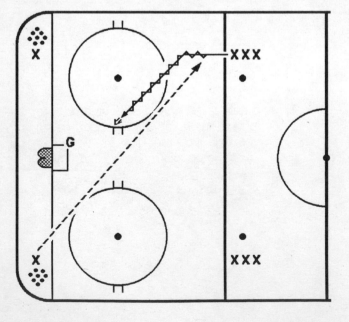

19. Along the ice drill: Variation of the pass out drill except the goaltender is without a stick and all shots are along the ice.

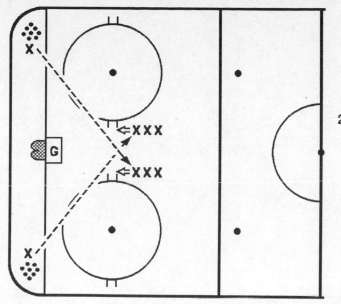

20. Pass out stationary drill: Players are stationary in the slot and shoot as soon as the puck is passed out. Alternate pass outs.
Variation: Pass from one corner and shoot. Pass from the other corner and shoot.

21. Pass across drills: Drills 7 to 11 can be performed with passes coming across instead of from the corner.

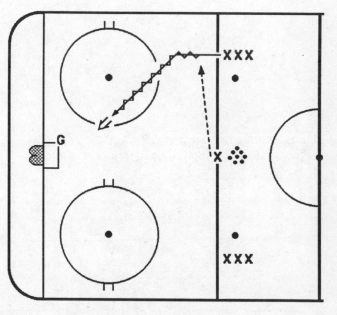

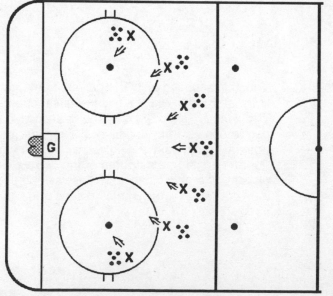

22. Semi-circle drill: The players are stationary in a semi-circle starting from the blueline. The players shoot in rapid succession. After each player has shot one puck, he retrieves it and moves in five feet using wrist shots only.
Variation: Shoot alternate rather than in succession (left side, right side, next left, etc.)

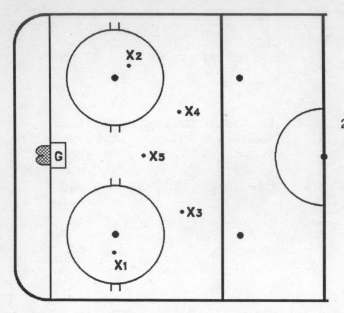

23. Each player has a puck and shots are from different angles. The players shoot by numbers in order. The goaltender should know the order as well. Move players into different positions to create new angles.

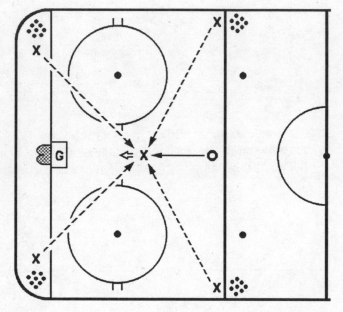

24. Pucks are passed from different angles with the last shot chased by a checker. Rotate positions.

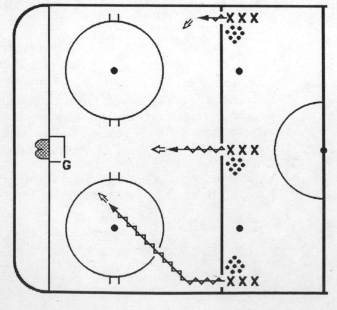

25. Variation shooting drill: The players form three lines and move with a puck simultaneously. The winger shoots from the blueline, the centre shoots from the high slot straight out from the goal and the other winger shoots from an angle at the bottom of the circle. The players alternate lines and halfway through the drill, the long shots come from the opposite side.

26. **Moving Slot Drill:** The centreman skates to the centreline and passes to the winger. The winger moves down the boards and passes the puck back to the centre (after he passes the pylon), who then shoots from the slot area, one timing it or shooting without stopping. The forwards alternate positions of the centre and wing. Work only with the centre and one winger alternating from one side to the other.

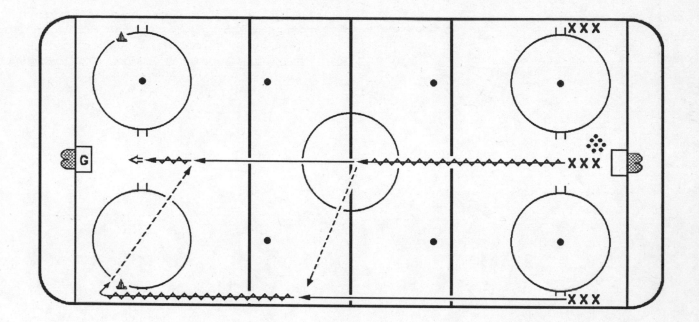

27. **Shooting under pressure - chase the rabbit:** The puck carrier says "go", skates the length of the ice outside the pylon and shoots with the checker starting two steps behind him and on the inside of the pylon.

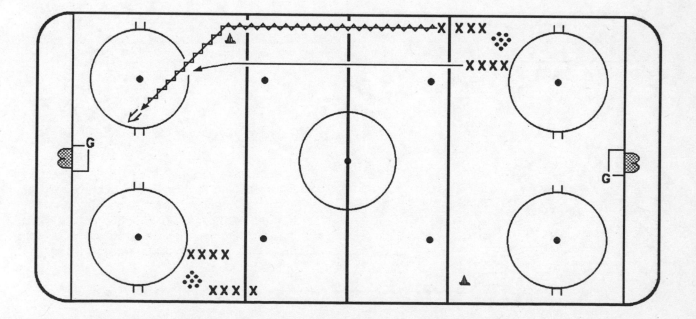

28. Shooting under pressure: The same drill as 27 except the shooter receives a pass from centre ice.

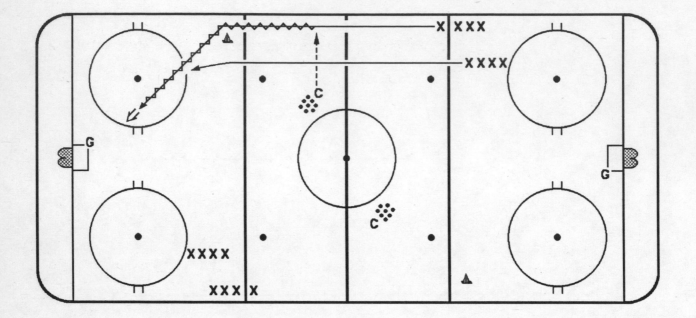

29. The player skates the length of the ice, shoots and then chases the player coming from the side as he skates the length of the ice and shoots. Work both sides of the ice.

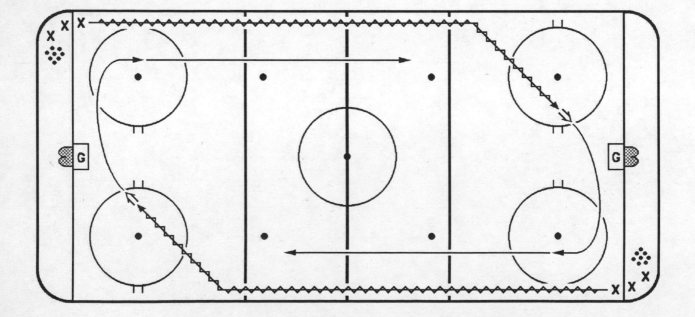

30. Shooting under pressure: The player skates from the corner with the puck, cuts around the pylon and shoots. As soon as the puck carrier hits the far blueline, the checker from the opposite side cuts across and attempts to stop the player from shooting.

Variation: Same drill but this time a pass is made from the neutral zone to the player coming up the ice.

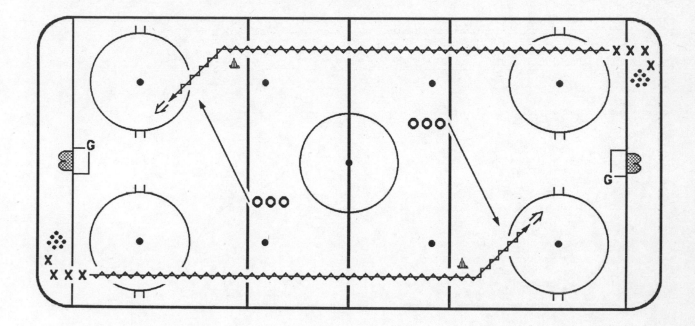

31. Continous shooting drill: The player skates down one side, cuts around the pylon, shoots, goes for the rebound, turns, receives a pass going in the opposite direction, skates down the centre of the ice, and shoots. Work the drill from both directions.

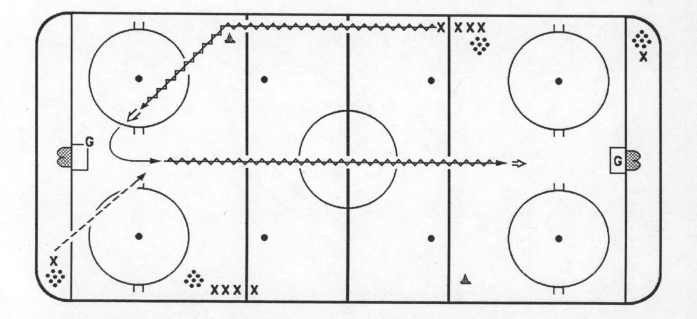

32. Group shooting drill: The first player in group 1 skates diagonally across the ice, receives a pass from the first player in group 2, skates around the pylon, and shoots on goal. Group 1 player moves to group 4 and group 2 player moves to group 3. The type of shot can be predetermined. Work the drill from both directions.

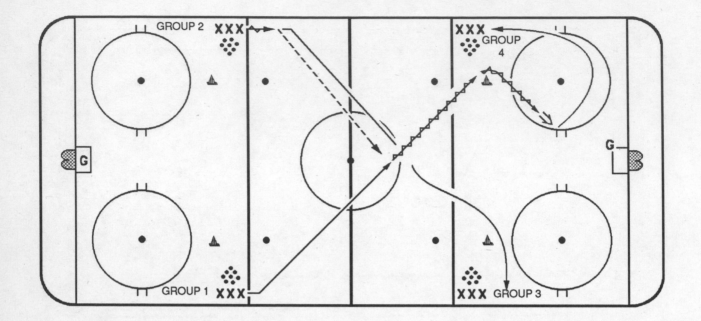

33. The player passes the puck to a player who has come from the other side of the rink and skated around the centre circle. The player receiving the puck goes in for the shot. After passing the puck, the player skates around the circle and receives a pass from the other side. The players return to the same side they started on.
Variation: Have two men starting together for a two-on-none. Then progress to three at the same time to create a three-on-none.

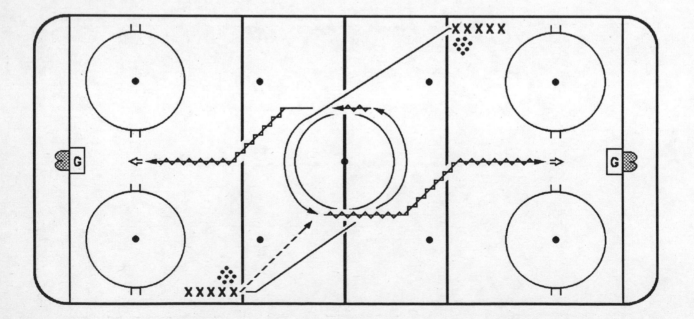

34. The puck is passed from corner to corner and then passed to the player skating around the centre circle from the other end. The player receiving the pass then goes in and shoots. The players rotate following the puck. After shooting, the player returns to the corner where he started.

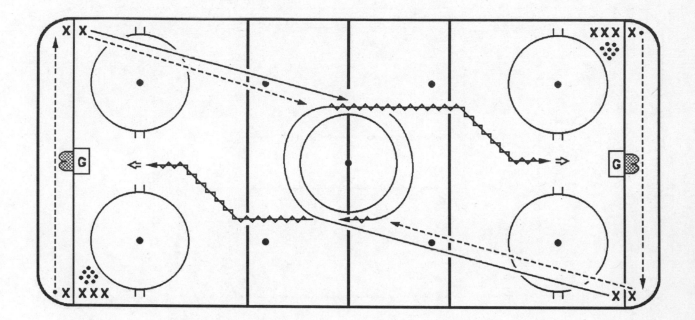

35. Variation of shooting warm-up circling centre ice. After taking the pass, skate backward to the blueline, then turn and skate forward and shoot at the net.

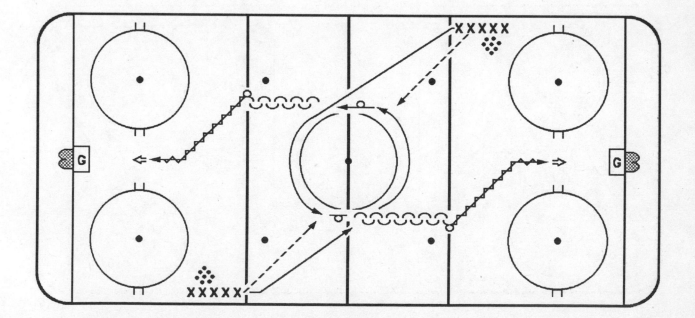

36. The puck is passed from the forward to the defenseman, then defenseman to defenseman, and back to the forward who then goes in and shoots on the goal. The forward returns to the same line he started in.

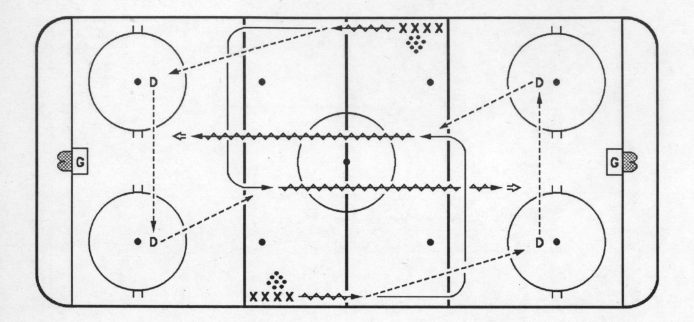

37. The player skates in on the net, takes a pass from the preceding player, picks up a puck in the corner and passes the puck across to the next shooter. A pylon may be added for the player to skate around before shooting.

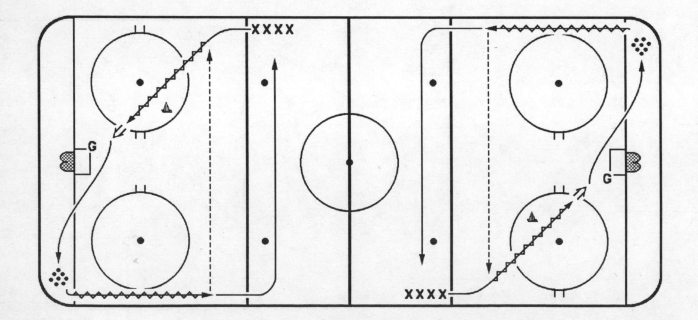

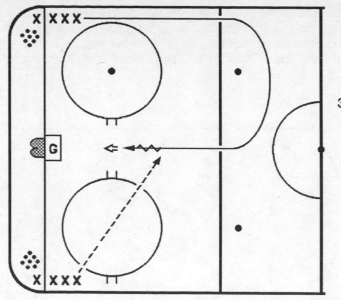

38. The player shooting the puck comes out of one corner, cuts in the middle of the ice at the blueline, receives a pass from the opposite corner, and proceeds to shoot on the goaltender. The player passing the puck then becomes the next shooter and receives a pass from a player in the opposite corner.

39. Tip-in drill: Tip-ins should be executed from a stationary and moving position and from the short or long side. The drill can be run faster by having the defensemen shooting directly from the blueline without receiving a pass out. All shots should be on the ice or low.

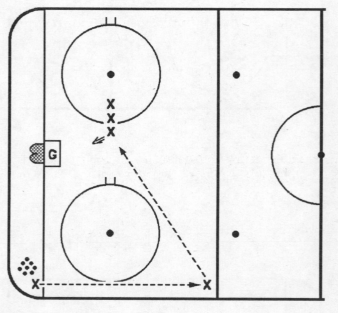

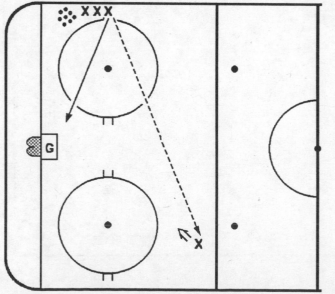

40. Tip-in variation: Player passes the puck from the far side and moves for the tip-in.

41. Tip in drills for young players: Much time can be wasted with young players when they attempt to tip in pucks shot inaccurately from the blueline. A variation for tip in drills can be worked in pairs with one player shooting the puck at the boards and the other player tipping the puck to the boards at certain spots. The shooter should be 15 feet away from the tipper. Change positions every few shots and tip from both sides.

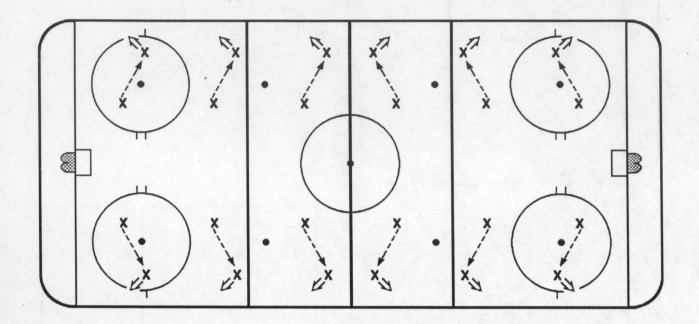

42. Flip shot drill from defensive end: Skate around the net and flip the shot high in the air down the ice. Try not to let the puck go over the goal line. Execute this drill from the backhand and forehand side.

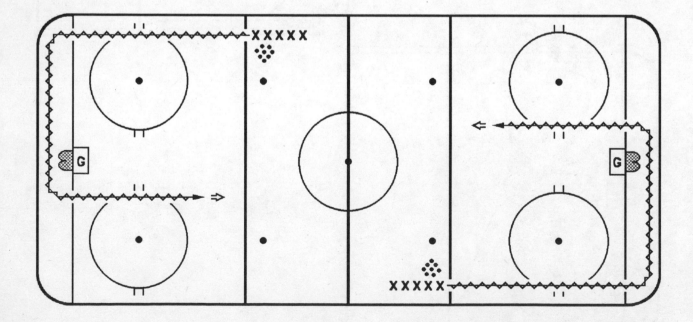

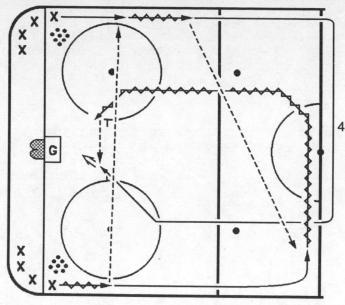

43. Players skate from two corners, pass the puck diagonally across, turn and work a two-on-none. The players return to the opposite corners.

44. Two-on-none: The puck is passed to the player at the blueline. The forward goes behind the net and receives a return pass for the two-on-none.

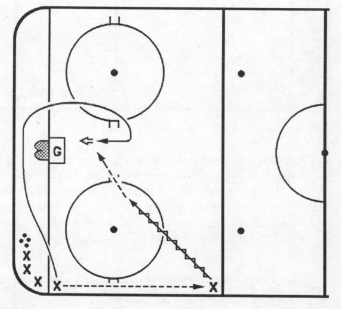

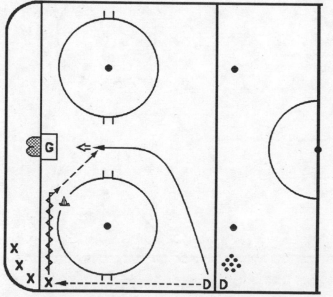

45. Two-on-none: The defenseman passes the puck to the forward. The forward then skates around the pylon and passes to the breaking defenseman for a shot on goal.

46. Flip shot drill for shooting in the offensive end: Skate to centre ice and flip the shot into the offensive end toward the goal or in the corner.

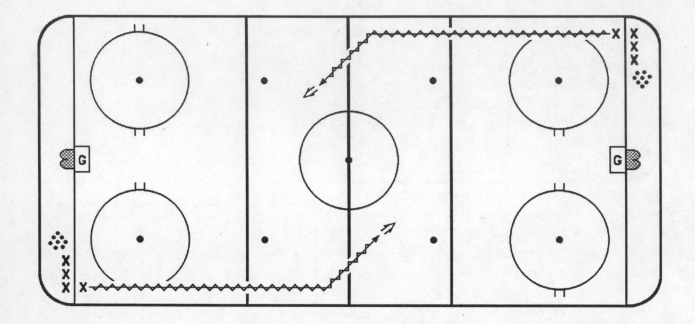

47. The first player shoots and goes to the corner. The second player follows for a rebound and then turns and takes a pass. He skates to the other end and shoots. The person giving the pass follows the shooter for the rebound, turns and takes a pass, skates to the other end and shoots.

NOTE: Combination drills - Combine many types of shooting drills using the entire ice surface, whenever possible. Rotate from group to group. Be innovative.

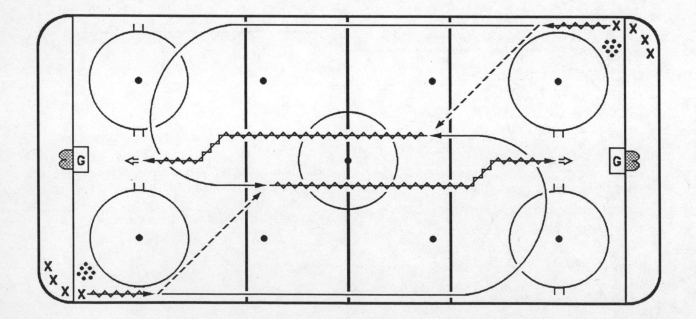

8. STICKHANDLING AND PUCK CONTROL

Stickhandling is important for a one-on-one, manoeuvering at close quarters, or close-in on a goaltender. The puck is passed whenever possible and stickhandling should not be used in open ice or on a breakaway.

METHODS OF STICKHANDLING AND PUCK CONTROL

Remember the following points whenever practising stickhandling and puck control:

Keep the head up. Your peripheral vision allows you to keep the puck in view.

Cup the puck in the centre of the blade, cushioning it while you stickhandle. Be sure to roll your wrists.

Slide the blade of the stick along the ice but do not bang it. There should be little or no noise created by the stick hitting the ice.

Try not to shift the lower hand down as it will tip off the opposition that you are about to change to a shooting position.

Goaltenders should be involved in all stickhandling drills.

SIDE-TO-SIDE STICKHANDLING

Stickhandle with the puck in front of the body and move it from side to side, forehand to backhand.

Be sure your weight is over the top of the puck. That is, if the puck is off to your right, then your body weight should be to the right. The same goes for the other side.

BACK-TO-FRONT STICKHANDLING

This is the same as side-to-side stickhandling except that the puck is moved off to the side of the body.

BACKWARD STICKHANDLING

This is the same as side-to-side and back-to-front stickhandling except you are skating backward.

The puck must be drawn toward the body in the side-to-side action or the player will lose control of it.

This is an essential skill for the defensemen. Remember to keep the head up.

STICKHANDLING WHILE CUTTING IN

The stickhandling principles are the same. Keep the feet moving when turning and try to eliminate gliding.

DRILLS FOR STICKHANDLING

1. **Stationary stickhandling**

   Direct team into three lines, ten feet apart. Have the players watching the instructor's hand.

   If the arm is straight up, stickhandle in front. If the arm is to one side, stickhandle to that side.

2. **Stickhandling while moving**

   Divide three lines ten feet apart. Stickhandle down the ice at half speed. This is a puck control drill and skating speed is not essential.

3. **Stickhandling while stationary and moving**

   Start stickhandling while stationary.

   Move on the command at half speed.

   Stop on command and continue stickhandling in a stationary position.

   Repeat these movements for the length of the ice.

4. **Stickhandling around the rink**

   Players skate around the rink in one direction outside the pylons. Change direction halfway through the drill.

5. **Stickhandle and breakaway**

   Stickhandle to the red line and then push the puck to the goal line, eliminating stickhandling in open ice.

6. **Stickhandling in both directions**

   Two groups: one skates in one direction, the other in the opposite direction. The players must keep their heads up to avoid collisions.

7. **Stickhandling in all directions**

   All the players have pucks and stickhandle in all directions. The ice can be divided in three areas and each group must keep the puck in that area.

8. **Backward stickhandling**

   Drills 1 through 7 can be used while stickhandling backward.

9. **Forward-backward stickhandling**

   Skate forward while stickhandling and then stop and stickhandle while stationary. Then skate backwards while stickhandling. Use a whistle or a verbal command to change direction. This drill can be done in lines across the ice or while the whole group is skating around the ice.

10. **Forward-backward stickhandling**

    Stickhandle forward to the red line, backward to the blueline, forward to the far blueline, backward to the red line, and forward to the end of the rink.

STICKHANDLING DRILLS CHANGING DIRECTION

The following drills are used with pylons.

Pylons in a straight line

Four pylons in each of four lines. Skate through the pylons, first without and then with the pucks.

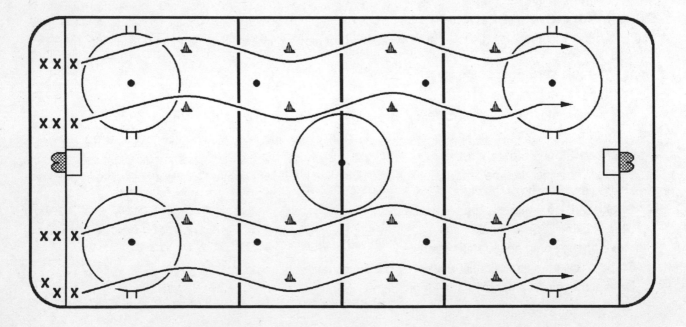

12. Stickhandling while changing directions and using pylons: Player stickhandles forward to the first pylon and then stickhandles backward to the second pylon, etc. Execute the drill without a puck first.

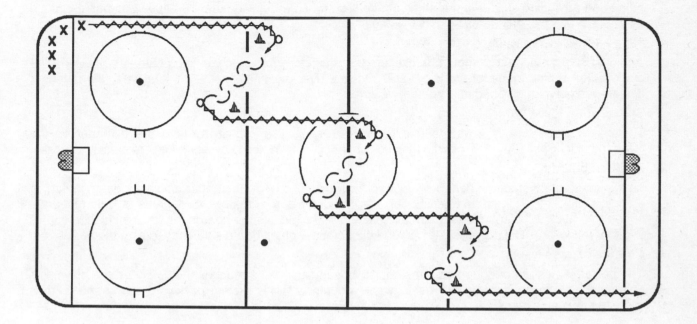

STICKHANDLING AROUND A MAN

It is important that a player knows when to stickhandle and when to pass to beat a man. Many plays are broken up by the defending team when a player attempts to stickhandle around a man instead of passing.

Generally, a player should attempt to stickhandle around a man when he does not have a teammate in a position for a pass, or when the player is in close quarters and a pass cannot be made, or in a one-on-one situation with no trailing teammate. A cardinal sin in hockey is to attempt to stickhandle around a man in your own end of the rink or if you are the last man. Ascertain the defender's speed, direction, whether he is sweeping his stick, looking down at the puck, off balance, reaching slowly, as all of these positions can be taken advantage of. Don't use the same move all the time (i.e. going to backhand side). Analyze the situation and make an appropriate move.

1. **Forehand shift**

   The puck is shifted to the forehand side. The arms are fully extended, the puck is brought out slightly back and away from the defender. Use the body as much as possible to protect the puck. Keep the head up. Speed is important in this move. As the skill is learned, set up the move with a slight move to the backhand and/or a head-and-shoulders fake to the backhand side. As an advanced skill, the lower hand can hold the stick while the upper hand is used to ward off the defender.

2. **Backhand shift**

   The puck is shifted to the backhand side. The arms are extended. The body can be used to protect the puck. The head is up. The move can be set up with a fake to the forehand side.

3. **Slip through**

   The puck is pushed forward between the defender's stick and skates or between the skates. The defender should have slowed down, the head should be down and a large space should be between the legs or between the stick and skates.

4. Slip across

In the slip across, as opposed to the slip through, the puck travels across the forward direction instead of straight ahead. Set this move up by a shift to one side to get the defender to shift weight on that side. The puck is slipped across between the defender's skates and the heel of the stick. The player shifts directions and picks up the puck on the other side of the defender.

5. Double slip across

This is an advanced skill. It is the same as the slip across except the puck is slipped across a second time and ends up on the same side as the original shift.

6. Fake shot (shift to backhand or forehand)

An initial slap or wrist shot motion is executed. A shoulder drop or lower hand side is beneficial. The puck is then shifted to the forehand or backhand side. This move is especially useful when the defender has slowed down or stopped in his defensive zone.

7. Spin around (delay)

The player stops quickly, close to the defender. The puck is kept away from the defender on the forehand side. Spin 180 degrees with the puck on the backhand and accelerate forward quickly or pass.

8. Puck off boards

This is used to advantage when moving out of your own end and a defender, usually a defenseman, is standing still. The puck should be shot off the boards at approximately 45 degrees at only moderate speed (the puck will come off the boards at the same angle it hits the boards (angle of incidence equals angle of reflection). The player skates around the defender on off board side and picks up the puck.

9. Change of pace

The player skates under control at three quarter speed. Just as he reaches the defender, the player accelerates. This move is especially useful when a defenseman is skating backward slowly and there is room to move on either side.

DRILLS FOR STICKHANDLING AROUND A DEFENDER (One-on-One)

1. Stickhandling across the ice against a stationary object: First practise the stickhandling move against a pylon. Next practise stickhandling first against a stationary player without a stick, and then against one with a stick.

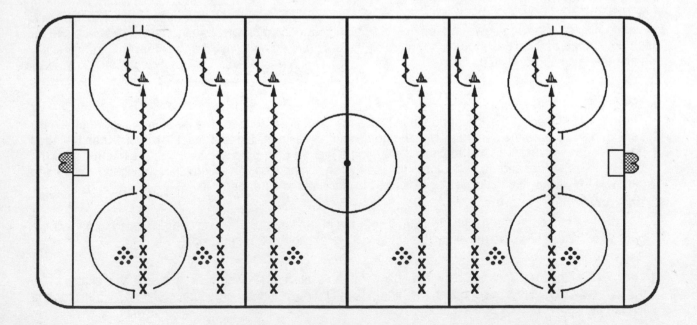

2. Stickhandling across the ice in pairs: One player acts as an attacker and the other acts as a defender. Change positions coming back across the ice. Execute the drill at half speed and passively at first. This allows the player to beat the defender with a move. Execute the drill at full speed. If you have a large number, divide pairs into two groups. One group moves across the ice then the other group follows.

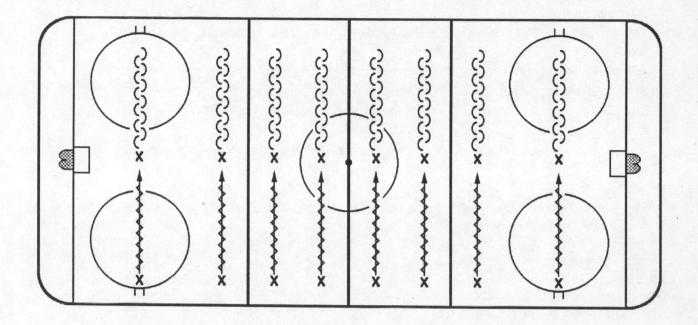

3. One-on-one in both directions: The defender is with the puck on the blueline. The offensive man is at the top of the face-off circle. The defender passes the puck to the offensive player and the one-on-one begins. Change positions moving back in the opposite direction with the forward acting as a defenseman and the defenseman acting as a forward.

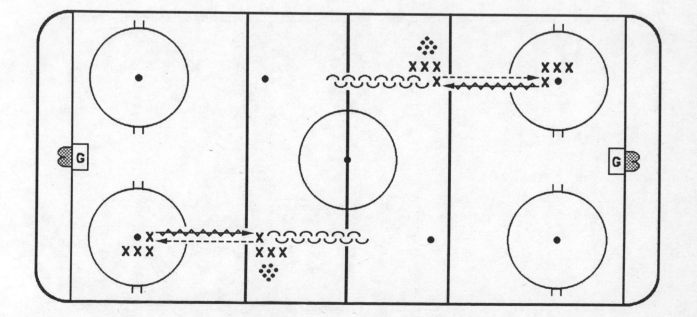

PUCK CONTROL USING THE SKATES

The skill of controlling the puck with the skates is difficult and requires long hours of practise. The Soviets and other European players are highly skilled in this area and make use of soccer for carryover application of this skill. Receiving a pass on the skates is discussed in the Passing and Receiving section

1. **Between skates**

   The puck is passed from one skate to another, always kicking the puck in a forward direction.
2. **Skate to stick**

   The puck is kicked ahead to the stick. Practise with both skates.
3. **Stick to skate to stick** (puck in front of body)

   The puck is passed directly back to skates and returned to stick from skates.
4. **Overskate the puck**

   Deliberately overskate the puck. Bring one skate behind the other and kick the puck up to the other skate. Practise with both skates.
5. **Stick to back skate to stick**

   The puck is drawn back and to the side of the body, then passed back to the back skate. The puck is kicked up as in overskating the puck.

DRILLS FOR PUCK CONTROL USING SKATES

1. Skate around the ice at slow speed practising various skills.
2. Skate around the ice at high speed practising various skills.
3. Skate the length of the ice practising skills.
4. Skate around the pylons using only the skates to control the puck.
5. Divide into three groups and divide ice into three sections. Have three games with the players not using sticks. A team scores by holding the puck against the opposite side boards.

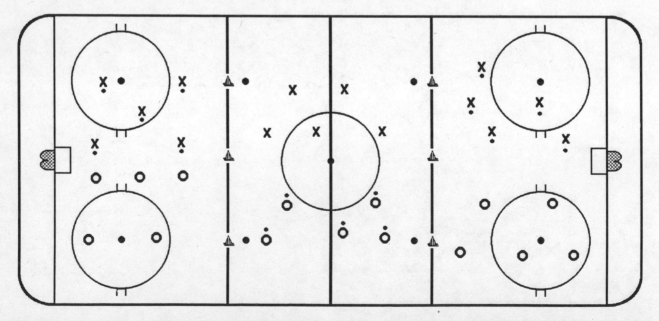

Soccer, ball hockey, lacrosse, etc. are all helpful for stickhandling and puck control. Kicking a ball on the ground is also helpful. The Europeans make great use of off-ice drills and games to develop these skills.

DEKING THE GOALTENDER

When a player breaks in alone on a goaltender, he must decide whether to deke the goaltender or shoot. When the goaltender is far out in the crease, this is an ideal time to deke the goaltender. Do not telegraph your moves by dropping your head or shoulder, or slipping your lower hand down the shaft to indicate a shot. Make your move quickly.

TYPES OF DEKES ON THE GOALTENDER

1. **Backhand shift**

   This was described previously. The puck is moved completely around the goaltender.

2. **Forehand shift**

   This was described previously. The puck is moved completely around the goaltender.

3. **Half backhand shift**

   The puck is shifted to the backhand side and then slipped between the goaltender's legs.

4. **Half forehand shift**

   The puck is shifted to forehand side and then slipped between goaltender's legs.

5. **Backhand - forehand shift**

   The puck is moved to the backhand side and then quickly moved to the forehand side. This manouver is effective when the goaltender moves with the first shift.

6. **Forehand - backhand shift**

   This is the opposite to 5

7. **Backhand drag**

   The player approaches the goaltender on his backhand side at a sharp angle. The player starts to cut across the front of the net. The puck is dragged behind with the top hand only on the stick and the puck is slipped in on the short side by the post.

8. **Fake shot and shift**

   Fake the shot to one side by dipping shoulder. Shift to the other side when goaltender makes a move.

DRILL

1. Breakaway drill: Line up players in three lines and break in on the goaltender. Have the players switch lines as they come back.

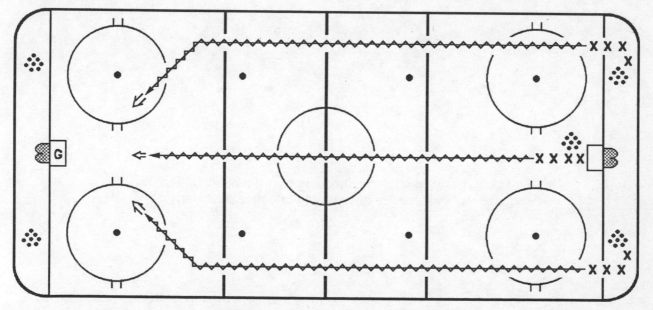

**It is important in all body checking that the head be kept up.
Agility and balance are essential to effective checking.**

9. CHECKING

Checking is a very important aspect of hockey and in many cases it is neglected in practice sessions. Play-off hockey puts stress on checking but the skills of checking should be used in every game.

METHODS OF CHECKING

USE OF STICK

In all stick checking, the checker should watch the man, not the puck.

1. **Poke check**

   The poke check is often used by defensemen in a one-on-one situation or with a forechecking forward. Goaltenders use this skill in some situations. The elbow of the arm holding the stick is bent and close to the side. The head is up and one hand is on the stick. This move must be used when the opponent is in close quarters. The arm holding the stick extends quickly. Keep the body in a stable position and don't lunge at the opponent. The arm and blade of the stick do the checking. Hold the stick in until the opponent is in close range.

2. **Stick lift**

   Approach the puck carrier from behind and to the side of the puck. Lift the opponent's stick at the shaft near the heel of the stick. Take possession of the puck. Upper body strength is important in this move.

3. **Stick press**

   Press the stick down over the opponent's stick or lower arm. The approach is the same as the stick lift. Upper body strength is also important in this move.

4. **Sweep check**

   The checker approaches the puck carrier from the front in a semi-crouched position. The stick is swept in a flat position to knock the puck from the offensive player's stick. The head is kept up in anticipation of a body check if the sweep check fails.

5. **Hook check**

   The hook check should be used only when the puck carrier cannot be fully overtaken. Approach the puck carrier from behind with one hand on the stick. Go down on the inside knee, extend the arm holding the stick after obtaining the puck. The weight is on the other skate so a quick pivot can be made. Turn the blade of the stick flat on the ice towards the puck and hook the puck back. Regain balance, get up off the knee, and resume skating stride.

6. **Diving poke check**

   This check is used as a last resort when the offensive player is in a breakaway situation. Skate as closely behind the player as possible and keep inside of puck carrier and approach from an angle. Leave the feet in a diving motion when the offensive player reaches 30-40 feet from the net. Extend the arms and put the stick flat on the ice. Aim the stick and body at or ahead of the offensive player's stick and attempt to knock the puck away. Do not knock the opponent's feet away, as this could cause a tripping penalty or penalty shot.

BODY CHECKING

It is important in all body checking that the head is up and the eyes are on the opponent's chest area, not on the puck. Getting the proper handle and speed when checking an opponent will allow an opponent to be taken out of the play regardless of size. Agility and balance, including lateral and backward skating ability, are essential in good checking.

1. **Shoulder check**

   A player should be able to use either shoulder. The point of the shoulder hits the opponent's chest. Knees are bent and extend on contact. The skates are turned outward and dig in, shoulder width apart. The drive is off the back leg. One hand is on the stick with the other flexed to the side. The hand is close to the body to prevent injury. The push is up and through on contact. Keep the head up and don't commit too early. Watch for an opponent with his head down. This is a good time for the shoulder check.

2. **Riding the man out of the play**

This check is used mainly along the boards. The checker stays between the offensive man and the goal and is even with or slightly ahead of the man. Body contact is made with the side of the upper body and hips. If possible, extend the inside arm across the body of the offensive man. Cut the offensive man off and angle him toward the boards. Ride the man off and go for the puck.

3. **Hip check**

This is used mainly by defensemen along the boards. When mastered, it is an effective mid-ice check. The check is started by skating backward, usually one hand on the stick. Pivot and push off the far side foot and move into a low crouch position. Swing the hips at 90 degree angle and drive sideways into the puck carrier. Timing is extremely important in this skill.

4. **Back checking**

Back checking is an essential skill for all forwards. It assists the defensemen by allowing them to stay up and force the play. The back checker should stay at least one stride ahead of the offensive man and within a stick's length away. The man, as well as the puck, should be watched using peripheral vision. The checker should not let the offensive player get ahead of him. As the man moves closer to the goal move tight with the opponent's forward progress. Always stay on the wing and do not chase a puck carrier into the centre area and leave your check, as the defensemen will pick up the centre area.

FORECHECKING (One-on-one)

Forechecking is an important defensive skill and can also become an offensive skill if possession of the puck is gained in a scoring position. The forechecker must always keep his head up and play the man, then go for the puck. The stick may be held in one hand in order to poke the puck away. Angle the man toward the boards and cut off his skating space. Do not approach the offensive man straight on. Do not chase the man behind the net unless you are very close to him. Agility is important. A good forechecker can stop quickly, change direction, pivot, skate backward, sweep, and poke check effectively.

TAKING A CHECK

It is important that all hockey players be able to take a body check to prevent injury or to recover quickly to get back into the play. When an opponent is moving toward a player to body check, the player taking the check can tense his muscles and gain momentum by moving toward him. As momentum equals mass times velocity, the smaller the player the more important speed is in head on contact. It is important to spread the body check force over a large area against the boards. Consequently the whole body should be against the boards and the body should give on contact and spring off the boards from the check. Keep in a semi-crouch position and do not use the hand or wrist to cushion a blow. Learn to fall properly, quickly regain your feet, and start skating again.

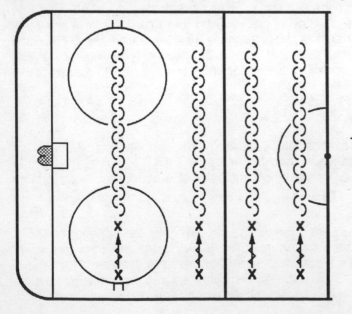

DRILLS

1. One-on-one drill moving across the ice: Use the various types of stick and body checks. Work at half speed passively and then work at full speed. Use the full length of the ice.

2. One-on-one drill using the length of the ice: Same as one-on-one drill moving across the ice (1), except there is no more space to maneouver. Players switch from offense to defense.

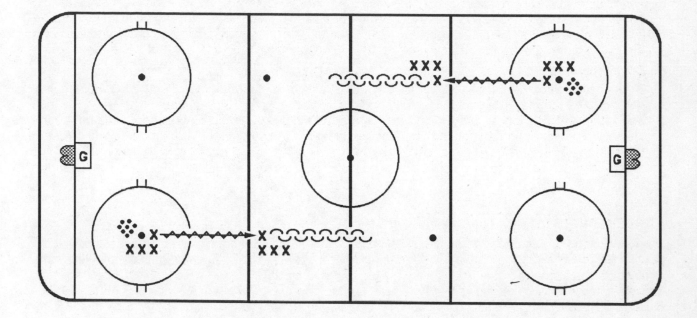

3. One-on-one swing drill: The forward (X) skates to the far blueline, turns and receives a pass from the opposite side. The defenseman (D) skates forward around the centre circle and turns backward. The forward goes one-on-one against that defenseman. The player who passes the puck then goes around the centre circle and turns backward. The forward starting beside him skates inside the far blueline and takes a pass from the defenseman.

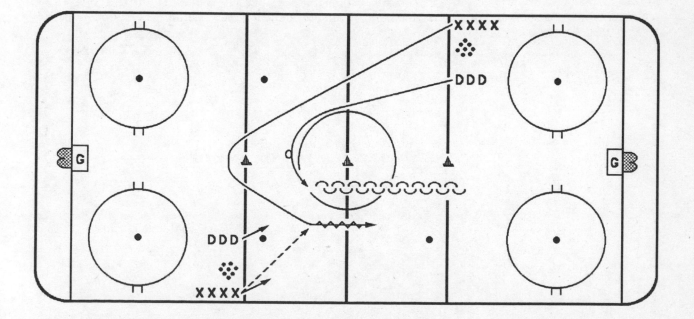

4. Checking the player stopped behind the net: The puck carrier carries the puck behind the net and stops. The checker stops in front of the net. The puck carrier then moves to either side and the checker moves with him. The puck carriers then become the checkers and the checkers become the puck carriers.

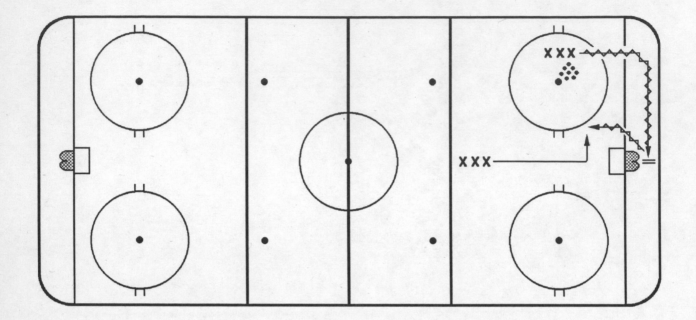

5. Checking the player moving behind the net: Same as 4 except the puck carrier does not stop behind the net and moves out the far side. The checker moves in at an angle and attempts to force the puck carrier to the corner.

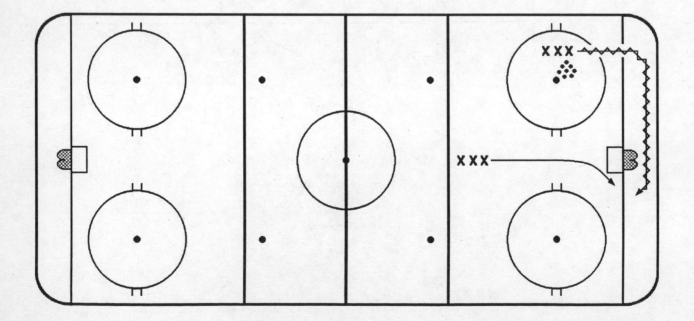

6. Checking the winger: On a command, the winger starts down the boards with the checker starting slightly behind. The winger receives a pass from a centre, cuts around the pylon, and moves in on the goaltender. The checker stays on the inside of the pylon and attempts to check the winger. The drill is worked in both directions.

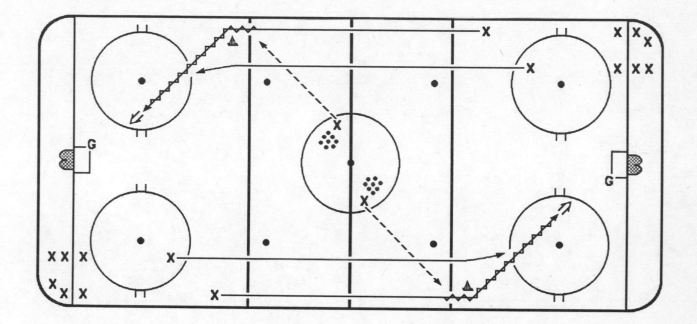

7. Chase the rabbit: The puck carrier says "go" and skates to the outside of the pylon the length of the ice and shoots with the checker starting two steps behind him and to the inside of the pylon.

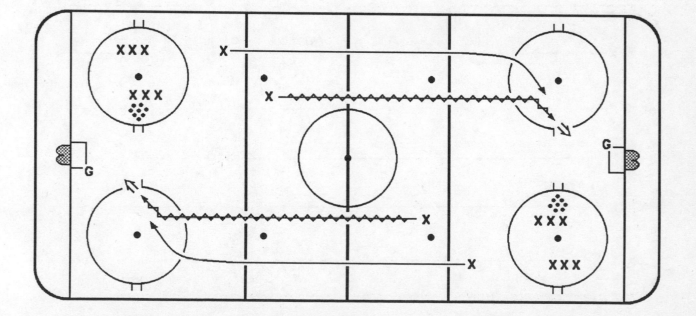

8. Work in pairs around the boards taking and giving a body check.

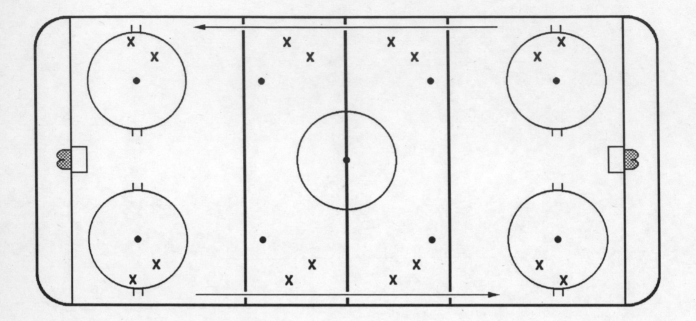

9. Practise falling front rolls, side rolls, falling to one knee and recovering the skating stride. Do a different manoeuver between each set of lines.

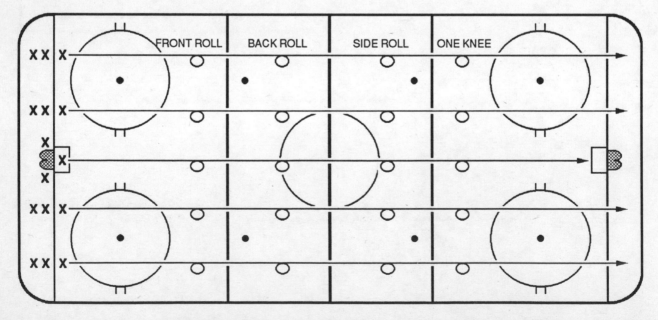

FRONT ROLL   BACK ROLL   SIDE ROLL   ONE KNEE

10. Diving poke check drill: Practice leaving the feet and diving at an angle at a puck carrier in the clear cutting in from the wing. (Not Shown)

10. OFFENSIVE TEAM PLAY

Offensive play begins when a team gains possession of the puck in its own end. Offensive play can be divided into three catergories:

1. Moving the puck out of the defensive zone (breakout).
2. Moving through the neutral zone.
3. Playing in the offensive zone (attack).

MOVING THE PUCK OUT OF THE DEFENSIVE ZONE

The following are standard methods of moving the puck from the defensive zone when the puck is shot in by the opposition or possession is gained by the defensive team, usually by the defensemen.

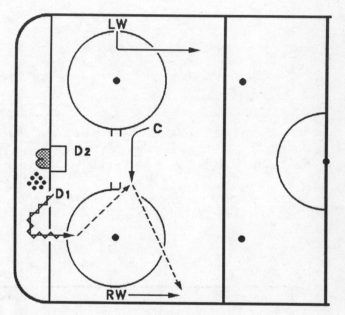

1. The defenseman turns quickly with the puck. D1 can pass to the centre, right wing, or carry the puck himself. If D1 passes to the centre, the centre then makes a quick pass to the winger. The wingers move as soon as the defenseman turns with the puck and the centre cuts across in position for a pass.

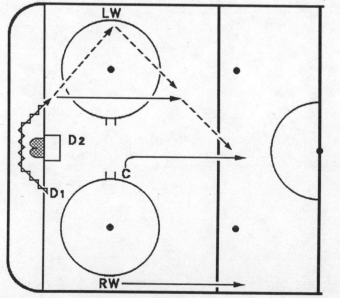

2. The defenseman skates behind the net without stopping. D1 passes to the winger. who in turn passes the puck to the centre, who has curled and is starting to break up ice.

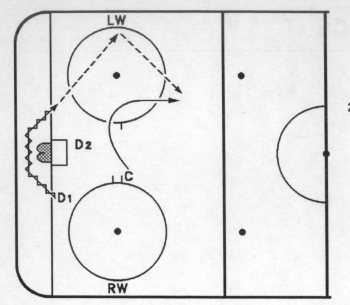

2A. The defenseman skates behind the net without stopping. D1 passes to the winger who returns the pass to the defenseman on a give and go. The centre cuts straight up the middle of the ice. The winger takes the position of the defenseman after he returns the pass.

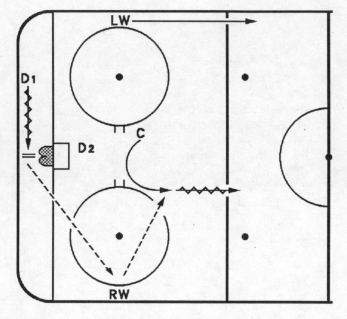

3. The defenseman stops behind the net. D1 passes to the winger. The winger passes to the centre. D2 stations himself in front of the net.

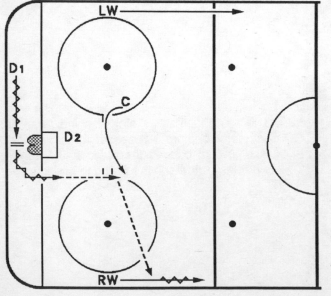

3A. D1 passes to the centre. The centre passes to the winger. D2 is in front of the net.

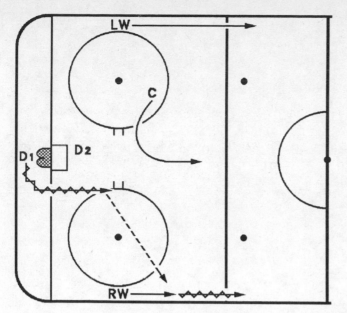

3B. D1 carries the puck and passes it to the winger or the centre. D2 trails the play.

4. D2 moves to the corner when D1 is in full possession of the puck. The winger moves up the boards. D1 passes to D2. D2 passes to the centre. The centre passes to the wing.

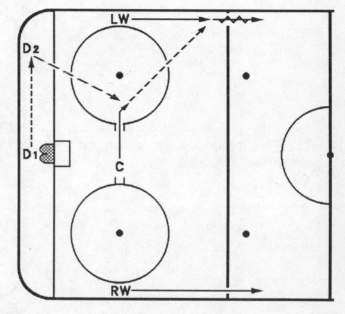

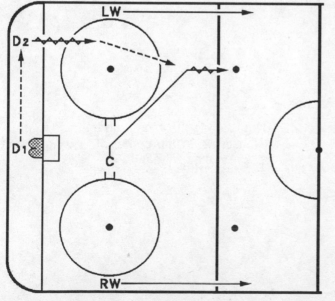

4A. D1 passes to D2. D2 skates with the puck and then passes to the centre or the winger.

93

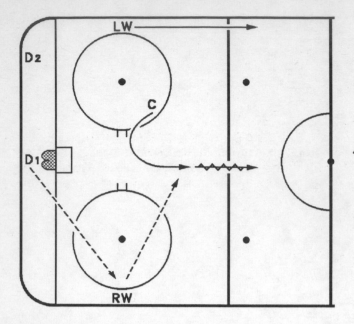

4B. D1 passes to the offside winger, who passes to the centre.

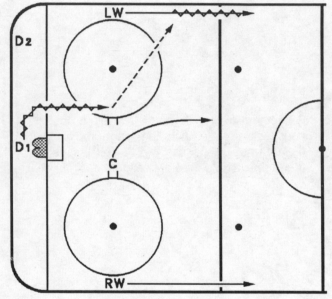

4C. D1 carries the puck up the centre of the ice and then passes to the winger.

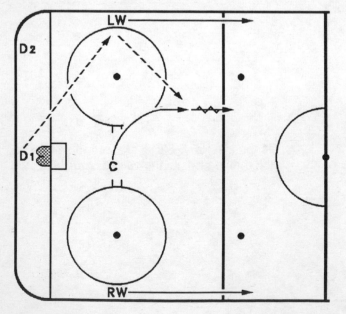

4D. D1 passes to the winger on the side with the defenseman in the corner. The winger then passes to the centre.

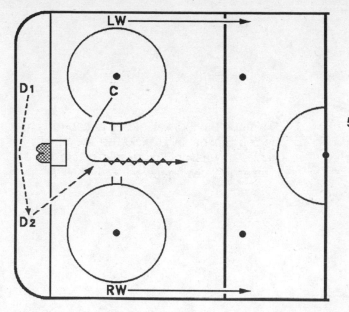

5. The defenseman passes the puck off the boards to the other defenseman. D1 passes the puck off the boards to D2. D2 passes the puck to the centre. The centre passes the puck to the winger.

5A. D1 passes the puck off the boards to D2. D2 passes the puck to the winger. The winger passes the puck to the centre.

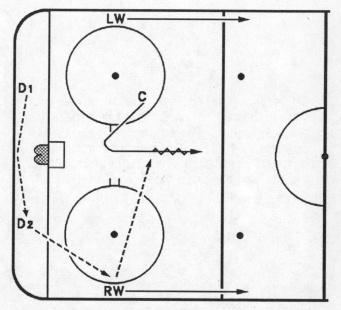

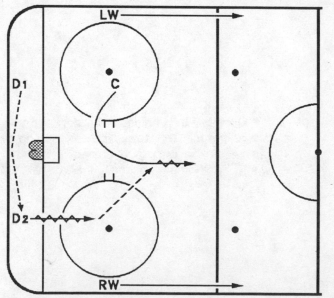

5B. D1 passes the puck off the boards to D2. D2 skates with the puck and then passes to the centre or winger.

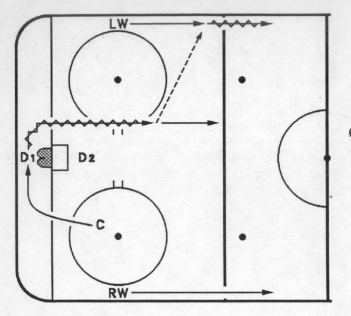

6. D1 stops behind the net. The centre comes behind the net and picks up the puck. The centre moves up the middle of the ice and passes to the winger.

6A. D1 stops behind the net. The centre swings wide to the corner and drops the puck back to the defensemen. The winger on the puck side pulls off the boards. The centre moves up the wing. D1 passes to the winger coming off the boards or passes to the centre, or D1 can carry the puck.

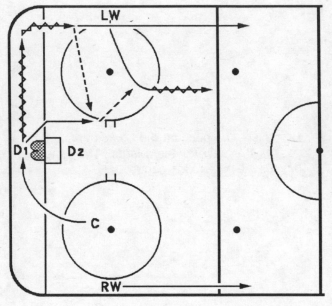

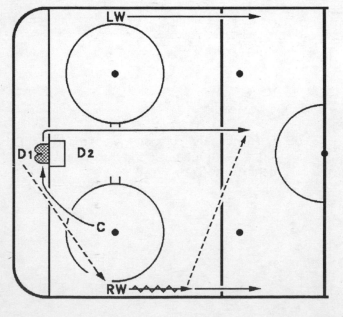

6B. D1 stops behind the net. The centre circles behind the net. D1 allows the centre to go by but keeps the puck and passes it to either winger. The winger passes to the centre.

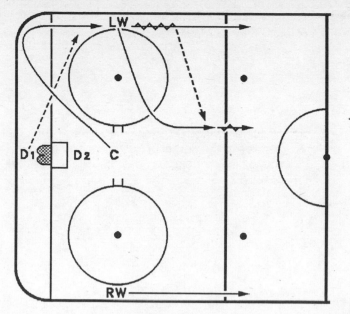

7. D1 stops behind the net. The centre circles to the corner and the winger on the puck side cuts across to the middle area of the ice. D1 passes to the centre. The centre passes to the winger in the middle area of the ice.

7A. D1 stops behind the net. The centre circles to the corner and the winger on the puck side pulls off the boards to the middle area of the ice. D1 passes to this winger.

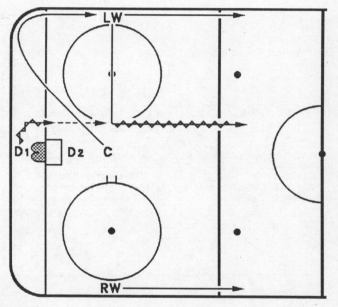

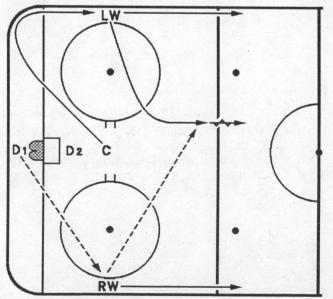

7B. D1 stops behind the net. The centre circles to the corner and the winger on the puck side pulls off the boards and moves to the middle area of the ice. D1 passes to the offside winger, who passes to the other winger.

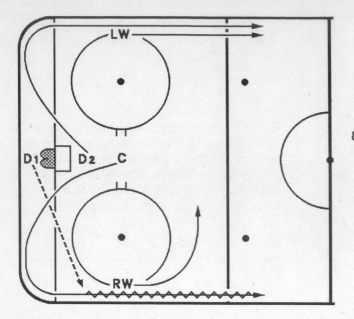

8. Double swing: D1 stops behind the net. D2 moves to the corner. The centre swings to the opposite corner. D1 passes to D2 or the centre.

9. Around the boards: The defenseman shoots the puck around the boards and the winger picks the puck up on the move. This play is usually used from a face-off or when the puck has been shot directly in the corner and the defenseman is being chased.

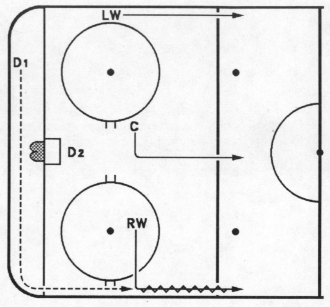

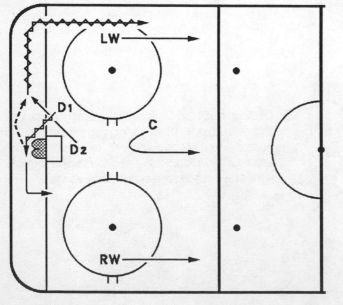

10. Defense reverse: D1 carries the puck behind the net and is being chased by a forechecker. D1 drops the puck back to D2, who has moved from his position from in front of the net. The defenseman in front of the net always calls the reverse.

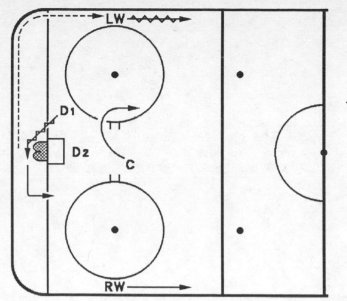

11. Reverse to the winger: Same as the defense reverse except the defenseman passes the puck back to the winger who is stationed at the hash marks. The puck is passed on the ice along the boards. The winger should not be too high up on the boards. He can receive the pass moving or standing still.

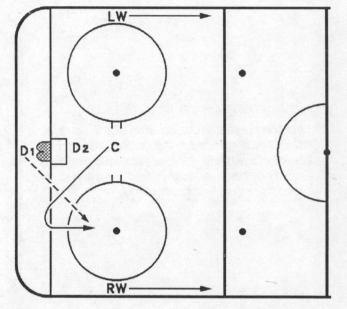

12. The centre tight turn: The centre makes a tight turn at the goal line. The defenseman passes the puck to the centre.

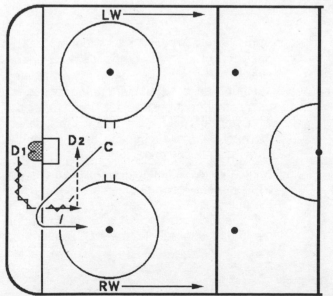

13. Variation of the centre tight turn: Same drill as 12 except instead of passing puck to centre, defenseman moves out from behind the net and passes to the other defenseman. This pass must be made with caution.

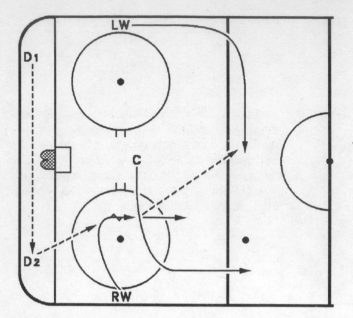

14. The centre and winger cross: D1 passes to D2. The offside winger goes high and cuts across the middle outside the blueline.

MOVING OUT OF YOUR OWN END

1. Line the players up by position at the blueline. The puck is shot in by the centre and the first player in each line moves in to bring the puck out. The coach designates the method of bringing the puck out of the end.

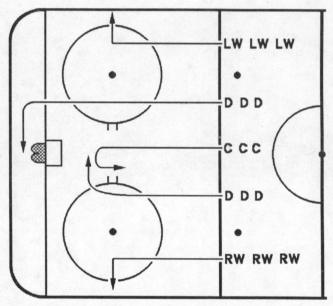

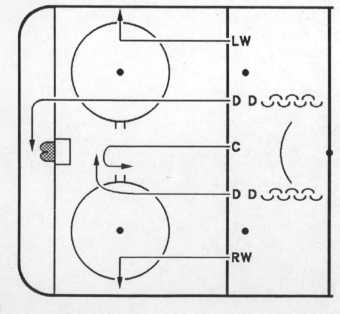

2. Same as in 1 except the breakout progresses offensively the length of the ice as a five-on-two. When the offensive play is completed, another breakout starts from the opposite end using another offensive line. The defense pair who start the play follow it down the ice and then act defensively for the next five-on-two from the opposite end.

A variation of the offensive play can be done by having the forwards pass the puck back to the points if a direct play is not made on the net. The forwards should go to the front of the net to deflect or screen the shot coming from the point.

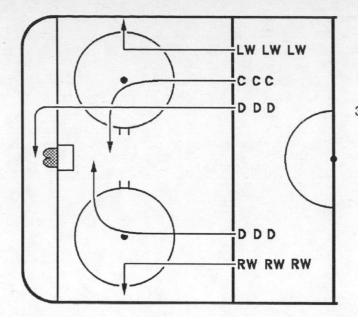

LW LW LW

C C C

D D D

D D D

RW RW RW

3. The players line up in lines and defense pairs against the boards outside the blueline. The centres line up on the boards with either wing. Lines and defense pairs go in order and the puck is shot into the defensive zone by the coach. The coach states the method of bringing the puck out of the end.

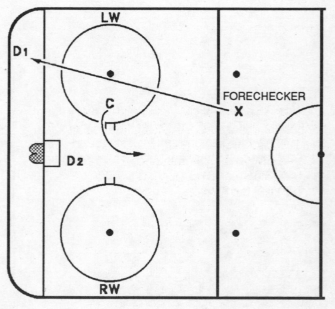

LW

D1

C

FORECHECKER

X

D2

RW

4. Execute drills 1 and 3 with one forechecker moving on the puck.

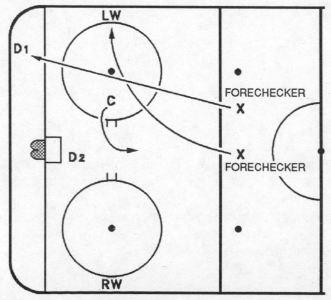

LW

D1

C

FORECHECKER

X

D2

X
FORECHECKER

RW

5. Execute drills 1 and 3 with two forecheckers moving into the zone.

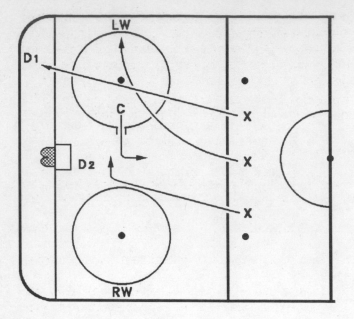

6. Execute drills 1 and 3 with a complete forward line forechecking.

7. Work five-on-five drills with one team forechecking and the other team attempting to bring the puck out of their own end. Each team has a forward line and two defensemen. The puck is shot in by the forechecking team from the red line.

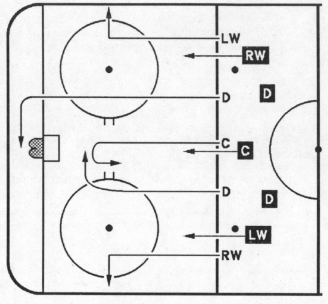

PLAY IN THE NEUTRAL ZONE

Neutral zone regroup has been used extensively by European teams to take full advantage of their wide ice surface. More recently, North American teams have adopted this system of play.

The Soviets were probably the first to make use of the neutral zone by devising special plays for that area. Now, it's a major part of the game for all European teams and successful North American teams.

The neutral zone regroup is used offensively when a team is unable to penetrate the opposition's blueline. Instead of shooting the puck in, the offensive team keeps possession by turning back, passing the puck to the defence and regrouping to attack the opposition's blueline again.

After passing back to their defence, the three forwards swing back up ice, going for open space and gaining speed for another attack.

While the Soviets are now varying their system by shooting the puck over the blueline more than they used to, the regroup is still a major part of their game, especially on their own side of centre ice.

Because it represents a change from straight line hockey, there may be some confusion if the neutral zone regroup, which involves swinging across the ice rather than staying strictly in lanes, is not practised first. Players have to learn to switch with their linemates so they don't all end up in one part of the ice, leaving one or more lanes wide open. They have to find the right timing, so that they swing and regroup as a unit, ready for a quick, simultaneous attack from a good position.

It's an organized system rather than a chaotic, every-man-for-himself scramble across the ice. Once mastered, it can be used by almost any team provided the defensemen are fairly adept at handling the puck and passing well.

These are the principles of practising the neutral zone regroup:

- Pass the puck back to the defense. The receiver then passes across to his defense partner. They should be positioned so that they are slightly staggered, with one deeper in the defensive zone than his partner.
- As the puck is passed back to the defense, the forwards move to open ice by swinging back toward the defense.
- The forwards must skate under control with their sticks on the ice, getting themselves into position for a pass. They should fill all three lanes of the ice.
- If a forward is not open for a pass and the defense cannot move the puck up immediately, the man in possession should make a return pass to his defense partner. The forwards must then swing back again to be in position to receive a pass.
- Assuming the defense receives the pass back at the defensive blueline, the three forwards should cover the following areas: near the defense; mid-ice; past mid-ice.
- If no forward is open for a pass, the defensemen should move forward with the puck themselves.

The following progressive drills can be used to teach the neutral zone regroup. The objective is to initiate the player to the idea of swinging across the ice from his wing and regrouping with his linemates for an organized attack. This sounds simple enough but may not be a natural move for someone schooled in the straight-line, up-and-down-the-wings approach to hockey. Note: these are progressive teaching drills with no checking involved at this stage.

1. Forward swing: Players, including defensemen, line up along the boards. On the whistle, the first man in the line skates down the wing, swings inside the offensive blueline, receives a pass from the first player in the other line and moves down to the other end for a shot on the goaltender. He then returns to the back of the line from which he started, while the first player in the other line takes his turn.

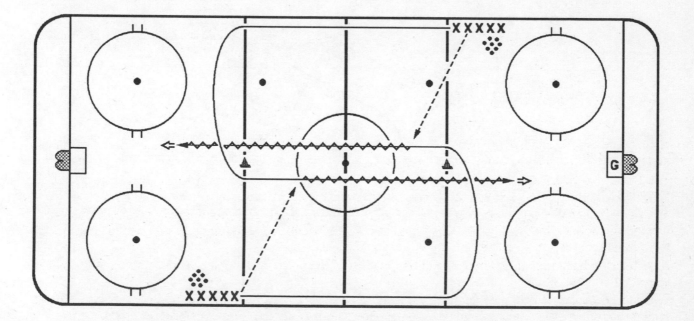

2. Forward passes back to the defense and swings: Same as drill 1 except two defensemen are included. They don't check but receive and give passes. They should be staggered with one deeper in the defensive zone than the other.The first forward skates across the blueline, passes the puck to the near defenseman who then relays it across to his partner. The forward swings either in front or behind the first defenseman and up centre ice to take a return pass from the other defenseman. He then goes up for a shot on goal. Drill continues, each side going in turn.

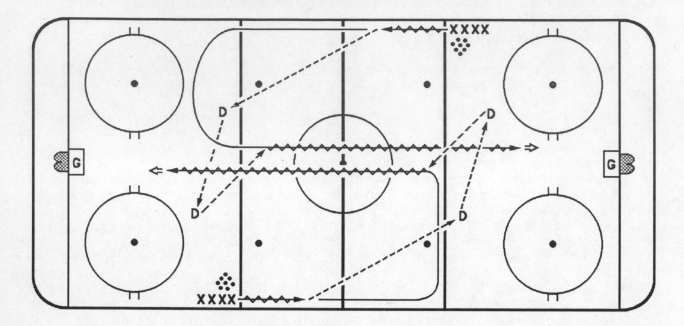

3. Two forwards swing from the same side: This teaches forwards to swing together so they don't interfere with each other. Each must look for open ice rather than bunching together. The first two men come down the wing and swing across, one in front of D, the other behind. The first forward passes the puck to D who then relays it to his partner. The forward takes the return pass and goes up ice with his teammate for a shot on goal. If his teammate goes wide, he should go up the centre; if the teammate chooses centre, he should swing wide.

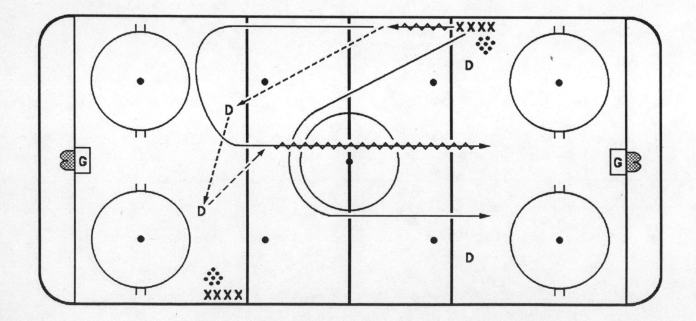

4. Two forwards swing from opposite sides: This is the same as drill 3 except the two forwards swing from opposite sides of the rink. One swings near the defense or behind it, the other swings in the centre ice area. Alternate coming from one end and then the other.

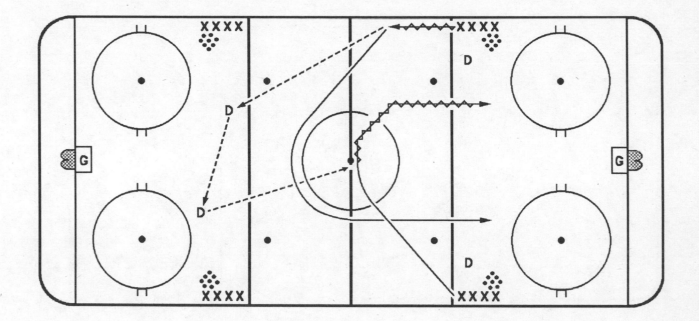

5. Three forwards swing, two from one side, one from the other: This drill combines 3 and 4, using three forwards. They should cover the areas near or behind the defense, the centre line, and the far blueline. Alternate ends.

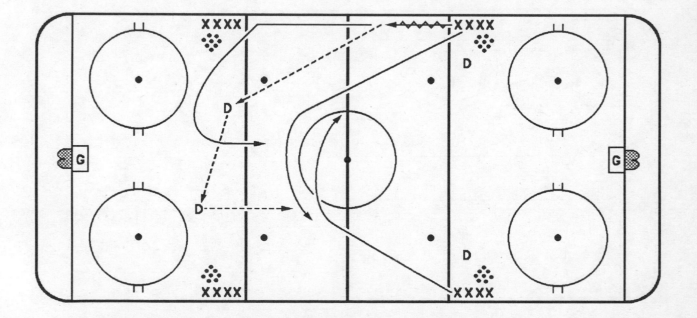

6. Neutral zone regroup, attack the goal twice: Three forwards start at the blueline, pass the puck to the defense, swing, and receive a return pass. They skate to the far blueline, pass the puck to the defense, regroup, receive a return pass, and attack the goal, three-on-none. They then return to the starting point. Forwards should try to find open ice so they're not all jamming the same area at the same time.

Remember: Depth is a factor. Swing so that zones near the defense, mid-ice and past mid-ice are covered.

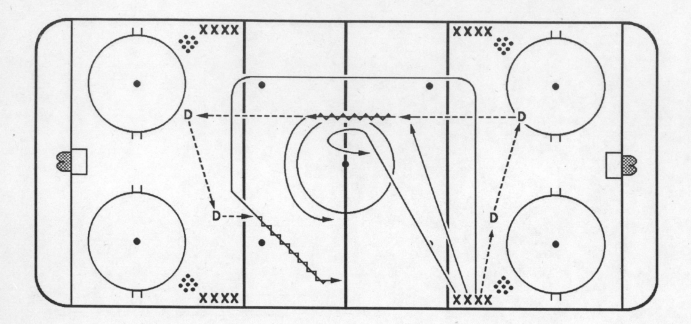

7A. Break-out: There are now five players (three forwards and two defensemen) working as a unit. The forwards dump the puck in from outside the blueline. The defense retrieves it and they all break out, five on two, using whatever system the team has been practising. Drill continues in (7B).

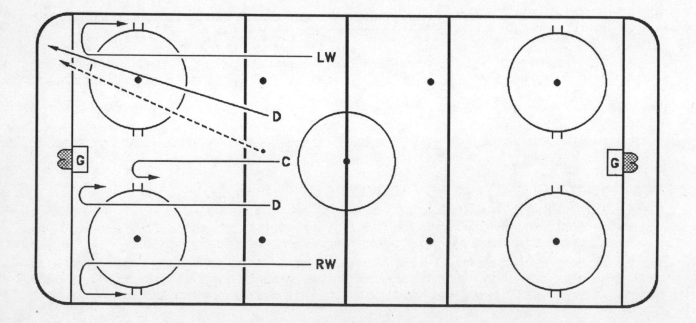

7B. Neutral zone regroup, second neutral zone regroup, attack the goal three-on-two: When the forwards reach the far defense, they pass to them instead of attacking, as they did in drill 6, and regroup with that defense pair. This is the first regroup. Meanwhile, the first defense pair has skated back into position for a five-on-two attack by the group that now has the puck. When the forwards reach the blueline, they again pass to the defence and regroup again. This is the second regroup. The forwards now skate down to attack the goal three-on-two, and the next group starts from the other end.

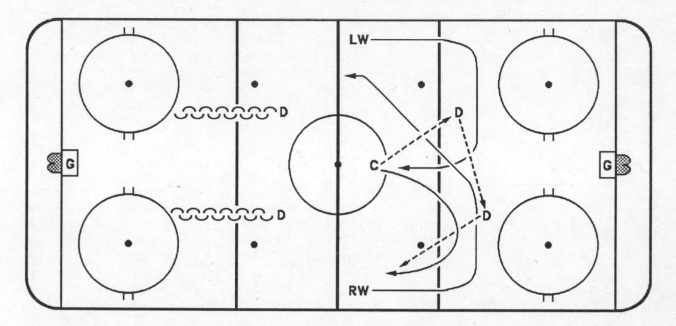

When they have mastered all these drills, the coach can set up a scrimmage in which they try to use the neutral zone regroup whenever it is appropriate; that is, when they can't carry or pass the puck across the opponent's blueline. Instead of dumping the puck in, they swing back, regroup and attack again.

To make sure the neutral zone regroup is done correctly, watch for the following points:

- When players swing, they should skate for open ice. Make sure they fill all three lanes.

- Players should think about what they are doing and be under control. It's not a helter-skelter skate across the ice. They have to try to get into position to receive a pass.

- Although the players may swing out of their lanes, the lanes still have to be filled. This means they have to be ready to alternate, i.e., if the centre moves over to the wing, that winger should move into the centre, etc.

- During the regroup, players should also cover different depths in the neutral zone, as we pointed out earlier (near the defense, mid-ice, past mid-ice). This adds a dimension to the regroup systems and requires each player to read and react quickly to what his linemates are doing.

PLAY FROM THE NEUTRAL ZONE INTO THE OFFENSIVE ZONE
(Basic three-on-two plays)

Plays made by the offensive team into the offensive zone are usually made from the neutral zone just as the play approaches the opposition's blueline. The play then continues until a scoring opportunity.

The basic concept in offensive team play is that one forward should be driving for the net at all times to create an opening or to draw a defenseman with him. The forward, other than the puckcarrier and the driving man, should trail the play. This is sometimes referred to as the one-two-three principle.

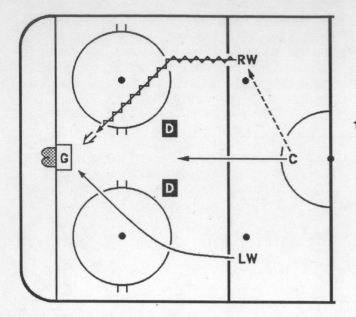

1. The centre passes to the winger. who cuts around the defenseman and shoots. The offside winger cuts to the far post for a rebound. The centre trails the play in the high slot area.

2. The centre passes to the winger. The centre trails the play slightly to the side of the puck carrier. The winger goes wide to take the defenseman over. The winger passes the puck back to the centre who either shoots, or passes to the other winger who shoots.

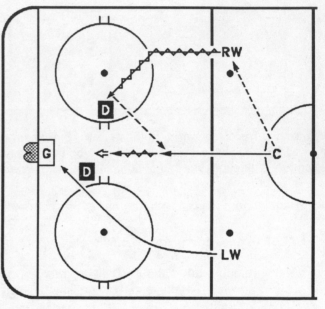

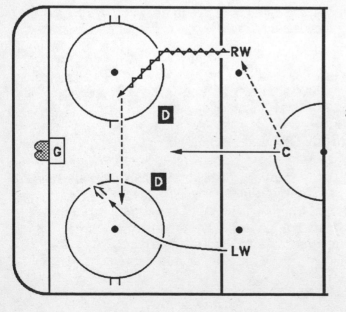

3. The centre passes to the winger. The winger cuts behind the defenseman and passes across to the opposite winger. The opposite winger shoots. This play works well if the opposition defensemen are well out toward the blueline.

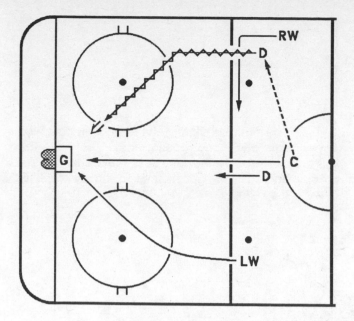

4. The winger, ahead of the play, skates parallel to the blueline. The defenseman on the winger's side moves quickly up the boards. The centre passes to the defenseman. The defenseman cuts in and shoots or drops the puck back to the trailing centre who shoots. The left winger goes to the net for a rebound.

5. The centre passes to the winger and the winger cuts wide and goes behind the net. The centre trails the play and moves to the slot area. The winger passes to the centre who then shoots.

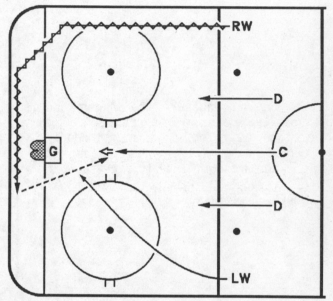

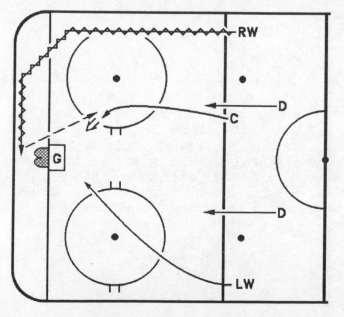

6. The winger drives hard behind the net and passes the puck back on the same side. The trailing forward tries to shoot quickly as the goalie tends to move from the post because he believes the winger is continuing behind the net with the puck.

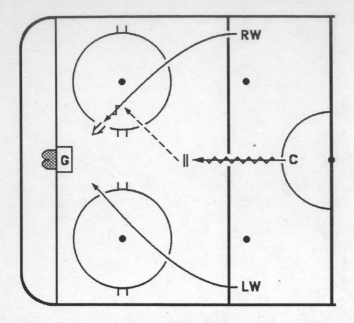

7. The centre is slightly ahead of the winger who cuts wide and goes behind the net. The centre trails the play and moves to the slot area. The winger passes to the centre, who then shoots.

8. The centre is ahead of the wingers when crossing the blueline. The centre cuts across to either wing. The winger on that side cuts behind the centre. The centre drops the puck back to the winger. The winger passes to the offside winger, who is cutting for the net. The offside winger shoots.

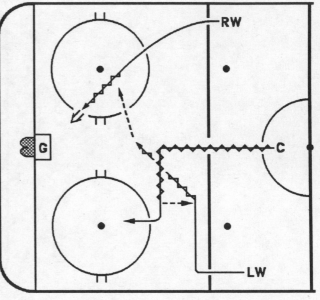

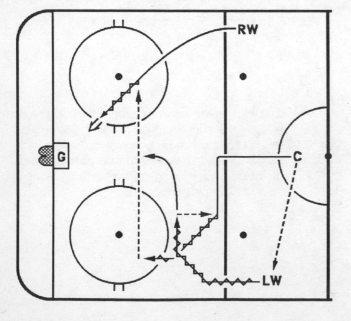

9. The winger cuts across over the blueline. The winger takes a pass from the centre and cuts toward the middle of the ice in front of the defenseman. The centre cuts behind the winger and is in a position to go wide with a return pass. The offside winger may cut wide or cut toward the centre of the ice.

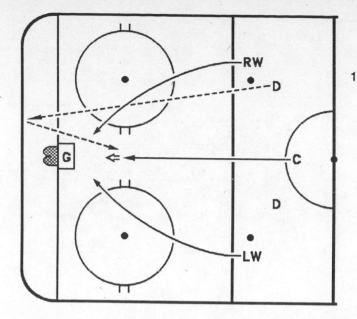

SHOOTING THE PUCK IN

10A. The puck is shot off the end boards: This play is used when the wingers are covered and a play cannot be made or if one offensive player is breaking quickly and can beat the defenseman to the puck. As an offensive play, it is imperative to gain control of the puck after it has been shot into the offensive end.

The centre or winger shoots the puck off the end boards. The centre and the winger on the puck side go for the rebound off the boards. The offside winger trails the play and moves into the high slot area.

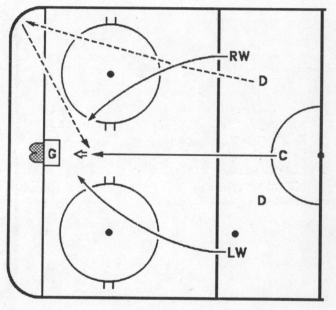

10B. The puck is shot in the corner: The centre or winger shoots the puck into the corner at an angle such that the puck will come out in front of the net. The centre goes for the slot area. The offside winger cuts to the front of the net.

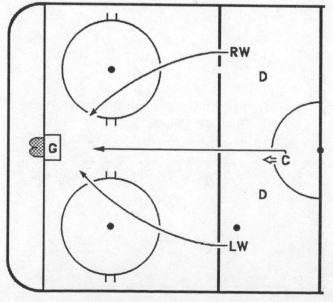

10C. The puck is shot at the net: The centre or winger shoots the puck at the goaltender, preferably a bounce shot to allow the forwards time to move in. The centre moves straight in. The wingers cut in for the goal posts looking for a rebound.

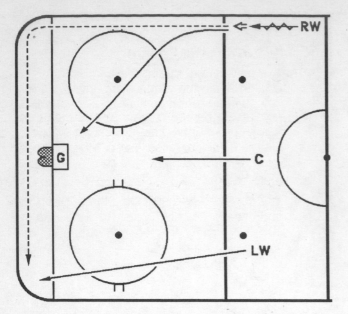

11. Rim the boards: The forward gets over the offensive blueline near the boards and shoots the puck around the rim of the boards to the far corner. The forward on the far side moves directly to the corner to pick up the puck. The puck should be shot hard and about one foot off the ice to prevent the opposition goaltender from stopping it behind the net.

12. Delay: The forward skates hard into the offensive zone and then does a tight turn (delay) and passes off or then drives again for the net.

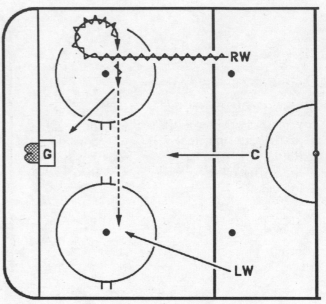

THE PUCK IN THE OFFENSIVE CORNER "OFFENSIVE TRIANGLE"

13. The winger moves into the corner for the puck. The centre trails the winger on the boards. The offside winger moves for the slot area.

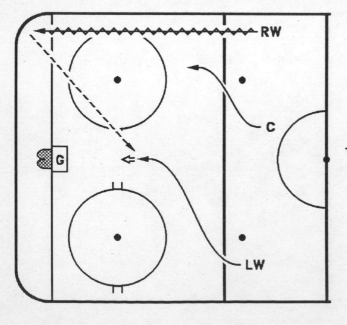

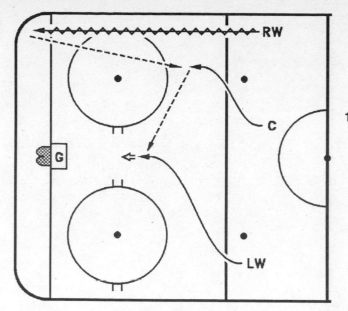

13A. The winger can pass to the offside winger or to the centre. If the centre receives the pass, he can shoot or pass to the offside winger moving to the net.

Note: The winger and centre on the puck side may alternate positions.

OTHER OFFENSIVE PLAYS

1. One-on-one: The offensive player should attempt to pull the defenseman away from the slot area. Having done this, the offensive player will try to move into the slot area by using a shift on the defenseman. Use the defenseman as a screen and shoot if the defenseman does not move from the slot area.

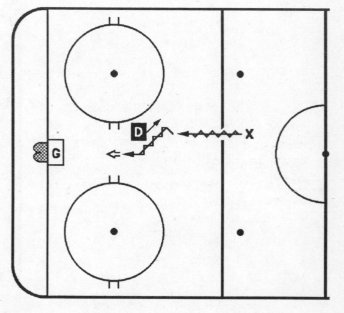

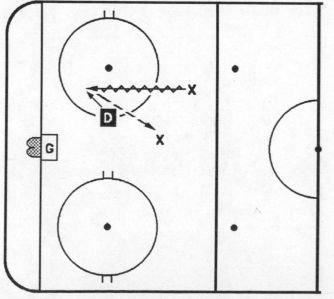

2. Two-on-one: The offensive player with the puck attempts to draw the defenseman over and away from the slot area. The player with the puck drops the puck back to the other trailing offensive player.

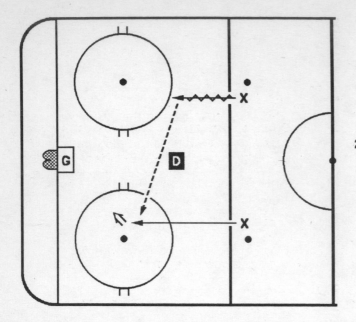

2A. The offensive player with the puck cuts wide. The other offensive player cuts behind the defenseman and receives the pass.

2B. The offensive player with the puck moves directly at the defenseman. The player with the puck drops a pass to the other trailing forward. After dropping the pass, the offensive player takes out (picks) the defenseman long enough for the other forward to skate to the goal.

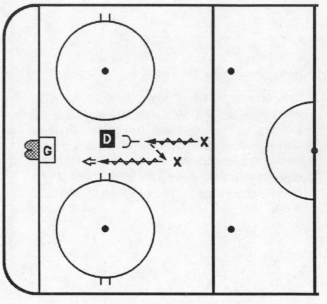

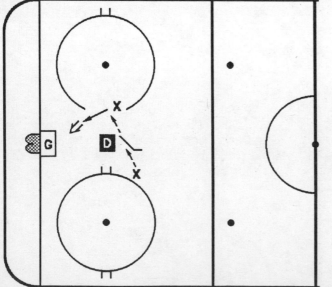

2C. The forwards are abreast with the defenseman between. The forward with the puck passes over the defenseman's stick or between his stick and skates to the other forward.

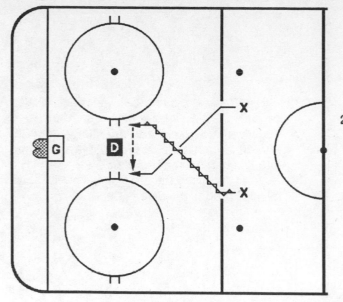

2D. Crossing pattern. The forward with the puck cuts across in front of the defenseman with the other forward cutting behind him. The pass is usually across or a drop pass may be used.

3. Two-on-two: An attempt to isolate one defenseman making a 2-on-1 situation. The offensive player with the puck moves wide and draws one defenseman over. The offensive player passes the puck back to the other forward and moves to the net for a rebound.

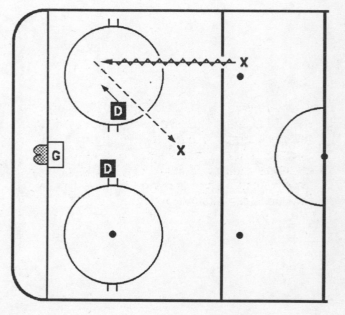

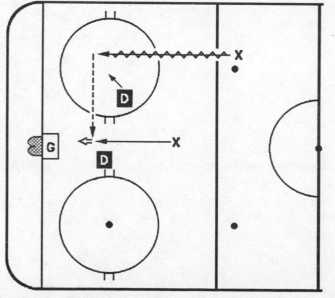

3A. The offensive player with the puck moves wide and draws the defenseman over. The other forward slips through the defence and receives a pass.

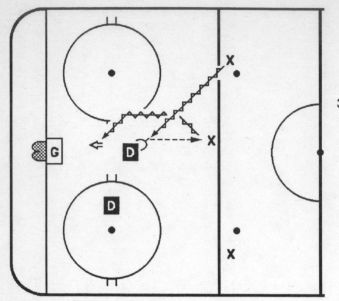

3B. The offensive player with the puck skates directly at the defenseman and then drop passes the puck to the other forward. After the drop pass, the offensive player moves into the defenseman to act as a screen. The forward receiving the drop pass either shoots or goes around the defenseman.

3C. The forwards cross in front of one defenseman and the pass is dropped with the man receiving the pass cutting to the inside or outside.

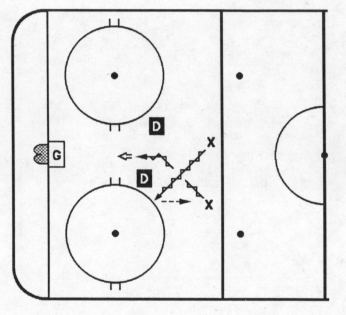

DRILLS FOR OFFENSIVE PLAY

ONE-TWO-THREE PRINCIPLE

These offensive drills are first started by a cross ice pass with the player receiving the pass driving for the net.

The first variation of the drill has the first player receiving the pass, driving for the net and shooting with the second player going down the middle of the ice and then driving for the net.

The second variation has the puck carrier passing to the trailing forward with the second man driving for the net. Thus, the one-two-three principle.

1. **Cross-ice pass:** The player receives a cross-ice pass, drives around the pylon and takes a shot on goal. After shooting, the player stays at that end on the same side of the rink. Alternate sides.

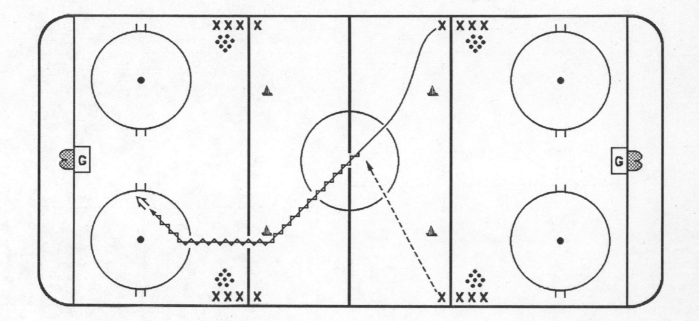

1A. **The first variation:** Two players leave at the same time from the same side. The first player takes a cross-ice pass and drives around the pylon and takes a shot on goal. The second player drives for the net. Alternate sides.

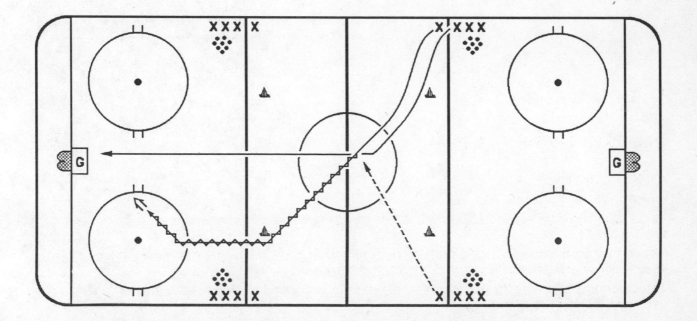

1B. The second variation: The players leave at the same time. The third player cuts around the opposite
pylon and trails the play. The second man drives for the net. The puck carrier passes to the trailer.

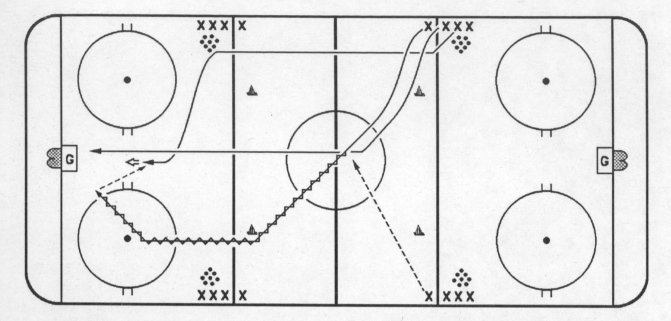

2. One-on-one: Drills 2 and 3 listed in Stickhandling and Puck Control can be used here.

3. Defenseman skates behind the net, turns up-ice and passes to a forward coming off the boards.
Another defenseman stands on the blueline and begins skating backward for a one-on-one. The defenseman passing the puck follows the play up to the far blueline and stops. The drill is repeated from the
other end with the defenseman who passed the puck from the one end acting as the defensive man
coming in the opposite direction. The defensemen, after passing and working defensively, return to the
end of the ice they started at. The forwards take the pass, then work offensively and stay at the opposite end on the opposite side of the boards.

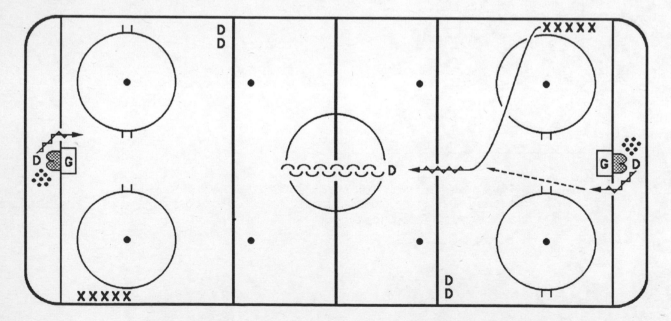

The objectives of the forwards are always to drive for the net, to occupy the slot, and to be in a position either to score or to screen the opposition goaltender.

Two-on-one drill: Work on two-on-one drills in both directions. The defensemen stay on the same side of the ice. The forwards work in both directions. Work both sides for defenseman by changing halfway through the drill.

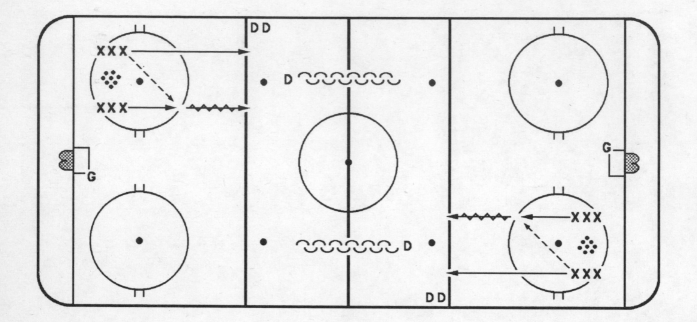

5. Two-on-one drill: Use the full ice surface. The forwards work from the corners with rink wide passes. The defensemen work the same end and the forwards work in both directions. The forwards working in the opposite direction do not start until a play has been completed on the net.

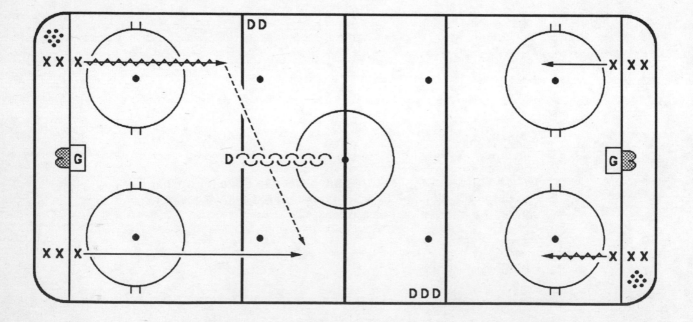

6. Drill 5 can be varied by having defensemen at both ends pass the puck to the forward by circling the net. Work the drill in both directions.

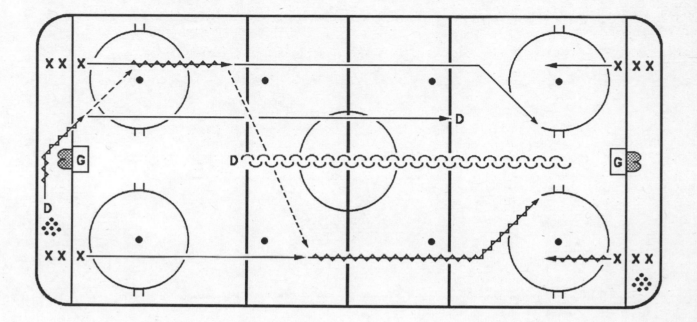

7. Two-on-one drill - one way: The forwards start from the two corners. The defenseman starts the play by circling the net and passing to either forward. Another defenseman is standing at the blueline and takes the two-on-one.

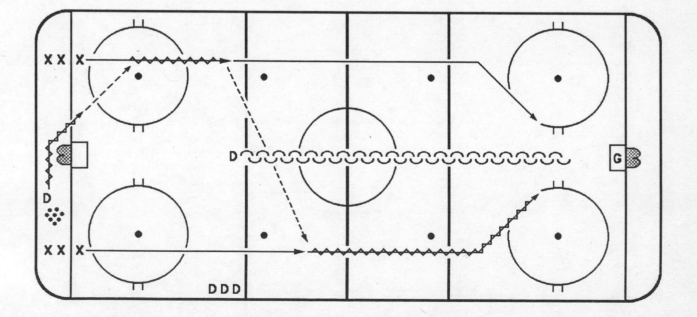

8. Two-on-one half-ice drill: This drill simulates a three-on-two situation where a centre and one winger are working on one defenseman. The other winger and defenseman are eliminated but the play is made on only one side of the ice as if it were a three-on-two. This drill can be worked in one direction or two.

One direction: The centre stays on the same side of the ice as the winger. The first centre goes with the right winger. The next centre goes with the left winger. The centre starts with the puck.

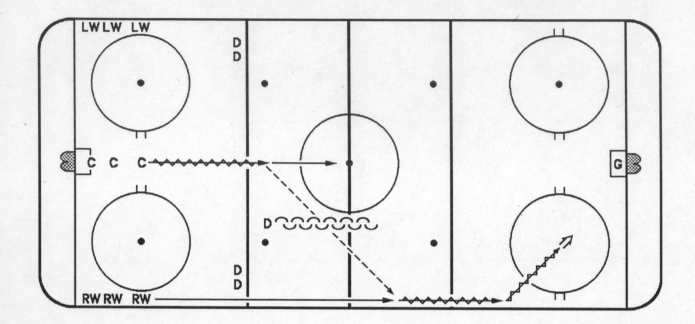

8A. Two-on-one half-ice drills in both directions: Switch sides halfway through the drill. The centres start with the puck.

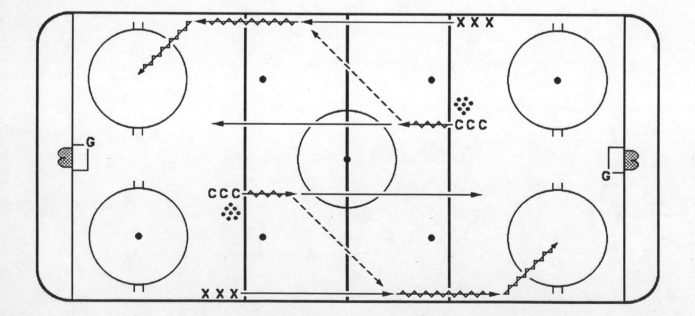

9. Two-on-one swing drill: Two forwards skate over the far blueline and receive a pass from a defenseman in that end. The defenseman who starts at the same end as the forwards skates around the centre circle, turns backward and defends against the attacking forwards. Once the defenseman has made the pass to one of the swinging forwards, the first two forwards and that defenseman start doing the drill the same way but coming from the opposite direction. Players return to the lines they came from.

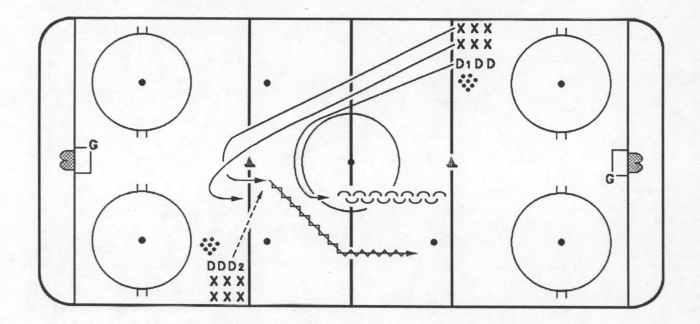

10. Three-on-two drill, one direction: The defenseman behind the net starts the passing for the three-on -two. The defence pairs take turns passing the puck up and working defensively.

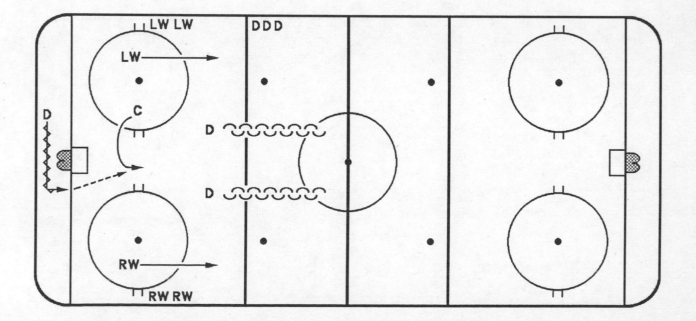

10A. Three-on-two drill, both directions: There must be a minimum of three forward lines and four defensemen for this drill. If six defensemen are available, have one at each end to start the play. Two forward lines must be at the end at which the drill starts. The forward lines stay at the opposite end after completing the rush and return in the opposite direction when their turn comes again.

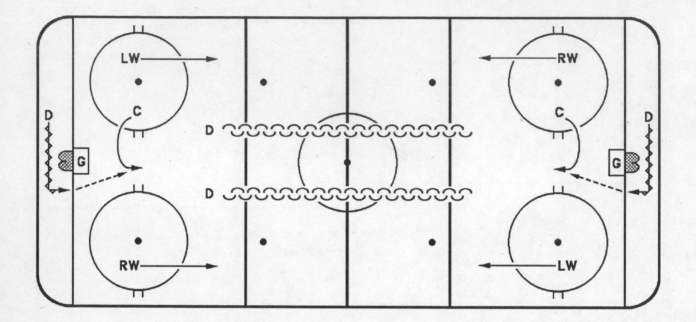

10B. Three-on-two drill, both directions with one line in succession. Same drill as 10 except the forward line, after making a play in one direction, immediately moves back in the other direction against another defence pair.

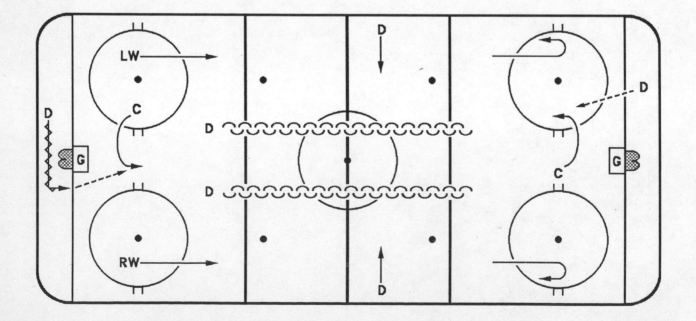

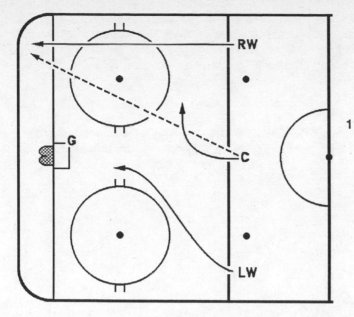

11. The offensive triangle drill: The forwards line up on the blue line and the puck is shot into the corner. The forwards work the various options of the offensive triangle. Shoot the puck into both corners.

12. Offensive triangle drill with defensemen: The defenseman on the side of the puck is shot into goes to the corner for the puck. The other defenseman goes for the front of the net.

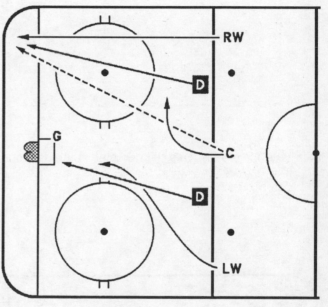

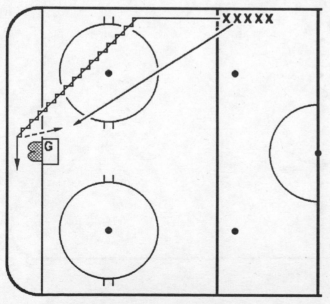

13. The first forward with the puck goes behind the net and passes the puck back on the same side to the trailing forward.

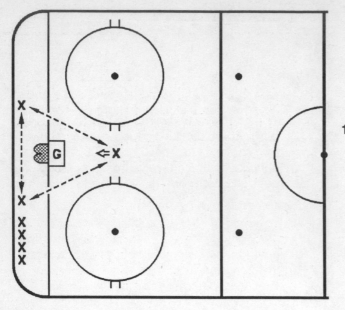

14. Offensive triangle drill: Three forwards pass the puck quickly around in the triangle and the forward in the slot takes a shot on goal. Rotate the players in and out.

15. Five-on-five drills: Use drill 10 listed in this section when moving out of your own end.

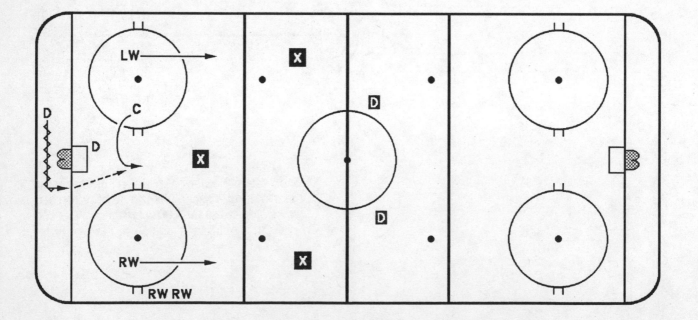

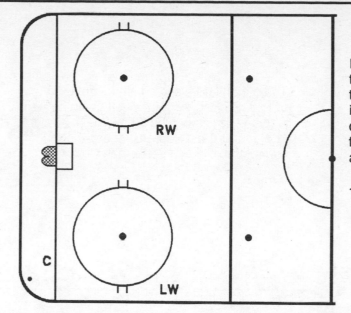

Defensive play is initiated in the opposition's end of the rink by a forechecking pattern. It continues through the neutral zone and becomes extremely important in the defensive zone. The object of defensive play is to gain possession of the puck from the opposition and therefore prevent a score and initiate the offense.

PUCK IN THE CORNER

1. One man in (1-2-2): In this system, only one forechecker moves in and the other two forwards pick up the opposition's wingers. The forechecker can be either the winger or centre, depending on which man is in first.

2. Centre in (1-2-2): This system is similar to 1 except the centre is always the first man in. Wingers pull up on the boards covering the opposition's wingers.

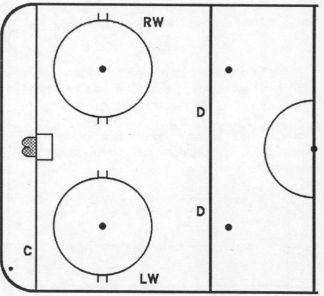

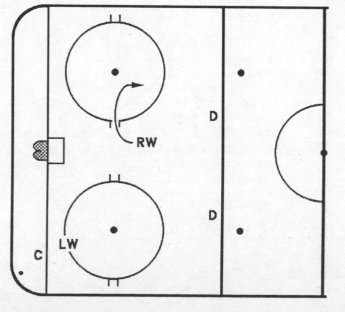

3. Two men in (2-1-2): The first forechecker takes the man out of the play with the second picking up the puck. The third offensive man stations himself in the high slot. If the opposition gains possession of the puck, the winger in front of the net skates back with the opposition's winger.

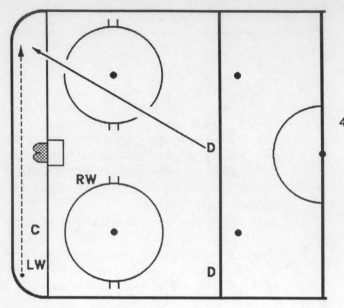

4. Three men in: This is an all out pressing type of forechecking system which could be used when a team is behind by one or more goals in a game. If the puck moves to the far side corner, the offside defenseman moves in.

5. 1-2-2 or 1-4: In this type of forechecking, one forward forechecks, the other two forwards pick up the wings and pull back as the opposition breaks out. The defense also pull back. This is used to protect a lead or forecheck a superior team in a defensive manner.

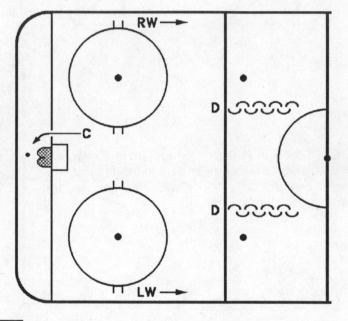

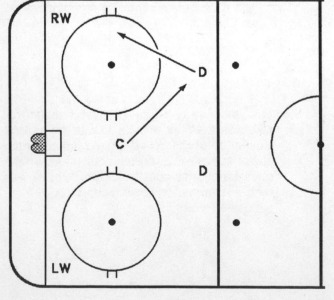

6. 2-1-2 (Defence may pinch): The wingers forecheck and the centre plays high in the slot area in this system. If a winger is slow in moving in, the centre switches positions with the winger. If the defenseman pinches in on the puck side, the centre takes the defence position.

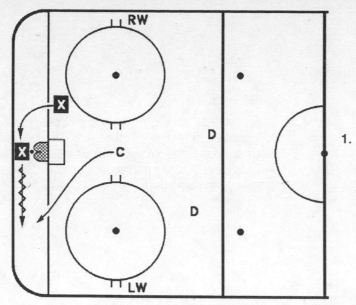

PUCK BEHIND THE NET IN POSSESSION OF OPPOSITION

1. The puck carrier is moving: One man cuts off the puck carrier. The forechecker cuts across the front of the net to ride the man out. The wingers pick up the opposition wingers on the boards.

2. Two men cut off the puck carrier: This is the same as 1 except the winger on the puck side moves in to help cut off the puck carrier. The defenseman on the puck side moves in to take the opposition wingers.

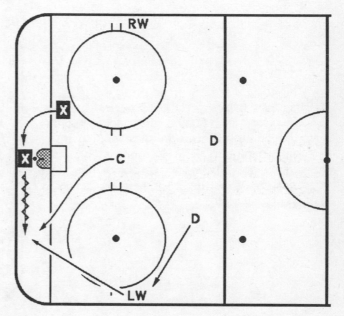

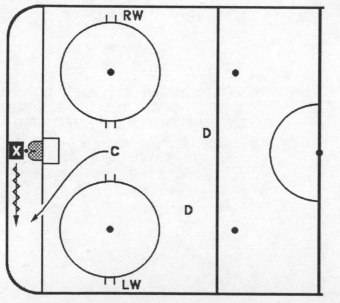

3. The puck carrier stops behind the net: The forechecker who stops in front of the net is the first man in, usually the centre or the winger. The other two forecheckers cover the opposition wingers on the boards. When the puck carrier moves, the centre moves with him. The wingers stay with the wings.

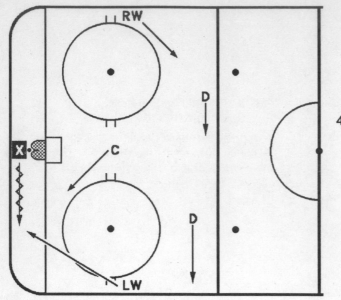

4. Variation of 2: When the puck carrier moves, the centre moves with the man and the winger moves in. The defenseman on the puck carrier's side moves in to take the forward to the boards.

5. The puck carrier is chased behind the net: This system sacrifices a forechecker in order to inhibit the opposition from setting up a breakout pattern. The winger on the puck carrier's side moves in to check him. The defenseman on the puck side moves in to cover the winger.

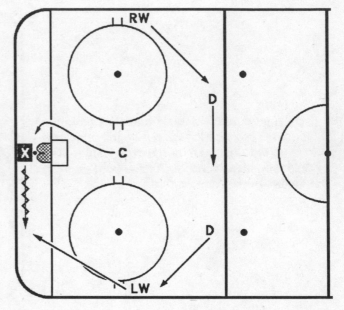

THE PUCK CARRIER STOPS BEHIND YOUR NET AND THE OPPOSITION DEFENSEMAN MOVES TO THE CORNER.

1. The forechecker stops in front of the net: The wingers pull back with the wingers on the boards. The winger on the defenseman's side moves in if the pass comes to the defenseman.

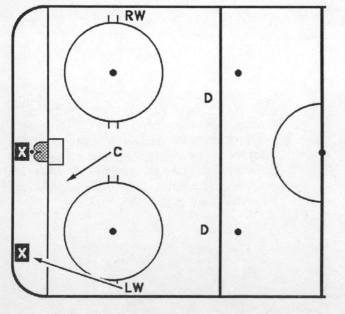

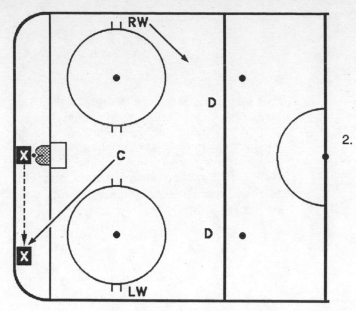

2. The forechecker stops in front of the net: The wingers stay on the wingers. The centre follows the pass to the defenseman.

3. Offensive triangle system: The puck moves from one side to the other side. The first man in chases the puck to the net and then swings out to the slot. The second man in moves across to the far side. The man in the slot moves to the corner where the puck has moved.

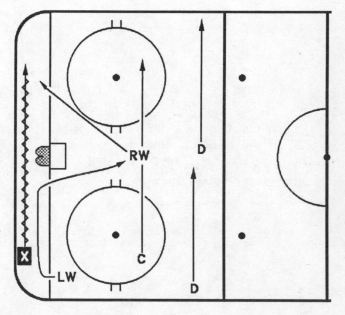

CHECKING SYSTEM FROM THE NEUTRAL ZONE INTO THE DEFENSIVE END

1. Wingers uncovered: The defenseman must back in, but attempt to give as little ice as possible. The first trailing forward picks up the slot area. The other trailing forwards pick up the wingers on the boards.

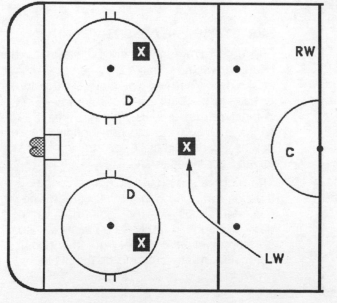

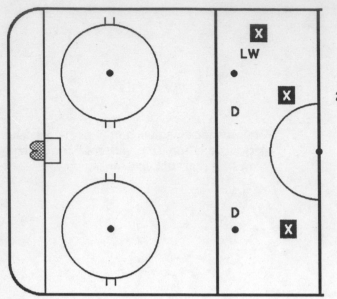

2. One winger covered, three-on-two: With one winger covered, the two defensemen attempt to make a three-on-three situation with the winger covering one man, keeping to the inside. The defensemen keep a short distance between themselves and the offensive men. The next trailing forward picks up the slot area.

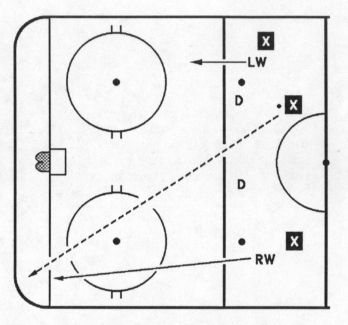

3. Both wingers covered, three-on-two: Both defensemen can stand up over the blueline and force the offensive man to make a play before the blueline. If the puck is shot into the defensive zone, the wingers should be the first to pick it up.

SYSTEMS IN THE DEFENSIVE END

The defensive wingers should stay with the offensive wingers until a play has been made on the net. When the play moves to the corner or back to the blueline then the system in the defensive end should go into effect. The centre usually trails the play coming into the defensive end and picks up a trailing offensive forward or defenseman.

1. The wingers are on the points, the centre is in the slot, the puck is in the left corner: The left defenseman is in the corner. The right defenseman is in front of the net. The wingers are approximately 15 feet from the opposition defensemen. The centre is on the puck.

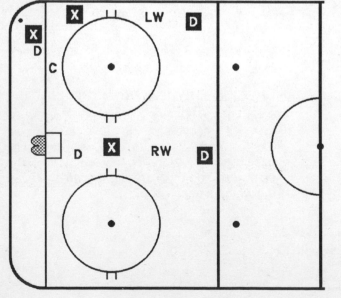

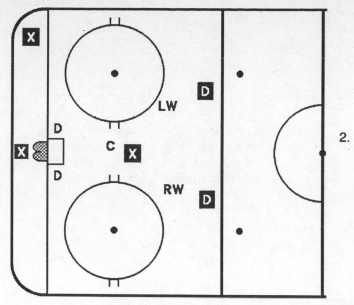

2. The puck is behind the net: The centre moves to the slot area. The defensemen position themselves off both goalposts.

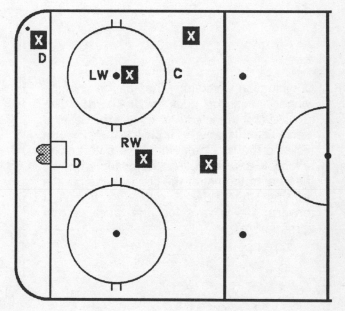

3. The puck is in the right corner: This is the same as in 1, but positions are reversed.

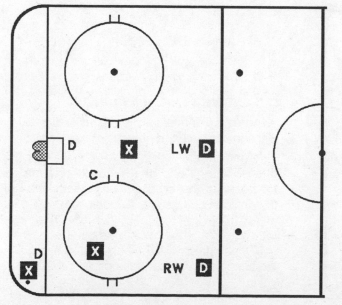

4. The wingers are on the wingers, and the centre is on the points: One defenseman goes to the corner on the puck carrier. The other defenseman stays in front of the net. If the puck is moved quickly to the offside point, the defenseman in front of the net moves on the point man if he skates in.

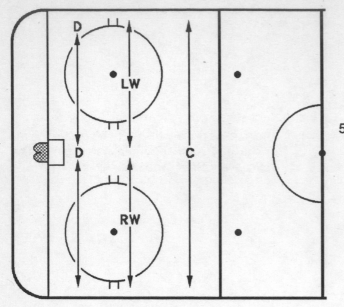

5. Sliding zone: The centreman covers the blueline area. The wingers cover from the board area to the slot. The defensemen cover from the front of the net to the corner.

6. Combination system: The centre or the winger is on the puck in the corner. The forward (not in the corner) covers the net side point. The offside winger covers the slot area first and the far side point, if the puck comes across to this man. The defensemen cover the front of the net or the corner if the puck is on the other side. A defenseman and a forward are always on the puck in the corners.

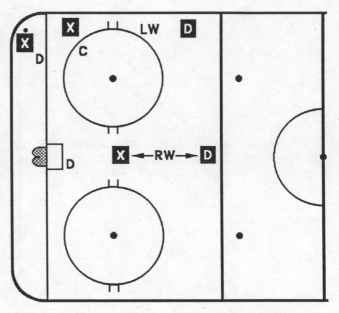

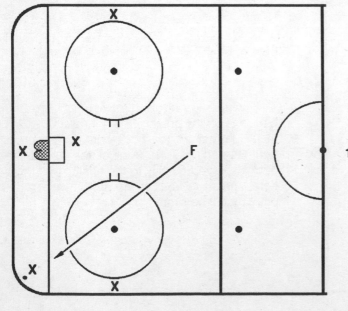

DEFENSIVE TEAM PLAY DRILLS

All forechecking drills discussed in Checking Section can be used here.

1. One-on-five drill: The puck is shot into the offensive zone and one forechecker attempts to break up the breakout play. Both ends of the rink can be used for this drill.

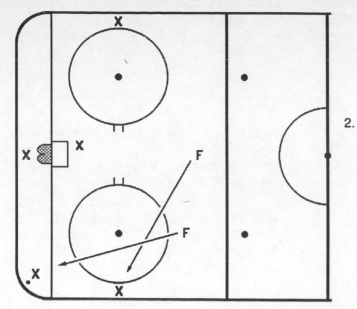

2. Two-on-five, three-on-five, five-on-five drill: Same drill as 2 except two forecheckers attempt to break up play, then three, then three forwards and two defensemen. The drill can be executed at both ends of the rink.

3. Defensive system still without opposition: Work a defensive system against no opposition. The coach can describe the situation and the players react by positioning themselves quickly, e.g. puck is in the left corner, the puck moves behind the net or the puck moves to the far corner. Also react to hand or stick signals by coach. The drill can be run at both ends of the rink as well as in neutral zone if you have three nets.

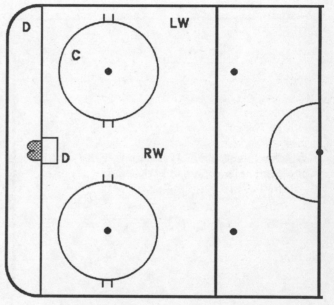

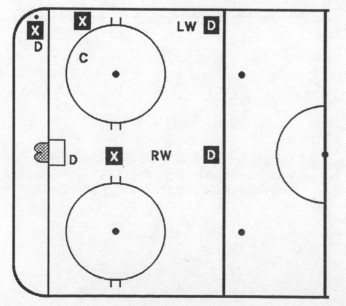

4. Defensive system drill with opposition defensive team without sticks: The offensive team moves the puck around with the defensive team without sticks, concentrating on positional play. Both ends of the ice can be used for this drill.

5. Five on five drill: This is the same drill as 5 except defensive players have sticks. The drill is worked in the defensive zone with the offensive team being given the puck in the corner or at the point and worked from that point. The play ends when a goal is scored, the goalie or players hold the puck or the puck is moved out of the defensive end over the blueline. The drill can be worked at both ends of the rink. (Not Shown)

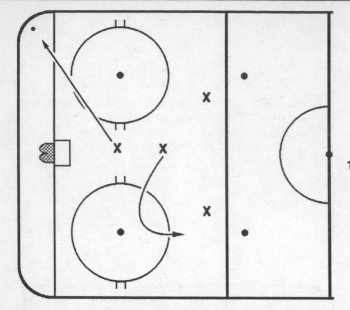

There are a number of penalty killing systems used in hockey.

FORECHECKING PATTERNS IN THE OFFENSIVE ZONE

1. One man short, stacked formation ("I"): The first forechecker moves to the puck side. The second forechecker swings to the opposite side and picks up the winger on that side.

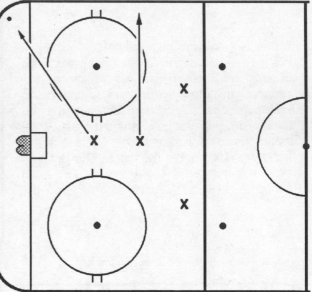

2. Stacked formation (variation): Both of the forecheckers move to the same side to attempt to break up the play.

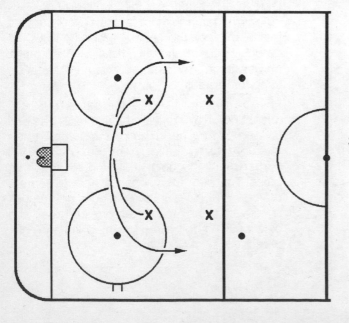

3. Forecheckers criss cross: First forechecker swings across to one side. The second forechecker swings to the opposite side.

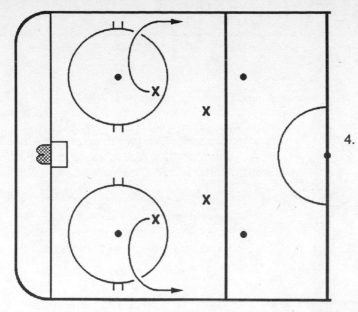

4. Forecheckers pick up winger on their side: Both forecheckers pick up their wingers on their side.

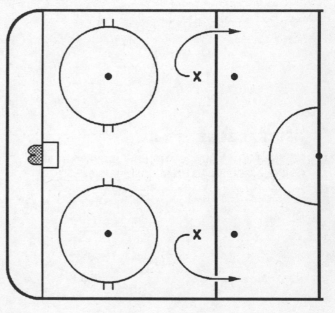

5. The forecheckers pick up the wingers at the blueline: The same as 3 except the forecheckers do not go further than just inside the offensive blueline.

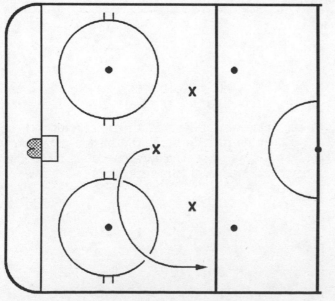

6. Two men short: The forechecker moves in and swings with the puck carrier and then picks up the winger.

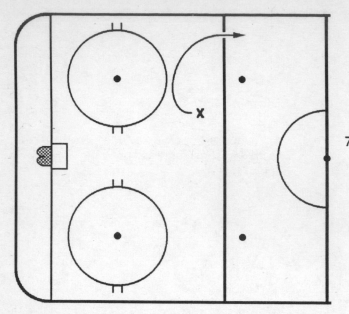

7. Two men short: The forechecker does not move in further than the blueline and then picks up either winger.

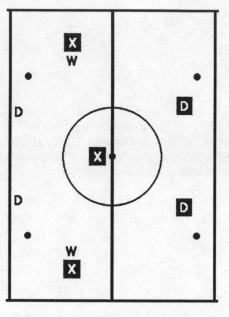

NEUTRAL ZONE

1. One Man Short: Wingers covered, the defensemen stand up at the blueline.

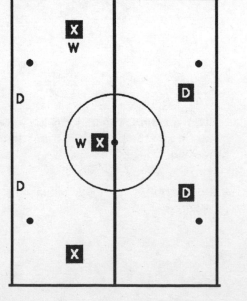

2. One winger covered, the other forechecker is in the mid ice area: The offside defenseman moves over. The forechecker in the mid-ice area moves on the puck carrier.

138

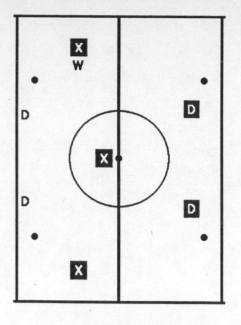

3. Two men short: The forechecker picks up either winger.

4. Two men short (variation): The forechecker picks up the centre area.

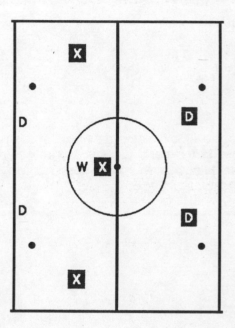

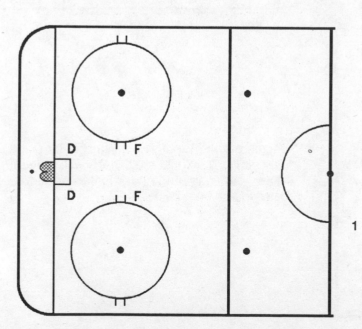

DEFENSIVE ZONE

In the standard box formation, two wingers and two defensemen force the play to the outside. The four defenders only move to the outside of the box for the puck if they have a 90 percent chance of gaining possession.

1 Standard box: The puck behind the net or in the centre area.

139

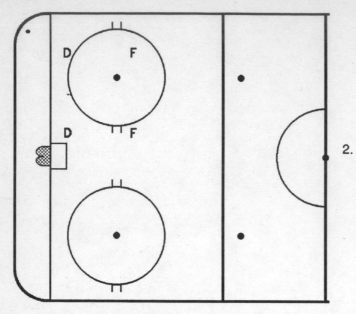

2. Standard box: The puck is in the corner or at the point.

3. Collapsible Box: Same as 1 except the box moves to the net area. The box moves out when the puck moves to the corner or back to the point.

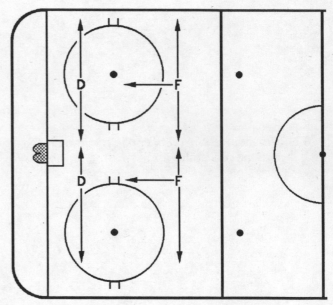

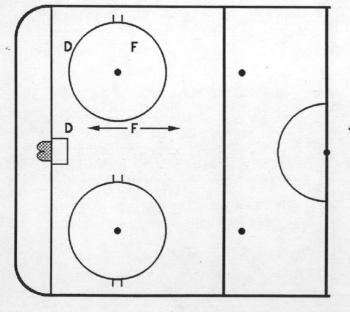

4. Sagging Box: The offside winger to the puck side moves back into the slot area. This man moves out again if the puck is passed to the defenseman on his side.

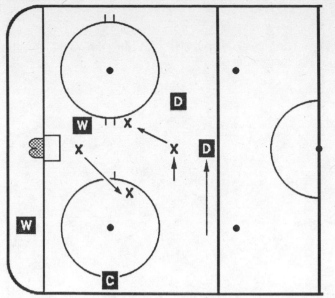

5. The Diamond (Rotating Box): When the opposition is on the power play, defenseman moves to the middle of the blueline. The penalty killing forward moves to the middle of the ice with the defenseman. The defenseman on the same side moves out and the offside defenseman moves to the front of the net. The offside penalty killing forward drops off to form the diamond.

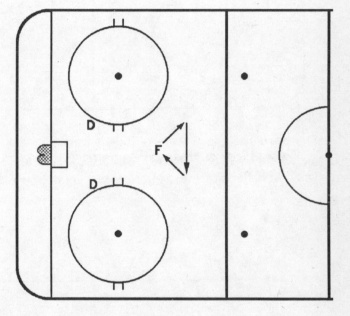

6. Two Men Short Standard Triangle: The forward at the top of the triangle moves from side to side covering the high slot area and the points.

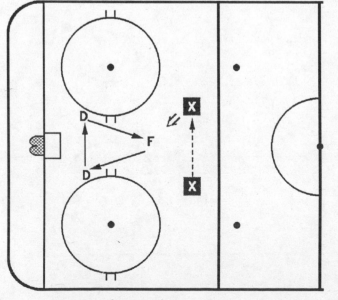

7. Rotating Triangle: This is the same as 1 except the defenseman moves out on the point man if the forward is trapped on the offside. The forward then moves back as a defenseman and the other defenseman moves to the offside. The defenseman who moves out becomes the top man in the triangle.

8. Sliding triangle (one defenseman, two forwards)

One defenseman stands in front of the net moving only from one side of the crease to the other depending upon the side the puck is on. The other two forwards move in and out eliminating the top man trapped which is the weakness of the normal triangle formation.

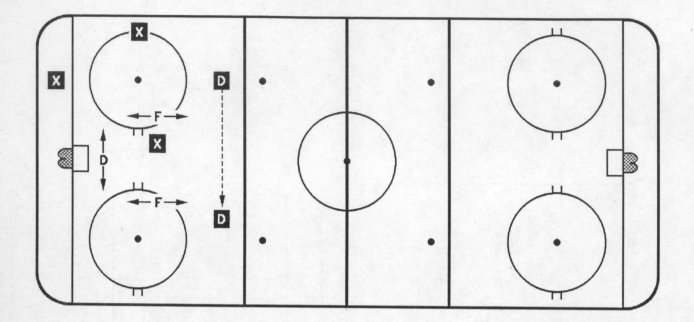

DRILLS FOR PENALTY KILLING

1. Work the box and the triangle without any opposition, reacting to the coach's hand or stick signals.

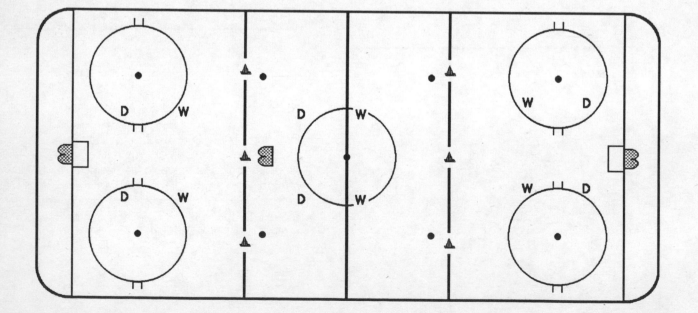

2. Work the box and triangle against any offense at each end of the ice. Work the box and triangle with the players, first without sticks and then with sticks.

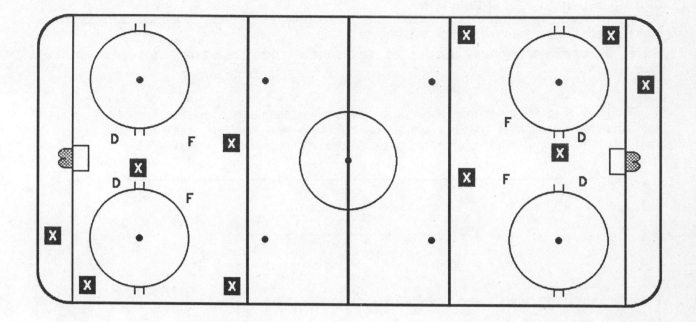

3. Work the forechecking forwards against the offensive team, bringing the puck out of their own end. This drill can be worked at both ends.

NOTE: Use the full ice surface to practise penalty killing. The puck can be shot into the offensive end by the coach and the offensive team attempts to start the play from there. Time limits for each offensive and defensive unit can be used.

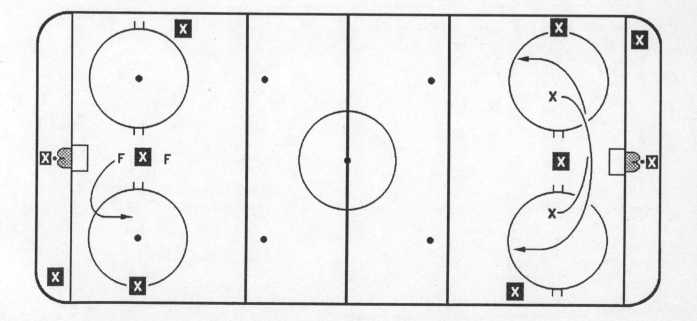

13. POWER PLAY

The objective of the power play is to move the puck into the defensive zone and maintain possession until an excellent scoring opportunity can be set up.

ORGANIZING IN THE DEFENSIVE ZONE
In many instances, the power play is initiated in the defensive zone after the shorthanded team has shot the puck the length of the ice from their defensive zone.

There are a number of different methods used to move the puck from the defensive zone of the team with the power play.

1. Set the puck up behind the net: The centre circles behind the net and takes the puck from the defenseman and moves straight up the centre of the ice. The defenseman in front of the net can move to the boards and follow behind the winger to set up a crossing pattern at the far blueline.

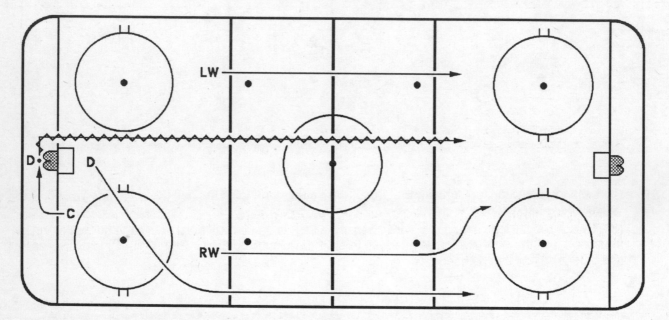

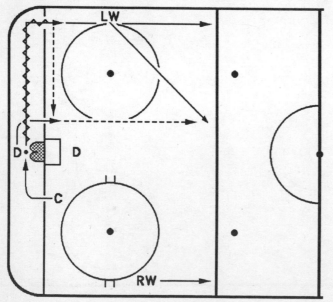

2. The centre circles behind the net, takes the puck and moves wide to the corner then drops the puck back to the defenseman. The defenseman moves straight up the ice or returns the pass to the centre who has circled back to the centre of the ice or to the winger cutting from the boards.

3. The defenseman stops behind the net with his partner moving to the corner. The centre makes a tight turn at the goal line on the opposite side to the defenseman in the corner. The defenseman behind the net gives the puck to the centre. The other defenseman in the corner goes straight up the ice to form a four-man attack.

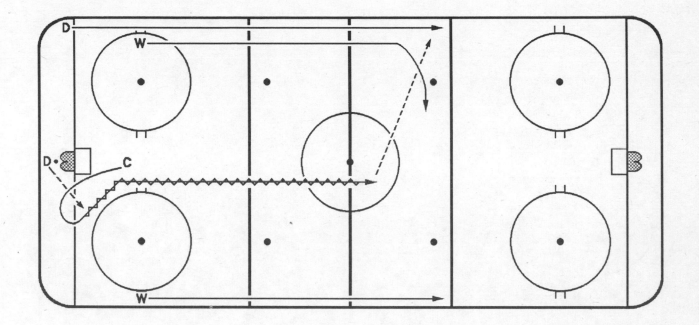

4. The defenseman stops behind the net with his partner moving to the corner. The centre makes a tight turn at the goal line on the opposite side to the defenseman in the corner. The defenseman behind the net gives the puck to the centre or the defenseman in the corner. If the puck goes to the defenseman in the corner, he will then take two strides with the puck and pass to the circling centre. The defenseman who was in the corner then moves down the boards and becomes the outlet man for the winger cutting across at the blueline.

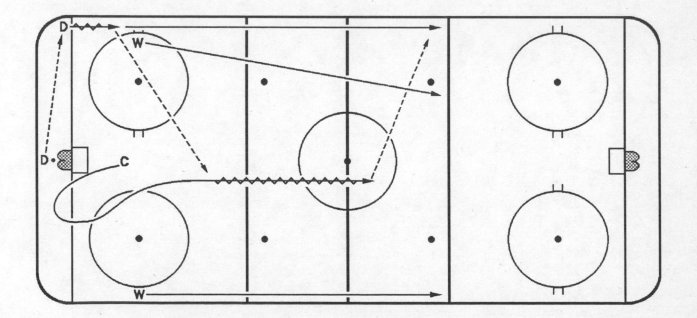

5. Any standard breakout play can be used in moving the puck from the defensive zone, such as a defenseman in the corner, or a centre swing to the corner.

6. Double swing - wingers high at the blueline: The defenseman and the centre swing to the corner. The wingers are high at the blueline, cut across, and are available for a pass from the defenseman or the swing man.

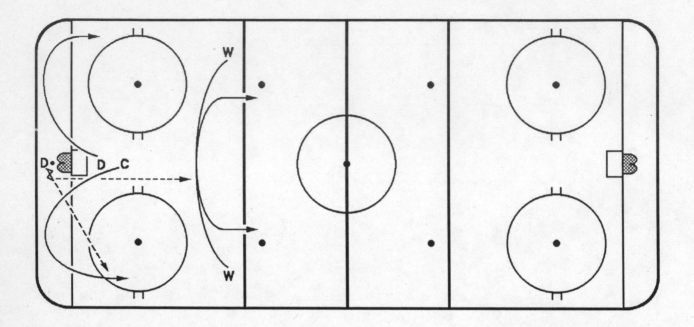

7. Double swing, one winger at the near blueline, one winger at the far blueline: The winger at the near blueline loops in and the winger at the far blueline cuts across for a pick or a pass as the play moves up the ice.

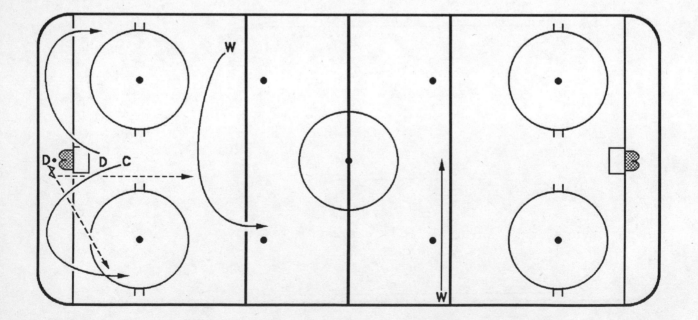

MOVING THROUGH THE NEUTRAL ZONE

In most cases, the team with the power play attempts to have a fourth offensive player involved in the play as the puck is moved across the opposition's blueline.

1. The centre carries the puck. The winger cuts in with the defenseman moving down the boards. One defenseman follows the winger up quickly on either side. The winger cuts to the centre area to pull his check with him. The centre passes the puck to either the defenseman or the winger.

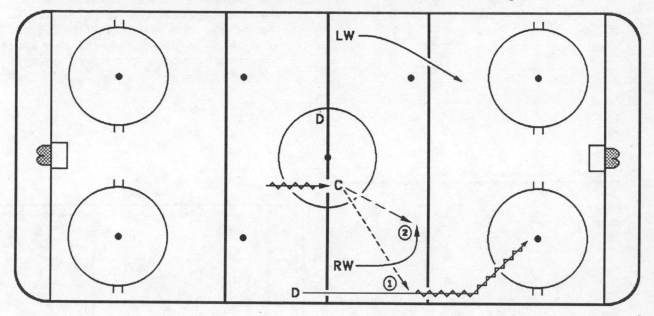

2. The defenseman carries the puck with the centre following the winger up the boards. The same play for the winger as above except the defenseman passes to the centre or the winger cuts across.

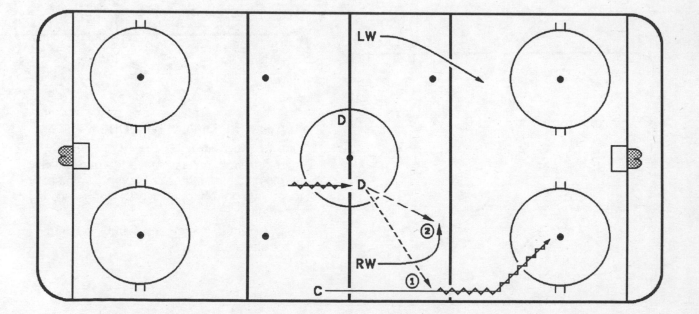

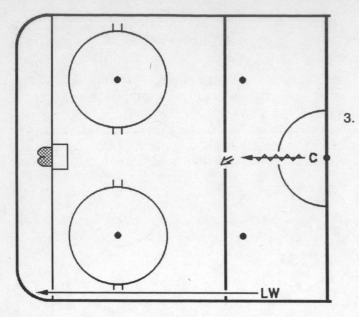

3. The puck carrier shoots the puck into the offensive zone. It is important that the puck is shot into the offensive zone with the wings in full flight. Getting possession of the puck after shooting is extremely important or the play is ineffective.

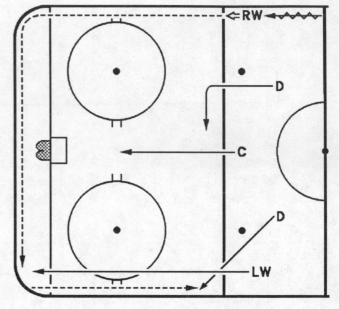

4. Rim the boards: The puck carrier moves down the ice close to the boards and shoots the puck in to rim the boards and to be picked up by the offside forward. The puck can then be passed quickly back to the defense to set up the power play.

   Any standard offensive line play can be used such as the centre stopping or cutting across inside the opposition's blueline.

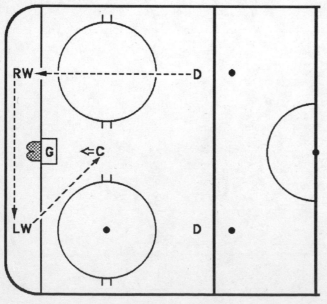

PLAY IN THE OFFENSIVE ZONE

One or two men shorthanded: The object in the offensve zone is to move the puck quickly and to place the offensive players strategically to set up in an open area for a scoring opportunity.

1. The wingers is in the corner and the centre is in the slot area.

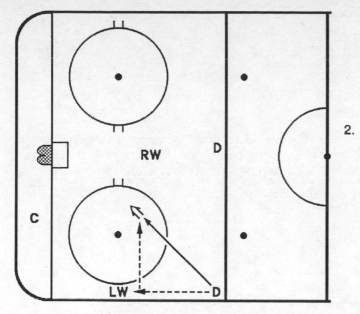

2. Give and go with defenseman: The defenseman passes to the forward in the corner and then moves to the net for a return pass.

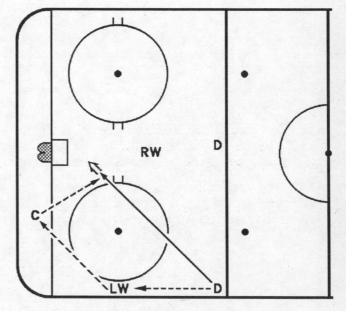

3. Give-and go (variation): If the defender moves with the defenseman, the forward can pass to another forward in the corner ...

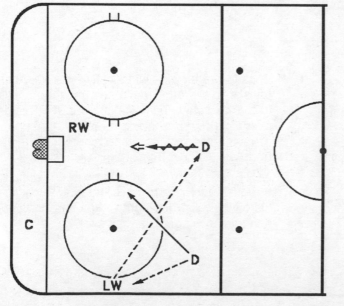

3A.   ... or to the offside defenseman.

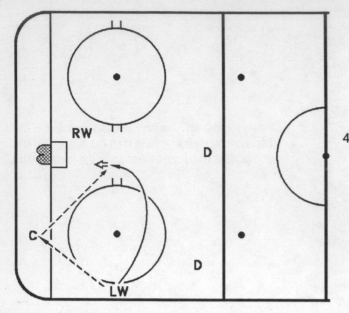

4. Two-on-one in the corner: The winger passes to the centre and then moves to the net for a return pass on the give and go.

5. Two-on-one in the corner (variation): If the defenseman moves with the winger, the centre can pass to the defenseman moving into the high slot.

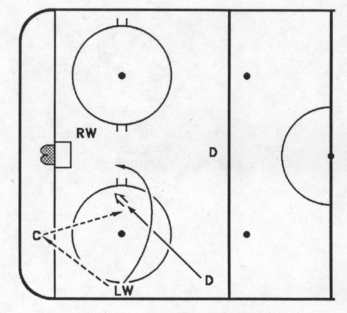

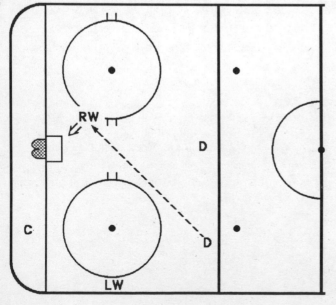

6. Pass to the far side winger: One defenseman passes to the other defenseman who passes to the far side winger stationed at the offside post. The forward takes the pass and shoots in one motion. The pass can come directly from the offside defenseman.

    NOTE: It is often an advantage in any pass to the offside winger to have the winger playing his off wing. i.e. the right winger is a left shot and the left winger is a right shot.

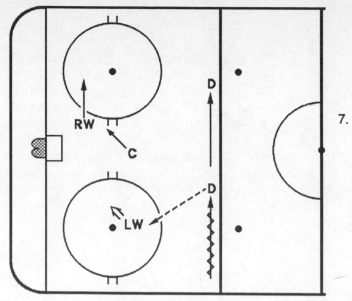

7. The defensemen move across the blueline. The one with the puck passes back to the winger. The object here is to shift the defensive box to one side and then pass back.

8. The centre moves to the front of the net to tie up the defenseman. The winger coming from the corner passes the puck across to the offside winger who is standing off the far side goalpost.

If winger coming to the net is covered, look for the defenseman moving down into the high slot.

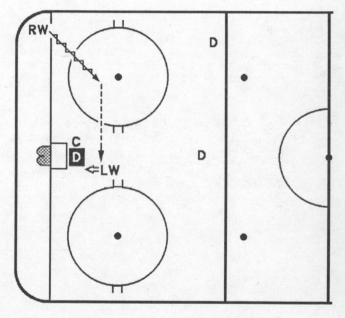

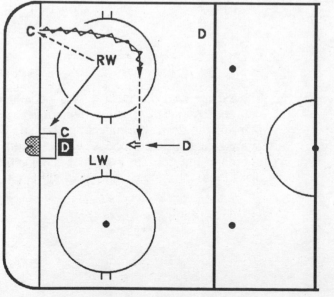

9. A two-on-one situation is set up in the corner with the other forward tying up the defenseman in the front of the net. The forward in the corner tries to pass to the offside defenseman moving in from the point.

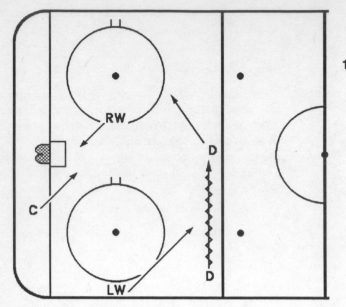

10. The point man with the puck at the blueline moves across the blueline and stops. The other point man moves in on the far side. The winger on the side of the puck moves out and the other winger and centre move to the front of the net to pick the opposition defenseman.

NOTE: The defenseman with the puck at the blueline can shoot or pass to the winger or the other point man. If the point man passes to either side, he can wait for a return pass or move through the centre and receive a return pass.

11. The centre with the puck moves around behind the net and circles in front to pass to the far side winger or shoots. The winger in front of the net picks the opposition defenseman on that side.

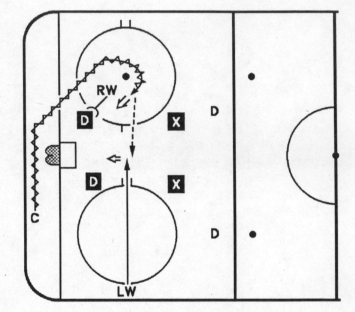

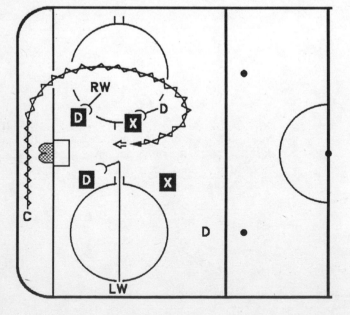

12. The centre with the puck circles behind the net, and continues out near the blueline, and then moves down the middle for a shot. The two wingers pick the opposition defensemen in front of the net. The near side defenseman picks the near opposition forward at the top of the box.

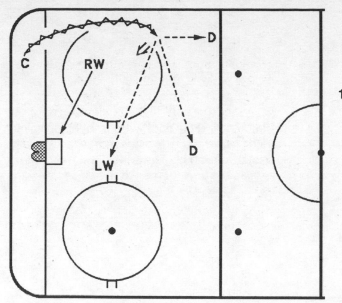

13. Combined system: From a two-on-one situation in the corner, the forward looks for the following possibilities in sequence:

    (1) Pass to the give and go man
    (2) Move out from corner for a possible shot
    (3) Pass to the offside winger
    (4) Pass to the offside point man
    (5) Pass to the near side point man

14. The puck is passed quickly around the outside from the C, LW, D, D, RW and then quickly across to the LW moving in for a direct shot.

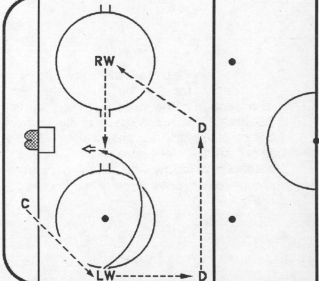

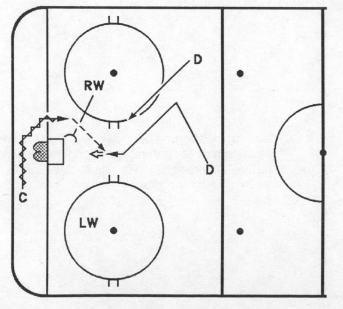

15. The centre moves from behind the net. The RW picks for the defenseman, the RD moves through the slot, and the LD moves over, takes a pass from the centre, and shoots.

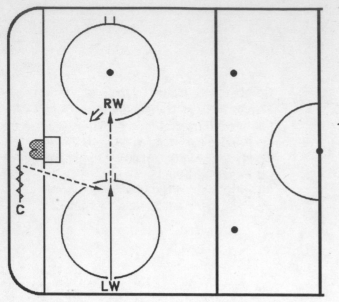

16. Pass back: The centre goes behind the net and passes back on the same side to the winger moving in. The winger either shoots or passes the puck across to the offside forward.

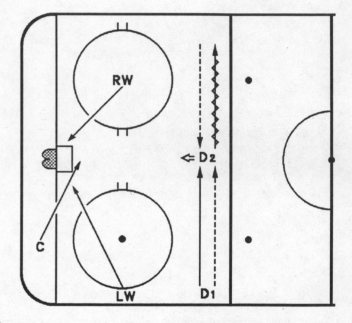

17. Defense moves to the boards: The defenseman takes a pass from the other defenseman in the middle of the ice. The defenseman receiving the pass then skates toward the boards and passes the puck back to the offside defenseman who has moved to the middle of the ice. The defenseman shoots and the other forwards go to the front of the net.

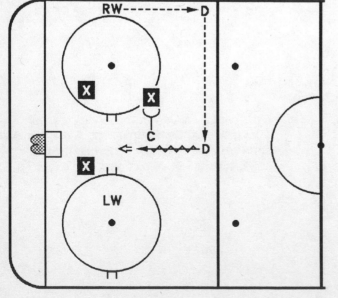

18. Two men short: The puck is passed from defenseman to defenseman and the centre picks off the top man in the defensive triangle.

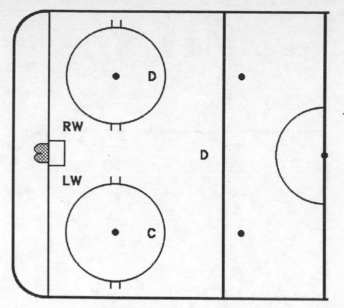

19. Two men short, defenseman to middle, two forwards in front of the net: The defenseman moves to the middle part of the ice, the offside defenseman and another forward form an umbrella (or outlets) and the other two forwards go to the front of the net.

DRILLS FOR THE POWER PLAY

1. Work breakout patterns and neutral zone plays with no opposition. The drill can be worked at both ends with the groups not passing the red line. Plays worked between the red line and offensive blueline can work between the defensive blueline and centre red line.

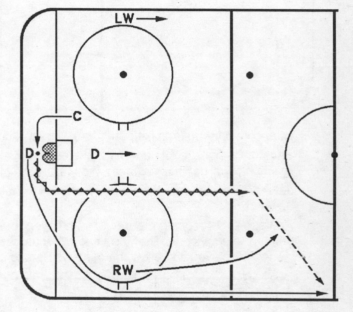

2. This is the same drill as 1 except two forecheckers attempt to break up the play.

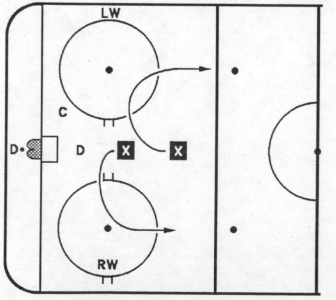

3. Offensive patterns against no opposition. Three areas of the ice can be used.

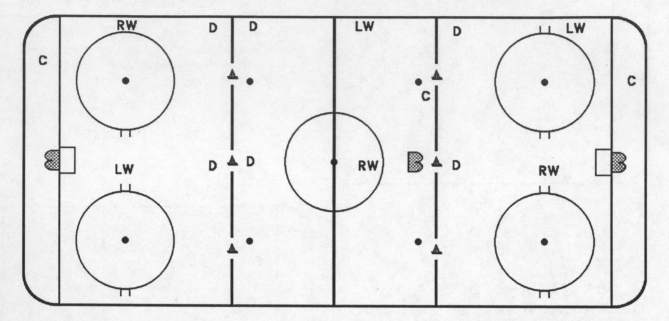

4. Offensive patterns against defenders without sticks. Both ends of the rink or three areas can be used.

5. Same as drill 4 except patterns are executed against defenders with sticks.

6. Full ice power play drill. Work against team one and two men short. The puck can be dumped into the defensive end and worked out against the penalty killing team. Time limits for each offensive unit can be used.

   An important teaching progression is to work the power play five-on-three. This allows the power play unit to have success. Then add a fourth man, first without sticks and then with. Once the power play is working well, you can allow the penalty killers to be more aggressive. Try to use all of your players.

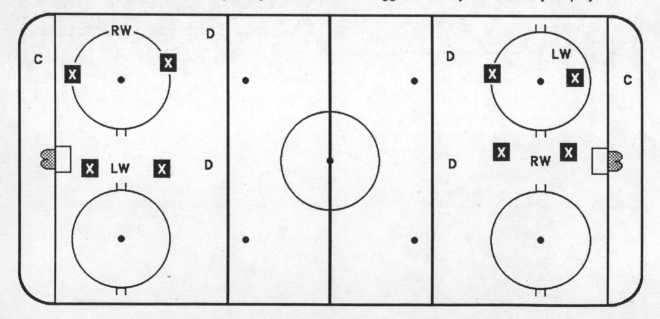

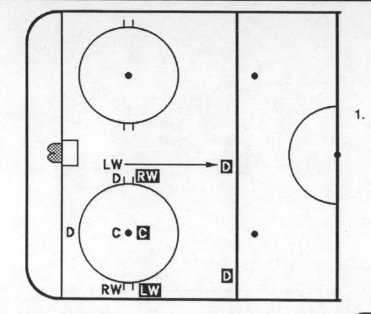

DEFENSIVE ZONE FACE-OFFS

NOTE: All face-offs are opposite for the opposite side of the ice.

1. Full strength

    Assignments:
    LW - Take right defenseman
    RW - Take left winger
    C - Take draw and centre
    LD - Take right winger
    RD - Take puck drawn back or centre moving to net

1A. Assignments:

    LW - Take right defenseman
    RW - Take left winger and then left defenseman
    C   - Take centre
    LD - Take right winger
    RD - Take puck drawn back or centre

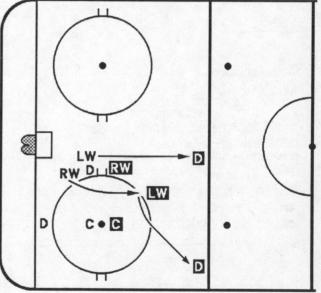

1B. Assignments:

    LW - Take right winger
    RW - Take left defenseman
    C   - Take left wing then right defenseman
    LD - Take centre
    RD - Take puck drawn back or centre moving to net

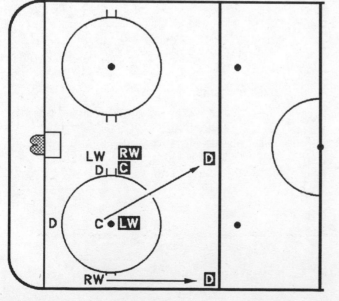

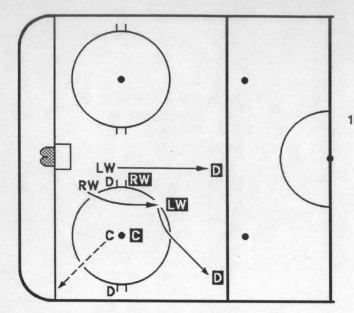

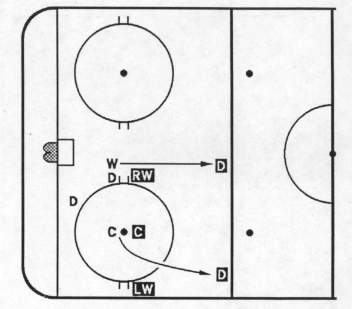

1C. Assignments:

LW - Take right defenseman
RW - Take left winger then near side point
C - Take draw and centre
LD - Take right winger or go to net
RD - Take puck drawn back or moves to net

2. One man short

Assignments:

W - Take right defenseman
C - Take centre and left defense
LD - Take right winger
RD - Take puck drawn back or centre moving to net

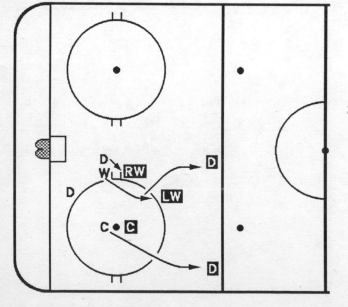

2A. Assignments:

W - Take left winger and then left defense
C - Take centre
LD - Take right winger
RD - Take puck drawn back or centre moving to net

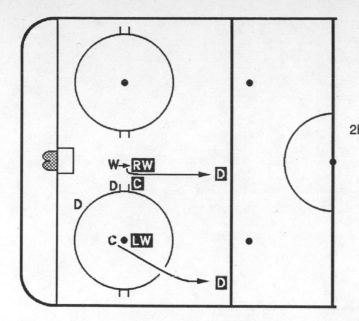

2B. Assignments:

    W   - Take right winger then right defenseman
    C   - Take left winger then left defenseman
    LD - Take centre
    RD - Take draw and left winger moving to net

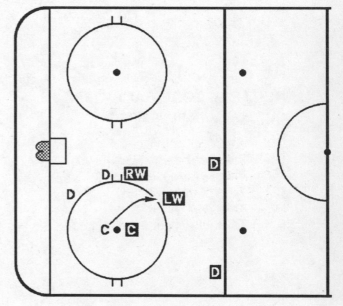

3. Two men short

Assignments:

    C   - Take centre then left winger
    LD - Take right winger
    RD - Take puck drawn back or centre
            moving to net

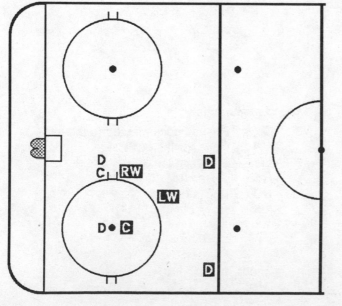

3A. Assignments:

    C   - Take left winger
    LD - Take right winger
    RD - Take centre

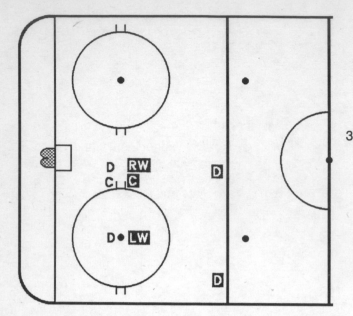

3B. Assignments:

   C   - Take centre
   LD - Take right winger
   RD - Take left winger

NEUTRAL ZONE FACE-OFFS
OUTSIDE OWN BLUELINE

1. Full Strength
   Assignments:

   C   - Pushes puck straight forward or to either wing
   LW - Take right winger or go for puck
   RW - Take left winger or go for puck

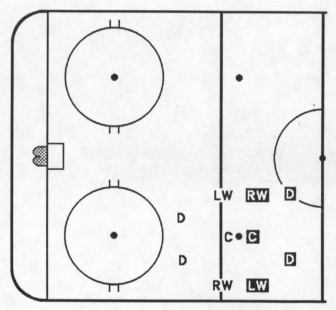

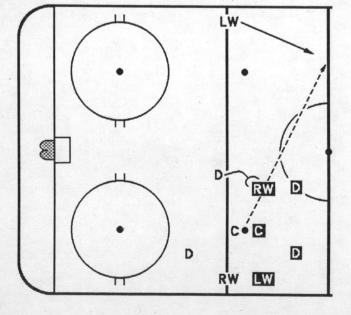

1A. Assignments:

   C   - Pushes puck forward to the left side
   LW - Goes for the puck
   LD - Moves to cut off RW
   RW - Covers LW
   RD - Backs up play

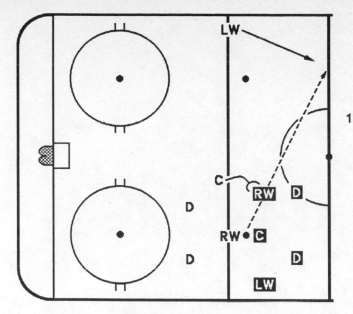

1B. Assignments:

LW - Goes for puck
C - Cuts off right winger
RW - Shoot puck to the left side
LD - Backs up play
RD - Covers left winger

2. One Man Short

Assignments:

W - Takes right winger
C - Takes centre
LD - Backs up the play
RD - Takes left winger

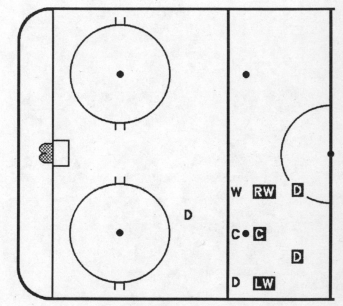

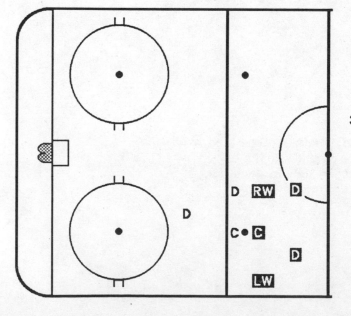

3. Two men short

Assignments:

LD - Takes right winger
C - Takes centre
RD - Backs up play and watches left winger

The player taking the face-off needs good peripheral vision to watch the puck in the referee's hand and the opponent's stick at the same time. Quick reaction time is essential.

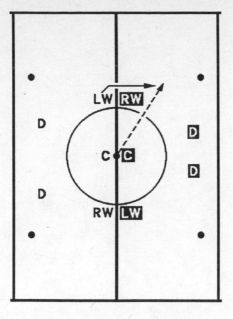

1. Full Strength
    Assignments:

    C   - Shoots puck forward to left or right winger
    LD
     or
    RD   - Backs up play
    LW   - Goes for puck
    RW   - Goes for forwards

1A. Assignments:

    C   - Draws puck back to left defenseman and gets in position to receive puck from right defenseman

    LD   - Receives puck and passes to right defenseman

    RD   - Passes puck to centre

    LW   - Covers right winger

    RW   - Covers left winger

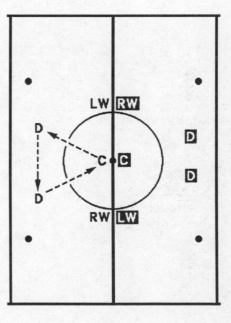

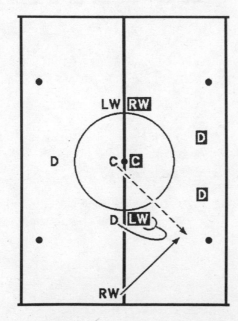

1B. Assignments:

    LW   - Takes right winger

    C   - Shoots puck to right winger

    RD   - Cuts off left winger

    RW   - Goes for the puck

    LD   - Backs up the play

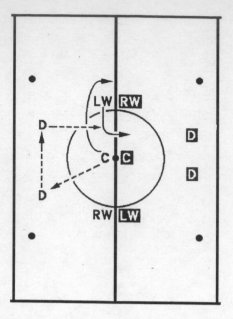

1C. Assignments:

C - Draws puck back to right defenseman and crosses with centre
RD - Passes to left defenseman
RD - Crosses with centre
LD - Passes puck to crossing left winger

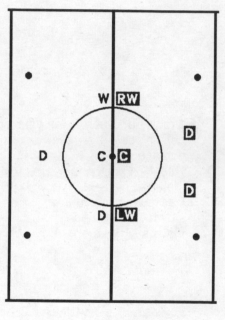

2. One man short

Assignments:

W - Takes right winger
C - Takes centre
RD - Takes left winger
LD - Backs up the play

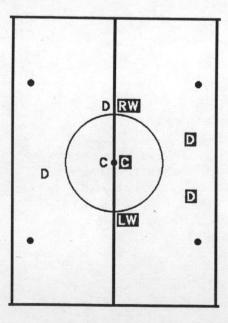

3. Two men short

Assignments:

LD - Takes right winger
C - Takes centre
RD - Backs up the play and watches left winger, or lines up opposite the left winger

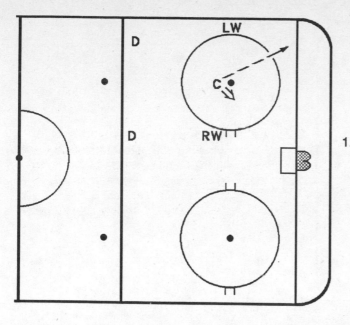

OFFENSIVE ZONE FACE-OFFS

1. Full Strength

   Assignments:

   C   - Shoots for net or draws to the left side
   LW - Goes for the puck in the corner
   RW - Goes for the net

1A. Assignments:

   C   - Draws the puck back to left winger
   RW - Prevents opposition from reaching left
          winger and then goes for the net
   LW - Takes the draw from centre and shoot
          for the net

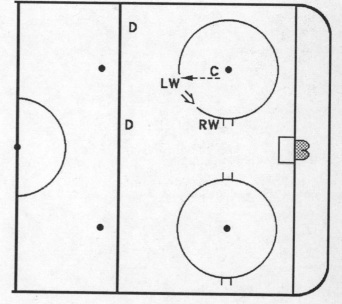

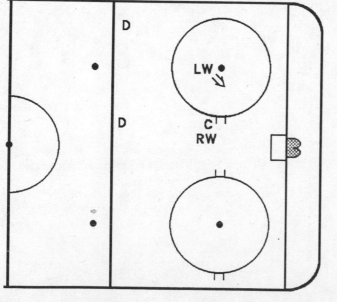

1B. Assignments:

   LW - Shoots for the net
   C   - Goes for the net
   RW - Goes for the net

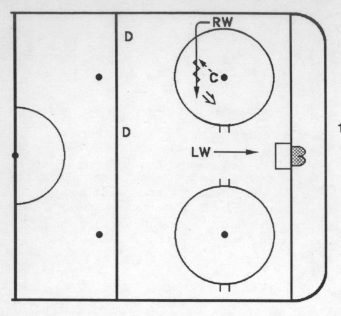

1C. Switch wingers with right hand shot on left side. RW moves across circle and shoots. LW blocks defensive player.

1D. Assignments:

C - Draws the puck back to left defenseman
LW - Goes for the net
RW - Goes for the net
LD - Shoots
RD - Backs up the play

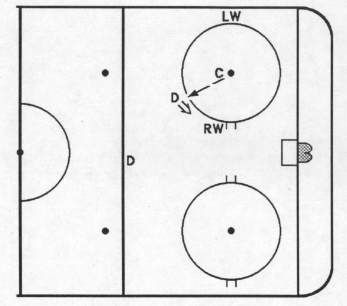

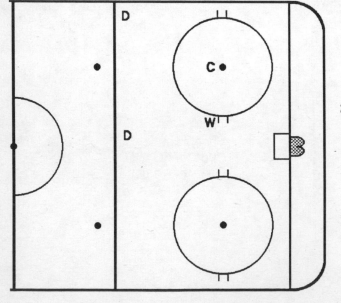

2. One man short

Assignments:

C   - Takes centre
W   - Takes left winger or go for the net
LD - Backs up the play
RD - Backs up the play

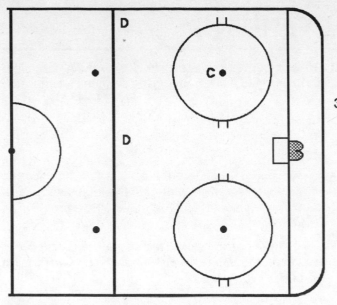

3. Two men short

   Assignments:

   C   - Takes face-off

   LD - Backs up the play and is in position to receive draw

   RD - Backs up the play and watches for a quick break

DRILLS:

Work in groups of three: One player drops the puck and the other two face-off. Rotate. Use all face-off spots on the rink.

Team face-off drills: Face-offs using various positions concentrating on defensive and offensive aspects. Practise one-man and two-men short drills.

15. GOALTENDING

Most hockey experts believe that the goaltender is the most important player on a hockey team. An excellent goaltender can make the difference on any team and be instrumental in improving the chances for success.

QUALITIES OF A GOOD GOALTENDER

Skating ability

It has been said by many that the goaltender should be the best skater on the team. The goaltender is required to complete many quick skating movements. All good goaltenders master the fundamentals of skating, such as start and stop, skate backward, forward, move side to side, drop to the knees and return standing, drop on the side and back and return to a standing position, pivot and make quick turns.

Reaction time

The goaltender must be able to react quickly to the movement of the puck and move the whole body, catching glove, stick glove or leg to stop the puck. Reaction time and movement time are improved through constant practice of the correct movement over and over at a high speed.

Playing the angles

As the position of goaltending is studied further, it becomes increasingly apparent that in certain situations the puck shot is faster than the body can react to stop the puck. Positioning the body at the optimal angle to reduce the openings in the net is one of the key areas for successful goaltending. It is important that the goaltender plays the angles evenly and does not over or under cover the short or far side. Experienced goaltenders stop many shots by body position alone.

GOALTENDING STANCES

Stand-up

The feet are apart so that the inside of the pads are barely touching. The stick is held in front of the skates with blade flat and at a 90-degree angle to the ice. The stick glove hand holds the stick slightly up the shaft from the wide part of the blade. The knees are slightly bent and the upper body is leaning only slightly forward from the upright position. The catching glove is held at the side at a point even with the top of the pad and slightly to the side.

Crouch

The crouch differs from the stand-up style in that the upper body is bent well forward at the waist. The legs are further apart and the knees are in a half squat position. The stick is held on the thin shaft next to the wide part of the stick and the catching glove is only slightly to the side of and half way down the pad.

Butterfly or "V" style

The legs are well apart and the feet are outside the width of the shoulders. The catching glove is usually only slightly below the waist and out from the pad. The stick is held in front of the opening between the pads and usually out from the pads and tilting slightly backward.

GOALTENDING SKILLS

1. **Moving side to side**

   The skate is pushed sideways off the near skate and the far skate is slid sideways to the far post all in one movement. The stick is pushed to the outside of the goal post to prevent a pass from the corner. The body faces forward and the head turns slightly to the side.

2. **Moving in and out**

   The skates turn outward slightly to glide forward. The skates turn inward slightly to move backwards. This move cuts down the angle of the shooter. The goaltender moves outside the crease while the puck is outside the blueline and moves back in as the puck carrier approaches the goal area.

3. **Skate save**

   The skate save is executed by rotating the leg outward and turning the foot to 90 degrees or better to the angle of the puck. The skate blade is kept on the ice and the leg continues to move sideways to deflect the puck to the corner.

4. **The full splits skate save**

The legs split apart and the skate save leg rotates outward and fully extends with the foot turned to 90 degrees. The other leg moves outward and slightly backward with the knee slightly bent. The catching hand is held upward. The stick is held between the legs. The full splits save is only used as a last resort to stop a puck shot low to the far side.

5. **The half splits skate save**

The skate save leg rotates outward and fully extends with the foot rotated to a 90 degree angle to the puck. The other leg bends and the pad is put flat on the ice. The goaltender can return to a standing position faster with the half splits than the full splits. The half splits save is used instead of a full splits save whenever possible as the goaltender is in a better position to recover.

6. **Double leg save**

The goaltender keeps both pads together and shoots both legs out to the side with one pad on top of the other. The glove hand is held high above the pads and the stick arm is extended above the head along the ice. This move is used when the goaltender has to make a fast move from the far post with the shooter at the far side of the net with the puck.

From the butterfly position, the goaltender extends his legs outward with the inside surface of the pads being on the ice. The blade of the stick is flat on the ice with the catching hand held high. This move is used for low and screened shots.

7. **Glove save**

The glove should be open and in a ready position to the side of the body. Try to catch all pucks to the glove side and release immediately to the corner or to a teammate. Do not let the puck hit the boards if possible. Bring the glove hand to the body if face-off is desired. Shots at the mid section should be controlled by the glove hand. Catch only the pucks on the glove side. Use the stick, pads and skates for low shots only and do not try to catch every shot on the net.

8. **Freezing the puck with the glove**

To freeze the puck with the glove, put the blade of the stick in front to protect the hand. Put the body directly behind the puck.

9. **Stick glove**

Shots to the stick glove can be either deflected to the corner or preferably covered and controlled by the catching glove. To deflect shots, the stick glove should angle only slightly to the corner and down. Pucks shot to the mid section of the body should be blocked by the stick glove and controlled by the catching glove.

10. **Block pass from corner**

Keep the blade of the stick outside the goal post to prevent the pass from the corner to the front of the net. Be in a position facing forward ready to save the shot if the pass is completed to the offensive man in front of the net.

11. **Stopping puck behind the net**

The goalie must be able to skate quickly from the net and stop the puck behind the net. The stick is held in one hand and the puck is left approximately 6" from the boards so that a teammate can easily take possession. If rushed by the attacking players, the puck should be shot back to the corner it came from. Once the puck is stopped, the goaltender should return quickly to the net. Until the goaltender has gained confidence, only shots from outside the blueline should be stopped by the goaltender behind the net.

12. **Passing the puck to a teammate**

The goaltender should attempt to clear all shots to a teammate. To pass the puck on the forehand side, use two hands on the stick and one hand for the backhand.

13. **Goaltender poke check**

The poke check can be used when the offensive player cuts across from the side of the net or moves straight in close to the goaltender. When the offensive man cuts across in front of the net, the goaltender should make the poke check with the bottom of the blade as the puck carrier draws even to the net. When the player comes straight, wait until he reaches to within extended stick length. This move is not advisable unless the puck carrier has his head down and is in close.

To poke check, push the stick forward and hold the stick at the end of the handle. Hit the puck with the bottom of the blade. The stick arm should be fully extended. The front knee is on the ice and the back leg is extended.

The goaltender must make sure that the puck carrier is in range before he makes the push with the stick.

14. Bounce shot save

Pucks shot at the stick should be steered to a teammate or to the corner by angling the blade to a greater angle than 90 degrees. The blade of the stick should not rest against the skates but should be held in front. Pucks hitting the skates should be steered to the corner. The pads should be slightly bent forward to allow shots to project downward instead of outward. Shots to the body should be controlled by both gloves. Shots to the stick glove should be deflected downward or to the corner or if possible controlled by the glove hand. Shots to the glove side should be caught cleanly and quickly thrown to the side or back to a teammate. If time permits, the puck in a glove save should be dropped to the stick and passed forward or to the side to a teammate.

15. Clearing the puck in front of the net

The goaltender must be quick to clear any pucks in front of the net to a teammate or to the corner. Either the forehand or backhand method with one hand on the stick is the quickest method. If time permits, a two hand forehand pass can be executed.

16. Screen shots

Keep low and move to try and get a view of the puck. Move out of the net to cut down the angles. The defenseman can help the goaltender by moving the players from in front of the net.

17. Breakaway

On a breakaway, the goaltender should stay well out as the player crosses the blueline. He should move back into the crease only as the player moves in closer. Stay out if the player has his head down.

18. Two-on-one, three-on-one, three-on-two

In a two-on-one, the goaltender should play the puck carrier and leave the open man to the defenseman. If the puck carrier moves right to the net, the defenseman then must move to prevent the puck carrier from cutting across in front of the net. The goaltender must play the puck being aware that the other offensive player may have moved to the slot area. The goaltender must play the puck at all times, in all other three-on-one, and three-on-two situations.

Covering the angles evenly and cutting down the target area is essential in all these situations. It is also extremely important that the goaltender know how his teammates will react. This can be accomplished by continued drill.

DRILLS FOR GOALTENDERS

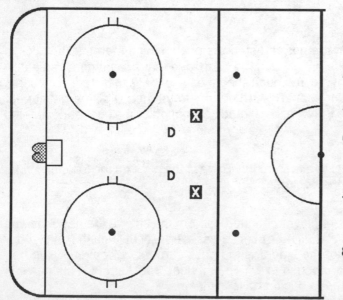

1. All drills in Shooting Section.
2. All drills in Skating Section.
3. Agility: knees and up. Goalie goes down on both knees and jumps up quickly to feet.
4. Agility: side to side. Goalie moves from post to post as quickly as possible.
5. Agility: in and out, side to side. Goalie moves in and out and side to side in his crease.
6. Agility: pick up pucks. Goalie without stick picks up puck from pile on one side, places it in the middle of crease, moves to the opposite side and repeats.
7. Practise the following movements on both knees: skate saves, full splits, half splits, double leg slides, butterfly pad saves.
8. Movement Drill (shown)
   Players pass the puck around and the goalie moves with the puck.

The goaltender must be able to react quickly to the movement of the puck. Positioning is also important: experienced goaltenders stop many shots by body position alone.

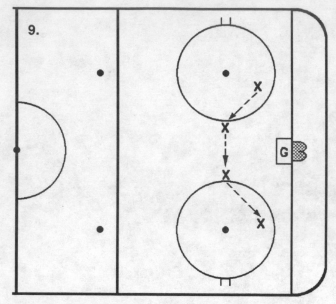

9. Movement drill
Players pass puck across in a semicircle in front of the net. Goalie moves with the puck.

10. Throw or shoot puck at goalie and have him steer puck toward corner.

11. Throw or shoot bounce shots at goalie.

12. Shoot on goalie and have him pass puck to a breaking forward; pass to both sides.

13. Shoot pucks around boards and have goalie stop them behind net.

14. Pass pucks from corner and have goalie stop pucks and clear.

15. Shoot pucks off the back boards so that they end up in front of the net; have goalie clear pucks either to corner or to a player.

16. Goalie lies on his side; coach kneels by his side and drops puck in front of pads; a player skates in and tries to shoot puck over pads.

17. Goalie lies on his side parallel to front of net or on his stomach perpendicular to front of net; coach has pucks in a semicircle in front; on command, goalie gets to feet as quickly as possible and stops shot by coach; repeat.

18. Agility: move on coach's signals all ways.

19. Agility: go across ice with short choppy steps.

20. Agility: move across ice with leg crossing side steps.

21. Angle drills: coach moves to various positions and goalie moves with him to cover angle for shot from that position; coach advises goalie if angle is correct.

22. Angle drill: players stationed at various positions with pucks; players shoot on command and goalie covers angle of shooter.

23. Skate around net with tight turn.

24. Skate around net with a tight turn and turn backward (Shown).

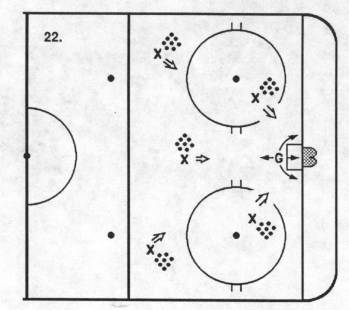

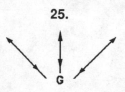

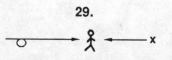

25. Agility: jump over stick, stop, backwards jump and stop.

26. In and out: poke check at puck.

27. Jump over stick waved two feet off the ice.

28. Rebounds and screen shots in close.

29. Agility: front roll, then stop a shot.

OFF-ICE GOALTENDING DRILLS

Off-ice training for goalies should emphasize flexibility, agility, speed, and strength training. Head and leg movements similar to those used in a game may also be simulated in off-ice training.

Flexibility
NOTE: Do all exercises slowly

1. Alternate toe touch
2. Double leg toe touch
3. Hurdlers stretch: forehead to alternate knees, forehead to knees together
4. Kneeling position: grasp the ankles, bend backwards
5. "V" sit
6. Bent knee sit-ups
7. Crouch, jump as high as possible with arms stretched

Agility

1. Jump back and forth two feet at once, holding the arms in goaltending position
2. Jump back and forth one to two feet
3. Jump sideways from one foot to the other
4. Butterfly position and up
5. Forward, backward, sideways running

6. Initial stance: front roll quick start, fast stop, move sideways and sit down on chair
7. Same drill: hit tennis ball at goalie after front roll and fast stop
8. Dive forward, come back to a crouch position
9. Front kip up, back kip up
10. Front roll to half-splits position
11. Cartwheel
12. Trampoline work: jumps, spins, forward and backward somersaults, knees up, etc.

Specific catching drills

1. Stand five feet from the wall with a tennis ball in each hand.
2. Throw the balls alternately and together against the wall and catch them on the rebound.
3. Work in pairs, throw two tennis balls back and forth.
4. Juggle two tennis balls.
5. Hit the tennis ball at the glove side and stick side.
6. Work in pairs, and throw a medicine ball or volleyball back and forth.
7. Two goalies in a butterfly position face each other; a tennis ball is dropped between them and the two players attempt to catch the ball.
8. The goalie with both stick and catching glove stands in front of a piece of plywood the size of a net; the instructor stands 15 feet away and hits tennis balls with a racquet high and low, trying to hit the plywood.
9. Same drill as 8 except a screening player stands in front of goalie.

16. PLAY OF THE DEFENSEMEN

The play of defensemen is an important topic when discussing the requirements for a successful team in today's style of hockey. Defensemen have to be as skilled as anyone on the team. Their traditional defensive role is still important but their offensive involvement is of increasing value. The good defenseman is expected to:
- work the defense;
- be big and strong to move people away from the front of the net;
- be quick and agile in moving the puck to initiate the play in the defensive zone.

In order to control the middle of the ice you need to have your most skilled players on the defense and at centre. If you don't have defensemen who can handle the puck well you may have to think about converting a forward. This is the type of player teams are looking for and few teams win without them.

Prepare defensemen for this style of play by:
- knowing the skills required for being a successful defenseman;
- using drills appropriate for learning the specific skills;
- being able to evaluate the learning efforts and offering feedback to the player.

SKILLS REQUIRED FOR PLAYING DEFENSE

TECHNICAL

Some say that teaching the technical skills is just for the young players, but this is not so. All age groups can benefit from technical improvement. Contrary to the way many coaches feel, even the 16 to 20 age group can make great progress if taught properly.

1. Skating

In hockey, defensemen have to perform the most skating skills. They have to perform many different skills, not just tight turns and quick starts, but backward skating, pivoting, and all the other skating skills. The skating skills that are particularly important for defensemen are:
- backward crossovers so that one can accelerate while skating backward while keeping in front of the puck carrier;
- turning - especially from backward to forward, as it means moving laterally to stop someone from going wide around them;
- backward stop and start;
- a tight turn and moving forward with quick acceleration;
- quick start.

2. Passing

If the defenseman can't pass the puck, all the basic ideas for breakouts are not going to work. Good passing is essential for getting organized in your own end and for performing the regrouping plays in the neutral zone. All passing skills should be constantly reviewed, using both the backhand and forehand, with some of the more important skills being:
- a sweep and snap pass while skating backwards and forwards;
- a sweep and snap pass coming out of a tight turn;
- "one touch" passing;
- a clearing flip pass.

3. Checking

The defensemen are expected to be good checkers, but often they are not taught the details of performing the various checks. The following are the basic checking skills used by the defensemen:
- poke check;
- shoulder check;
- hip check: In the past there have been some real masters of this check, but this still is seldom practised today. Interestingly, there are some coaches who feel that the hip check shouldn't be used at all,

especially along the boards because if you miss, then the opponent is home free. They would rather have the defenseman turn outside and face the man than to go in with the rear and risk missing him. The hip check, if executed properly, is really effective in the neutral zone.

- controlling the man along the boards;
- controlling the man in front of the net;
- a diving poke check. If a defenseman gets caught in a one-on-none and has been beaten, this check can be used in a last effort.

4. Puckhandling

- skating backward with the puck and then passing it, which often occurs in the neutral zone;
- making a pivot and then accelerating forward;
- stickhandling through tight turns.

5. Shooting

- quick releasing the puck;
- slap and snap shots, especially with low follow-throughs for low shot;
- wrist shot;
- "one timing" the shots.

INDIVIDUAL TACTICAL SKILLS

There are players who have reasonable technical skills but lack the ability to fully utilize them in games. Helping players use their skills effectively in a game requires constant work. Do not assume that a defenseman will know how to defend against a one-on-one unless it is practised. The following are the tactical skills that a defenseman should have.

SKILLS REQUIRED IN THE DEFENSIVE ZONE

1. Defensive Skills

- One-on-none: When a defenseman is beaten and is the last man, a diving poke check is necessary.
- One-on-one: head up, stick in one hand with elbow bent, poke check when in range but keep the head up and continue to take the man.
- Two-on-one: the last defender should think of an imaginary line running the length of the ice between the goalposts, and that is where he should play the opponents. Also, think of the situation as a two-on-two in which the goalie has the outside shots and the defenseman has the middle. When the puck gets within 15 feet of the net the defenseman goes for the puck carrier because the goalie can now move out to play the shooter. It is preferable that the defenseman use the marking on the ice as reference points when out to challenge the puck carrier.
- Two-on-two: most coaches would advocate staying on your own side and not crossing until there is a threat of scoring.
- Three-on-two: each defenseman plays half ice.
- Three-on-two (with one backchecker): defense closes the gap; defenseman with winger covered moves toward the middle of the ice.
- Three-on-two (with two backcheckers): defense stands up over blueline.
- Going into the corner to control the opponent.
- Covering the front of the net.
- Avoiding and fighting off screens.
- Intercepting passes and blocking shots: in blocking shots, make sure that the blocker is close to the shooter before going down, whether with a slide, one knee, or two knees.

2. Offensive skills

Emphasize the importance of moving the puck quickly, particularly in the defensive zone. In almost all instances this will mean making the pass while moving. Besides getting more power behind the passes, movement also means a greater threat to a forechecker or a defenseman who will often pull back when a puck carrier is moving toward them.

- Retrieving the puck off the end boards at high speed.
- Feigning moves to get the forechecker off the defenseman as he retrieves the puck off the boards.
- Being able to pass quickly and accurately coming out of sharp turns.

- Knowing how to support the play as the last man.
- Knowing when to pass cross-ice in the defensive zone (a very dangerous play!).

NEUTRAL ZONE
1. Defensive Skills
- Know how to look for the opponent who may have cut behind.
- Know how much room to give on attacking situations. e.g. 2 vs 1. 3 vs 2 with one backchecker, etc. start from the far blueline and maintain fast backward skating to be able to react to any situation.
- Know how to read the attack.
- Be able to force the attacker to play to the defenseman's strength.
2. Offensive Skills
- Puck handling skills to set up the regrouping plays:
    - passing laterally to the other defenseman;
    - making a pass to a curling forward;
- Moving up to support the forwards in carrying the puck over the opponent's blueline, the "second wave".

OFFENSIVE ZONE
1. Defensive skills
- Know how to "read" when to hold the blueline and when to retreat.
- Know when and how to "pinch".
- How to play the offensive man 1 vs 1 on the blueline.
- How to provide support for the other defenseman.
- Being able to identify and cover the quick counter attack.

2. Offensive skills
- Have good skating skills so as to be able to carry the puck in.
- Have good puckhandling and shooting skills to move in as a scoring threat.
- Know when and where to shoot from the blueline. It is preferable to make most of the shots from mid-ice. When a shot has to be made from the boards, keep it low and across the front of the goal so it can be deflected.
- "One timing" the shot from the blueline
- Making passes to open up the middle for the slot man

DEVELOPING THE SKILLS
Drills are the means for achieving the desired skills. Being able to show one or two new drills every practice is not as important as using drills that work. Use enough drills to keep things from getting monotonous but really concentrate on ones that emphasize the fundamentals.

The key to using drills properly is knowing what you want to achieve. If there is a particular problem or skill that you feel should be dealt with, then this should be the basis for selecting your drill. If the drill can also be made to simulate game conditions, it will eliminate one further problem of transferring what has been learned to using it in a game. When done with game intensity, it will also add a spirit and enthusiasm to your practice that is similar to what is expected during a game.

Besides setting up drills that are skill and game-specific, note what kind of learning is taking place. This is the mark of a good coach. Knowing the details of what is required and comparing it with what is actually being demonstrated by the players. Evaluating the outcome and offering constructive feedback is essential in the proper use of drills.

How much time should be spent on defensemen-related drills? Certainly there should be a component in every practice and many of the drills for the forwards could involve the defensemen. If the time is available, consider having a special practice once a week just for the defensemen.

Start all drills with the simplest one to build up the success rate and player confidence. Add to the complexity and get closer to game conditions.

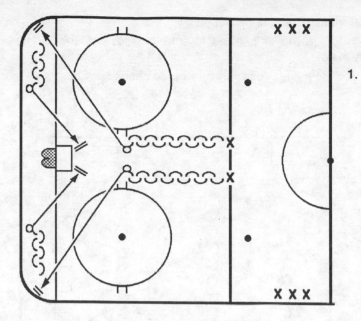

1. Backward turning, both sides: When the offensive team brings the puck into the defensive zone, the defensemen usually have to play their man by pivoting to the inside or outside.

   Players skate backwards from the blueline and at an ice marking or signal, turn to the outside and skate forward into the corner and stop. They then skate backward a few strides, turn in an opposite direction to their first turn, and skate to the net and stop. Switch sides after each time through.

2. Agility: During the game, the defensemen must be able to move quickly in a confined area, e.g., playing the "box" against a power play.

   Players skate forward from the goal line to the blueline, chop-step half way across the blueline, skate backward to the middle of the circle, turn to the outside and skate deep into the corner, make a sharp turn and return to the front of the net.

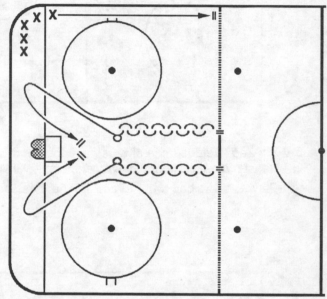

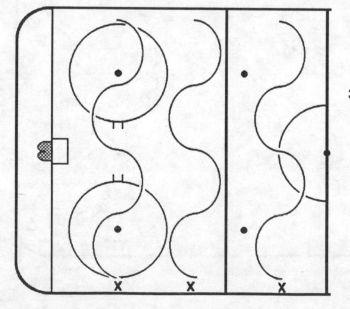

3. Cross-ice crossovers: Defensemen are expected to be able to skate backward, accelerating and moving side to side.

   Players move as a wave across the ice making three to four crossovers each way.

   Variation: The same exercise but change the direction in response to a signal and do it going lengthwise.

4. Defensemen must be able to stay face-to-face with an opponent while backing up.

   Players are paired off. Attacking players skate forward in a three to four crossover fashion. The defenders skate backwards attempting to stay in front.

   Variation: Attackers use a puck but the defenders do not aggressively attempt to check it away.

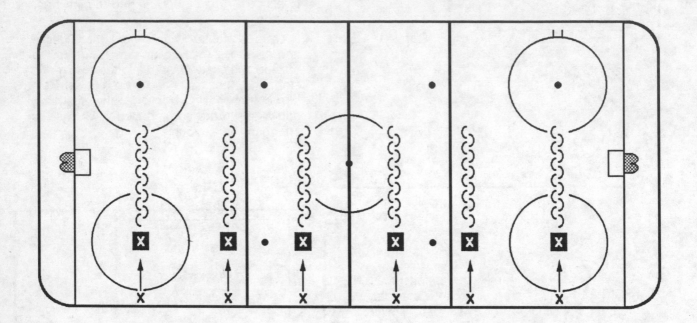

5. Zig-Zag: Defensemen always have the need for fast backward skating speed plus the ability to quickly transfer to sharp lateral movement to stay with an opponent.

   Players skate backward to each of the lines and then cross-step along the length of each line.

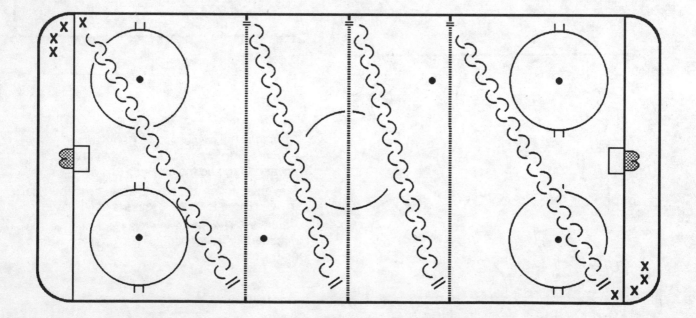

6. **Bringing the puck out:** Defensemen must be able to quickly retrieve a puck off the end boards under strong forechecking pressure, make a sharp turn and move the puck up ice.

Each player dumps the puck in the corner and retrieves it by making a sharp turn and quickly accelerating out with the puck. It is important to pick the puck up using manoeuvers that would throw off the forechecker. e.g., head fakes, a wave movement of the stick in the opposite direction. Add forecheckers later.

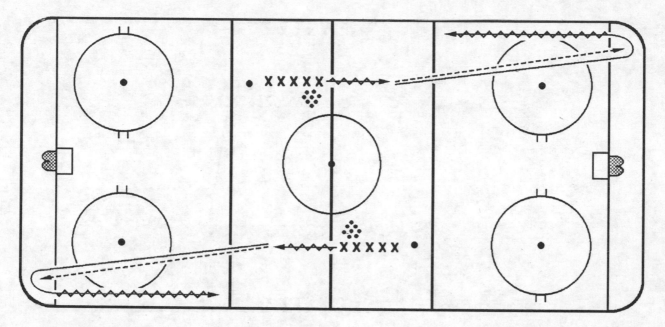

PASSING DRILLS

1. **Shuttle drill:** There are a number of occasions during a game when a defenseman has to make passes while skating backward or forward, and be able to convert these passes from receptions that vary from a puck sliding along the ice to a puck knocked down by a glove.

One player moves forward, the other backward across the ice. The puck is passed back and forth using different skills, e.g., flipping the puck and batting it down with a glove, "one touching" a return pass, etc.

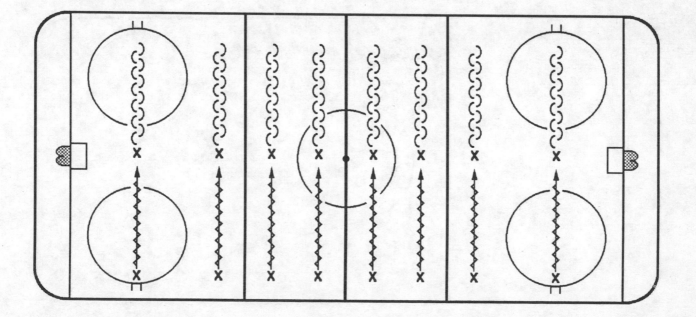

2. **Backward passing:** Skating backwards with the puck is very important in today's game. Good neutral zone play is difficult if the defensemen can't skate backward with the puck to help spread the forecheckers and give the regrouping forwards time to find open passing lanes.

The front player in each line (the one with the puck) skates to mid-ice and passes the puck to his partner. Both skate backwards to the goal, passing the puck between them.

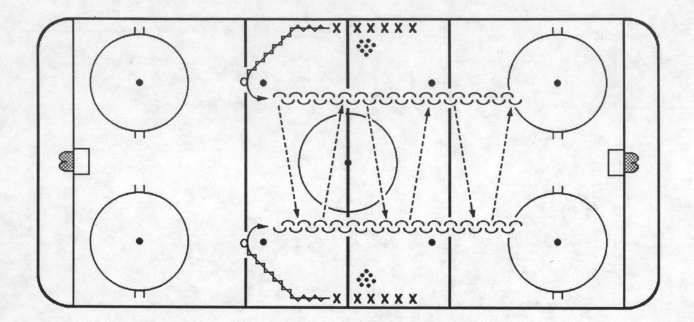

3. **Defenseman-to-defenseman warm-up shooting drill:** In neutral zone regrouping, it is often necessary for one defenseman to pass to the other before moving the puck to a curling forward.

The forward starts out with the puck and passes to the defenseman on his side. The defenseman skates backward with the puck and passes it to his defense partner who then gives the forward a pass as he curls around centre circle.

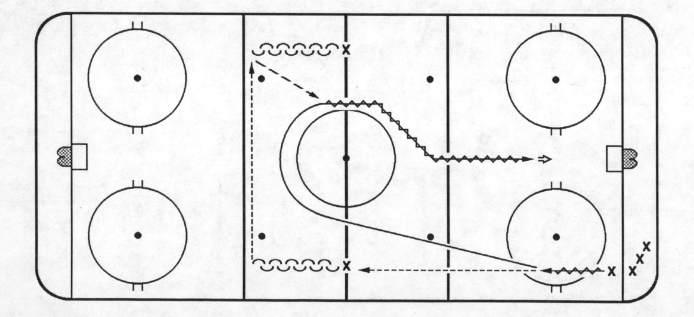

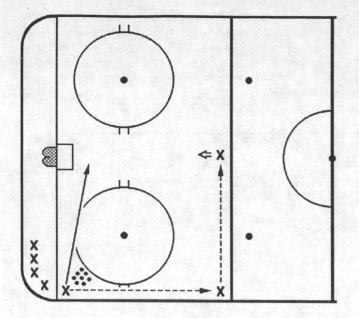

SHOOTING

Passout from the corner: Point men often have to make quick decisions on a passout or clearing a shot from a corner. To add to the complexity, the puck often arrives in a manner which is difficult to receive.

The player in the corner passes to the defenseman in different ways; off the boards, off the glass, bouncing, etc. He then goes to the net for deflections. The defenseman learns to play a variety of passouts. He relays a pass to his defense partner, as quickly as possible. He should look towards his partner before passing and not get in the habit of passing blindly. Slow passes likely will have to be returned to corner man in which case give-and-go from corner man can be made.

CHECKING

1. Hip check: Defensemen have to have many ways of checking. Sometimes hip checking an opponent is the most effective way at that moment. There is a tendency to ignore teaching this type of check which, if done correctly, can be very effective in taking a man completely out of the play.

    Start by practising along the boards, where the defenseman goes into the boards with his hip and checks the man. When some success has been attained, move out to open ice.

2. Diving poke check: Sometimes the defenseman is last man back and is beaten by the puck carrier. A diving poke check is often the only recourse available. Have players experience the different ways of sliding along the ice. Slide along the ice trying to touch the puck and the stick of puck carrier first

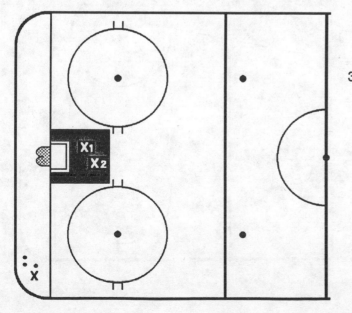

3. Controlling man in front of the net: It is necessary for defensemen to control the area in front of the net. Knowing how to tie up a man is an important part of this play.

    Player in the corner has three pucks and passes them out to forward in low slot. The forward must move around low slot area to try and get open for a pass for a shot on goal. Defenseman practices controlling in a legal manner by angling, blocking, pushing, or using his stick.

4. One-on-one: Defensemen should be aware that they can sometimes get beaten on a one-on-one. However, they shouldn't become so obsessed that they are caught leaving the blueline before they have to. The defenseman can keep the puck in if he moves in quickly and challenges the puck carrier before full speed is attained. The player starts from a corner with the puck. The defenseman should close the gap with the puck carrier by getting within stick length before too much speed is built up. D starts at the blueline and moves at an angle two strides inside the blueline to pick up the player coming from the corner. D now skates backward to play the one-on-one.

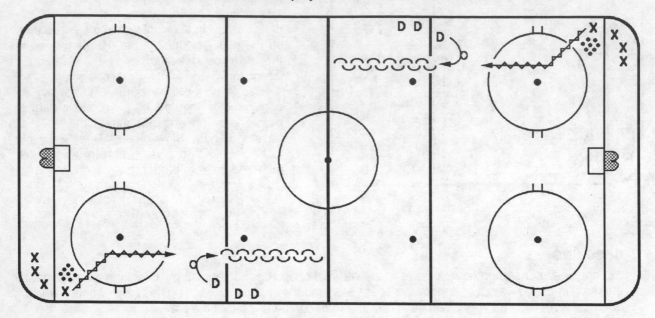

5. One-on-one from a circle: To improve backward skating speed of the defenseman. The player starts the play without a puck and swings around a pylon at the far blueline. He receives a pass from the corner and stickhandles down the ice in a one-on-one. When the original player who started the drill leaves, a player from the inside line leaves and swings around centre circle, pivots and plays the one-on-one. Rotate lines each time you come back.

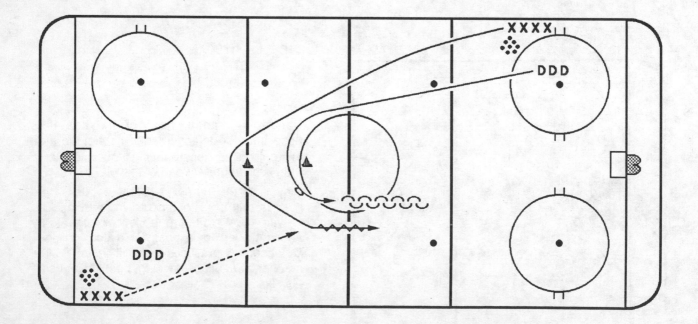

6. One-on-one flow drill: This forces the defenseman to stretch his backward skating speed to its maximum level. Player starts from the corner, without the puck, and receives a pass from the defenseman who swings around the pylon at the blueline. The puck carrier goes for the far net with game intensity. The defenseman skates around the pylon, pivots and plays the man one-on-one so that it will require all-out backward skating.

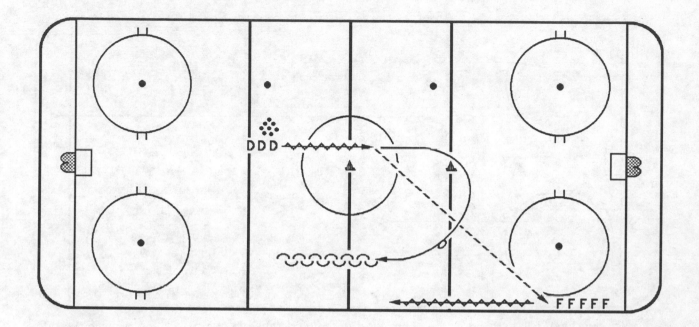

7. **Blocking shots**

Defensemen sometimes go down to block shots in the high slot and if they miss, they give the puck carrier an open road to the net.

Set up a drill in the low slot where you want a block to occur and, if necessary, build up the blocker's confidence by using tennis balls. Have the players practise different styles: the slide, one-and two-knee blocks. Experiment with each one to determine its blocking value and effectiveness in preventing the shooter from avoiding the block.

TEAM PLAY SITUATIONS

Defensemen should be starting all the team drills. The more they do this, the more they will have a chance to practise their passing skills. I'm not a believer in the two-on-nones or three-on-nones. Maybe they are good for a warm-up drill, but not for working on something that you are going to use in a game. Besides, a three-on-none is not a game-like situation. The defensemen should be in drills at all times. They should start the play and be in it all the way because that is what happens in a game.

Too often the defenseman on a two-on-one or three-on-one becomes over anxious and moves out of the mid-ice zone giving the attacker the inside shot. Preferably, the defenseman should stay in the middle and go no farther than the imaginary line between the posts on either side. When the puck gets back to within 10 to 15 feet of the goal, the defenseman has to play the puck carrier.

1. Two-on-one: The defenseman starts the play for two forwards with a breakout pass. The defenseman then skates hard for the far blueline and prepares to defend against a two-on-one on the return rush.

   The forwards execute a two-on-one rush. Upon completion of the two-on-one play, the defenseman defending the two-on-one play picks up a puck and starts a rush the other way.

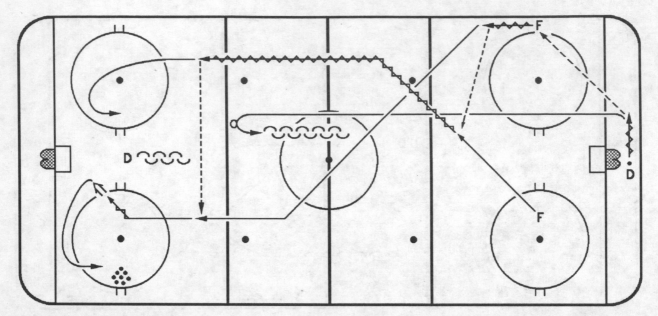

2. Back checking drill: In this drill, the coach tries to get the defense to stand up at the blueline. Start the drill with a D to D pass, a pass to a forward, and a five-on-four breakout. The two back checkers pick up the lanes, allow the defensemen to stand up at the blueline, and concentrate on the puck carrier. When the initial rush is completed, the flow is maintained with a five-on-two going the opposite way. Repeat two or three times.

   Variation: Use just one back checker or one forechecker in the offensive zone and one back checker in the neutral and defensive zone. Have back checkers vary their activity by filling lanes, covering a winger, or checking the puck carrier, so the defensemen can practise reading and reacting to different situations.

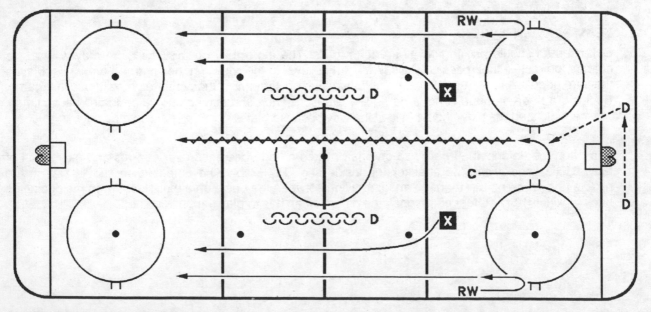

NOTE: These backchecking drills should be part of almost every practice. The flow and the variations also make it possible to build up the intensity and simulate game conditions.

184

17. PLAY OF THE FORWARDS

SPECIFIC ABILITIES OF FORWARDS

Wings

- Ability to cut in after taking a pass;
- Quick, hard, accurate, shot coming off the wings;
- Strong speed skater;
- Ability to take and give a pass;
- Ability to pick up a check.

Centres

- Good hockey sense;
- Able to pass well on forehand and backhand;
- Good stickhandler;
- Good skater with the ability to turn quickly and crossover while accelerating;
- Quick shot;
- Good checker;
- Better than average endurance;
- Good face-off man.

POSITIONAL PLAY

1. Defensive end

Wingers should station themselves near the boards with the stick in a position to receive and give a pass quickly. The centreman should be circling with his stick on the ice in a position ready for a pass. The puck should be passed to the head man as quickly as possible.

2. Neutral zone

Wingers should be skating down by the boards looking for an opening to put on a quick acceleration. The stick should be on or near the ice in a position for a pass.

3. Offensive zone

The winger should be in the corner if the puck is on his side. He should have his head up, take the man first, and then go for the puck.

If the winger receives a pass he should be able to cut in without losing stride and shoot or drop the puck in the slot. The far side winger should position himself in the slot area squared off to the net, ready to shoot.

The centreman should make the play, if possible, just as the winger hits the offensive blueline. The centre should trail the play or go on the forecheck if the puck has been shot in.

The section on Offensive Team Play describes the offensive play of the forwards.

FACE-OFF TECHNIQUES

The man taking the face-off should make sure that all players are in position before taking the face-off.

The player taking the face-off should be able watch the puck in the referee's hand and the opponent's stick at the same time by using peripheral vision. Quick reaction time is essential in this skill.

Players taking the face-off should have many methods of winning:

1. Backhand: This is the most common method. The player draws the puck at an angle or in some instances directly back on the backhand side.

2. Forehand: Anticipate the dropping of the puck. Rotate the body by a quarter turn. Come in front of, behind or under an opponent's stick.

3. Anticipate the dropping of the puck. As soon as the puck leaves the official's hand, hit the blade of your opponent's stick and then draw the puck back.

4. Hold and draw: Hold the opponent's stick with the blade of the stick until the puck has made contact with the ice. Then draw the puck back.

5. Lift and draw: If the opponent is attempting to slash the blade of the stick and is not going for the puck, lift the blade of the stick and then go for the puck.

6. Shoot: Shoot the puck directly from the face-off.

7. Skate through and shoot: The face-off man pushes the opponent's stick upward, skates through the face-off dot and kicks the puck to the stick.

DRILLS FOR FORWARDS

All shooting, passing, stickhandling, and checking drills mentioned in chapters 2, 3, 4, and 5 are excellent for forwards. Special emphasis should be placed on taking a pass in full stride and shooting quickly.

All one-on-one, two-on-one, two-on-two, three-on-one, and three-on-two drills with the winger or wingers covered should be emphasized. Individual face-off practice and team skill is also essential.

18. SCOUTING, GAME PREPARATION and BENCH MANAGEMENT

The saying "failure to prepare is preparing to fail" is a coaching truism. Careful planning and preparation for games gives the athletes and coaches a sense that they are ready for the contest. A well prepared team knows what to expect from the other team and this gives the players a feeling of confidence.

Game preparation can be divided into five areas: scouting the opposition, practise utilization for the opposition; pre game meeting; bench management during the game; and between period adjustments.

SCOUTING

Scouting the opposition should be done as close to the game date as possible. Trends, new personnel, changes in tactics, etc., are reasons why the latest game of the opposition team should be viewed. Usually, one or two members of the staff with the team should scout the game. The following is a scouting report that can be used to critique and analyze the opposition.

Opposition scouting

Scouted By	Score	Team Scouted	VS	Opposition	Score

Date	Place

FORWARD LINES	ORDER OF LINES	DEFENSIVE PAIRS
	1st 2nd 3rd	

Own end with puck
— How puck is brought out ....
— How they set up - centre circles ....
— Pass up the middle ....
— Defensemen carry ....

Opposition end with the puck
— Shoot or carry puck across the blueline ....
— Position of centre (net or slot) ....
— Good shooters ....
— Special plays ....

Power play
— How puck is brought out ....
— Centre come behind net ....
— Cetre pick up or leave for defenseman ....
— How they bring puck in over the blueline ....
— Special plays ....
— Shoot or carry across blueline ....
— Special plays in opposition end ....
— Position of centre in relation to box ....

Penalty killing

— Force play, how ....
— Pick up wings ....
— Defense up at centre for rush (at blueline
            or back in) ....
— Any forechecking pattern ....
— Box tight or loose ....
— Do they cover slot well ....
— Special face-off plays ....
— 2 men short ....

Own end (defensively)

— Who covers points ....
— Wingers up, centre back - or reverse ....
— Defence rough in front ....
— Weaknesses ....
— Face-off plays ....

Opposition end (checking)

— Who forechecks ....
— Position of centre ....
— Do defence hang in at blueline ....
— Weaknesses ....

Goaltending

— Rebounds ....
— Clearing puck ....
— Glove hand ....
— Stick hand ....
— Half splits ....
— Skate save ....
— Long shots ....
— Bounce Shots ....
— Conditioning ....
— Other comments ....

General comments

— Roughness ....

— How they start the game ....

— Face-offs (unusual) & best man ....

— Comments on lines ....

— Players to watch ....

— Unusual plays ....

— Other ....

The coach should be in total control of the bench. He must be ready to make quick decisions on personnel throughout the game and have a feel for which players are playing well.

GAME PREPARATION

Pre game meeting

It is useful to have a meeting to discuss the opposition's strengths and weaknesses. Such topics as playing style, power play, penalty killing, breakouts, forward lines, defence pairings, goaltending style, outstanding players, etc., can be discussed during this meeting. The scouting report can be used to discuss the opposition, and if short video segments are available on power play, breakouts, penalty killing, etc., they can be used at this time.

The pre game meeting should be no longer than twenty to thirty minutes. This should be more than enough time to highlight the opposition. Each player should be aware of such details as arrival time at the arena, the proper time to be in the dressing room, and game and warm-up times.

Pre game practice

The practice prior to the next game may also be used to prepare a team for the opposition. Practising against the opposition's style of forechecking, penalty killing, power play, and breakouts are some ways to prepare your team against certain systems.

A pre game meeting may occur before the practice or could be conducted on game day. Skate sharpening and preparation of sticks and equipment should be done after the last practice and before the game as the players' focus should be totally on the game when they arrive at the arena.

Arrival at the arena: Home games

Most coaches have a set time when the players must be in the dressing room. In most situations, players should be there a minimum of 45 minutes before the scheduled warm up. If dressing room stretching exercises are part of the routine the player should be prepared for this one hour before the warm- up.

Away games

A thorough knowledge of all details such as location of arena, parking, entrance doors, etc., will be important for the smooth preparation for a game. The location and size of dressing rooms, availability of a blackboard and chalk or rink diagram board is important information for the coach to know.

Other details include the size of the ice surface, shape of the corners, height of the glass around the rink (for pucks shot above the board level) type of ice (fast, slow, etc., especially near the end of a period) lighting, and the size and location of the entry gates to the bench. At the home arena, a good working relationship with the arena personnel is important for their cooperation in flooding the ice and cleaning of the dressing rooms, etc.

BENCH MANAGEMENT

Bench management is very important. The coach has to adjust to the opposition, as well as handle the team in an efficient manner during a game. Details such as the location of the gates on the players bench and the movement of players going on and coming off the ice are very important. In most cases an assistant trainer or other administrative personnel can open the gates. Some coaches prefer the defensemen to sit at the end of the bench closer to their own end of the rink with the forwards at the other end. Players usually come in through the gates and out over the boards (younger age groups should use the door at all times). Another useful idea is to have the players sit together in lines and defense pairs and move towards the middle of the bench. They are then ready to go over the boards when their names are called. This also allows the coach to be aware of those players who have not been on the ice recently or who have been sitting on the bench for some time as they will be on the middle of the bench. Some players may be on the bench by design of the coach or they just may have missed shifts due to penalty killing or power play situations.

It is important for a coach to plan before the game which players he is going to use in certain situations such as power play and penalty killing; how many lines he is going to use; which players will play more when behind or ahead in the game; and which players can be switched in event of injuries. The coach must also decide if he wants to match lines or cover certain players with a defensive-type player.

Having done all this the coach must be ready to make quick decisions on playing personnel throughout the game and must have a feel for which players are playing well on a certain night.

It is important that your players know who is going on the ice next. There are different systems for calling players such as by line and defence pairs, but in most cases the individual names of each player should be called for each line or defence pair up for the next shift. Little problems such as players with the same first or last name should be solved in advance by using nicknames. A good idea is to tell the players to turn and ask the coach if no names were called or if the players did not hear the names. The players should also be aware that they are responsible for replacing the position of the player on the ice and they must therefore be aware of which player on the ice is playing which position. In penalty killing and power play situations the coach may want to designate which player is being replaced on the ice. It is also the responsibility of the player on the bench to make sure that player on the ice is actually coming to the bench. Changing "on the fly" is something which should be practised. Most changes should be made while your team is in possession of the puck and the play is in the neutral or offensive zone. Some coaches time the on-ice shifts using a stopwatch with the alternate goalie or assistant coach doing the timing. This allows the players to get into a routine of quick changes and they will also be aware that the coach knows the length of each player's shifts.

If a delayed penalty is indicated and an extra man can be put on the ice when the goaltender comes to the bench, the coach should have a system for the player that replaces the goalie. Usually the coach designates one specific player or a specific position, such as the centre of the next line up to take the place of the goaltender.

The coach should be very aware of the momentum of the game and if his team is being outplayed badly, slowing the pace of the game down may be a good strategy. Coaches have been known to change the lines and defence pairs more frequently than usual, change goalies or even call a time out if this type of strategy is warranted in an attempt to change the momentum of the game.

The coach should also be in total control of the bench and, along with an assistant coach, should not allow negative comments about fellow teammates or yelling at the referee. The coach should be under control behind the bench but that does not preclude showing emotion or displeasure with a bad call by the referee. It is important that the coach keep control as emotions can allow him to get carried away and he may not then be ready for the next quick decision. Emotions, when used wisely, can sometimes be a motivational factor for the players.

Most teams have the head coach make the line changes and personnel adjustments while the assistant coach gives individual feedback to the players. It is important that the head and assistant coaches are coordinated and that each has a definite role behind the bench. A very important job of the coaches is to have the right players out at the right time and give feedback to the players during the game.

Between periods of the game

A good practice for coaches is to meet with the assistant coaches before going into the dressing room between periods. At this time, they could discuss the period statistics such as shots on goal and where they were taken; plus/minus; weaknesses of your team; strengths of the other teams; players playing well and poorly; and general strategy. After this has been done the head coach can go into the dressing room to discuss strategy and possible changes. Depending on the situation and how the team is performing, the coach can be positive or negative. If the team is playing well very little need be said. If the team is playing poorly, strategy changes, adjustments in style, personnel changes, etc. can be discussed. If the coach feels that the team is underachieving, it may be a situation in which the coach can be negative or use anger to motivate. If the coach has been negative, it may be wise to use some positive motivation just before the team returns to the ice to start the next period.

Post game review

After the game is over it is usual practice for a coach to enter the dressing room and make some general comments and congratulate the team on a win or make comments on a loss. The coach should let the players have a few minutes to cool down before making any comments. The coach could then review the schedule for the next practice or game. Some situations such as a big loss or poor play may require a team meeting. Some coaches have a team meeting after each game when the players are dressed and showered. It may also be necessary to meet individually with any players who are having problems or who may have caused a problem during the game.

In many situations, the head coach meets with the assistant coaches to discuss the games, analyze the statistics, and in some cases view the video of the game if this is available. If there are two or three assistant coaches, and if a video of the game is available, the job of breaking down and analyzing is done by the assistant coaches before the next practice or game. In some cases, the head coach may ask for certain video replays such as defensive breakdowns, power players, etc. In most cases the assistant coaches and the head coach will meet to discuss and view the video of the game. This can help the coaches to plan the next practice and work on apparent weaknesses.

A good coach is well organized and will have his team as well prepared as possible at all times. Remember, success comes more easily to those who are prepared.

19. STATISTICS

Statistics are a very important tool for the coach to assess what is happening during a game and to analyze what happened after the game is over. Over a longer period of time, statistics can show trends which will help the coach to assess the strengths and weaknesses of individual players and the team as a whole.

Although statistics may not be as meaningful with young hockey players, with older players and at higher levels of competition, statistics are important in the analysis of the total game or period by period. Strategy can be devised or altered depending on what is happening during the game. After viewing the statistics, a coach may notice tendencies in individuals or in the team as a whole which can be countered by a simple change in strategy.

Statistics point out individual and team errors which provide feedback to the coach. The coach in turn can now provide feedback to his players. In many cases the coach may have already spotted some or all of these errors but statistics serve to reinforce or change an idea a coach may have from observation. It is important for the coach in most cases to correct errors and use positive reinforcement. Although negative reinforcement can occasionally be used at the higher levels it is very important that statistics be used wisely by the coach and not become negative to the players by continually emphasizing what they are doing wrong. In most cases statistics can be used in a positive way to emphasize what a player is doing right.

After a thorough review of the game, the coach can also use the statistics to help plan his practices by emphasizing the weak areas of individual and team play. The practices may also be based on game strategy for the up coming opponent using the statistics of a previous game against the team as a basis for this planning.

Statistics can also be used as a motivational tool. Over a period of time, statistics can measure improvement and provide goals for both the team and the player. A large battery of statistics rather than just goals and assists will point out the importance of all aspects of the game and the value of different types of players on the team.

With younger players, game statistics may not have the same value as learning the basic fundamentals and having fun should be the most important aspect of the game. Emphasizing wins and losses, goals, and assists may mean that few if any statistics are used. Skill testing may be far more useful than spending time on complex statistics. Performance expectations have to be altered with the young hockey player with the major emphasis being skill improvement.

Statistics, however, do not tell the whole story of a game and it is important that a coach be able to quickly detect team and individual errors that are happening during a game. Statistics may confirm or change an opinion a coach may have reached by observation. It is the combination of an analytical eye and thorough game analysis that makes the complete coach.

Chart 1 describes the types of statistics that can be taken, the purpose of the statistics and how to use them.

There are many different methods of taking statistics. One or two regular reliable statisticians doing the job on a continuous basis is the best method for this task. People associated with the team such as friends or a parent, may be pleased to do this job. The statistician must also be able to compile the statistics after the game and keep a running up-to-date statistical record as well as point out trends to the coach. The statistician should report to the coach after each period and at the end of the game.

Chart 2 and Chart 3, are examples of a statistic sheet and a compilation of statistics for a team.

In conclusion, statistics are an important part of game analysis. They should be used positively to correct individual and team errors as well as to plan and change strategies before and during a game. If compiled properly and accurately, they can be an important aspect in the success of a team and the development of individual players.

CHART 1

STATISTIC	PURPOSE OF STATISTIC	YOUR TEAM	OPPOSITION
Shots attempted	To determine the number and location of shots taken by our own team and the opposition. These shots may or may not hit the net.	**INDIVIDUAL** Not attempting enough shots. Too many bad angles or outside shots. **TEAM** Not shooting enough. Too many outside shots.	**INDIVIDUAL** One player taking too many shots and not being checked closely enough. Player getting no or few shots. Reinforces good checking job. **TEAM** Too many shots from slot area and/or points. Team getting very few shots.
Shots on net Team opponents' totals Location of shots (team and opposition) Location of goals scored (team and opposition)	To determine the accuracy of the shooting. To determine the location of the shooter when the shots are on the net.	**INDIVIDUAL** Not shooting enough on net. Shooting from too far out. **TEAM** Very few shots on net. Too many shots from bad angles or from the outside. Not shooting from the slot area.	**INDIVIDUAL** One player getting too many shots on net. Player getting very few shots on net. Positive reinforcement on checking. **TEAM** Too many shots on net from the slot. Too many shots on net from the point or one side of the ice, e.g. right wingers or left defenseman getting too many shots.
Scoring chances	To determine how many direct scoring chances an individual or team is getting. Scoring chances are only counted when a shot is taken in from the high slot area and in toward the net.	**INDIVIDUAL** No chances means a player is not moving to the slot area for a scoring chance or a player is not being passed to in the scoring area. **TEAM** No chances means the opposition is clearing the slot and checking well or the team generally is not moving to the slot area.	**INDIVIDUAL** One player may be getting free in the slot area. **TEAM** Many good scoring chances means that the slot area is not being covered well.

STATISTIC	PURPOSE OF STATISTIC	YOUR TEAM	OPPOSITION
Shooting percentages	To determine the percentages of shots taken on goal and goals scored.	**INDIVIDUAL** To determine which players are the most proficient in the scoring area. **TEAM** To determine if the team's shooting acuracy adequate.	**INDIVIDUAL** To determine players who must be watched more carefully as the scoring percentage is high. **TEAM** High percentage shooting teams must be checked more closely.
Scoring statistics Goals	To determine the top goal scorers.	To determine the top goal scorers and get them on the ice at times when goals are needed, e.g., power play, behind one or two goals, pull the goalie, key face-off in opposition zone, etc. Period-by-period breakdown may show a trend.	Check the top scorers more closely. Get checkers out against the top scorers. Period-by-period breakdown may show weakness defensively at certain times in the game.
Scoring statistics Assists	To determine the best play-makers.	Should show best play-makers and good/ poor line combinations.	Top play-makers may be the key to a line and should be checked closely.
First goal, Tying goals Winning goals	To determine players who tend to get key goals.	To determine which players tend to score key goals. To know what players to use in critical situations in a game.	To determine which players tend to score key goals in games. To be able to defend against these players in critical game situations.
Penalties: - minor - major - unsportsmanlike - misconduct - match/gross misconducts	To determine which players are penalized, what type of penalties and which players are seldom penalized.	To determine which players tend to get more penalties than others. To determine when not to play players who have a high tendency to be penalized.	To determine which players tend to get more penalties than others. To try to draw a penalty from the highly penalized players.
Plus/Minus (full strength)	To determine the players who are on the ice when a goal is scored for or against while playing full strength.	A trend will develop if a certain defense pair or line is on for an unusual number of goals for or against. The coach may want to split up a weak defense pair or not play them in critical situations.	Detects strengths/weaknesses of defense pairs or forward lines that are high or low in this category. Close checking may be required against a high plus line. A stronger line may be sent out against a high minus line.

STATISTIC	PURPOSE OF STATISTIC	YOUR TEAM	OPPOSITION
Plus/Minus (power play and penalty killing)	To determine the players who are on the ice when a power play goal is scored for or against.	A trend will develop to identify best power play and penalty killing players and/or units.	To determine strong or weak penalty killing units of each opposition. Match your strength against strength and weakness against weakness.
Power play success %	To determine the overall success of your power play. 30 percent or better is considered quite good.	To determine the efficiency of your power play in general and against certain teams.	To determine the strength and scoring percentage of the opposition's power play.
Penalty killing %	To determine the efficiency of penalty killing. 80 percent or better is considered quite good.	To determine the efficiency of your penalty killing teams.	To determine the efficiency of the opposition's penalty killing teams.
Giveaways	To determine the number of poor passes in your zone that are intercepted.	To correct errors in thinking and/or execution in your zone. To determine poor passing skills and players who react well or poorly under pressure in your zone.	To determine poor passers or players who panic under pressure in their defensive zone. To know when and who to pressure in the opposition zone.
Body checks or take outs (hits)	To determine the number of body contacts made by the individual and team.	To determine which players are on or are not taking the man out and finishing the check. To determine the need for more checking drills and correction of errors in skill.	To determine if the opposition is a physical team or not. If a team is not taking the body, more liberties can be taken in the corners, etc.
Face-offs	To determine the number of face-offs won, lost, or tied in the defensive, neutral, or offensive zones.	If done poorly, work on face-off techniques should be increased in practice. Be able to put best face-off men out in critical situations. Be able to match against opposition face-off men. Be aware of a poor match-up of face-off men as the game progresses. Be aware of face-off men's efficiency in each zone.	To determine the strong and weak face-off men. To be able to match against strength and weakness.
Length of shifts	To determine the average length of shifts for each player.	To determine if shifts are too long or too short. Note if fatigue seems to be a factor.	To determine if the opposition has a marked tendency toward longer or shorter shifts. This will aid in line matching as well.

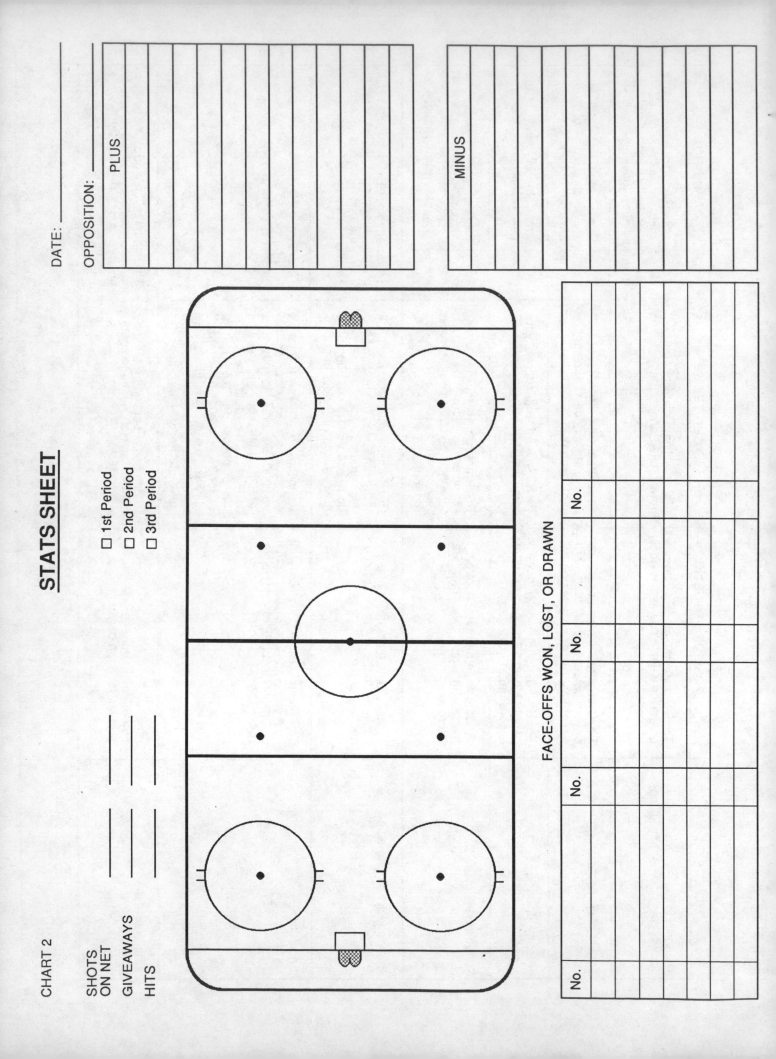

STATS SHEET

CHART 2

DATE: _____

OPPOSITION: _____

☐ 1st Period
☐ 2nd Period
☐ 3rd Period

SHOTS ON NET
GIVEAWAYS
HITS

PLUS

MINUS

FACE-OFFS WON, LOST, OR DRAWN

No.   No.   No.   No.

CHART 3

GAME SUMMARY

NO.	NAME	Games Played	Hits	Shots	Goals	Assists	Points	Minor Penalties	Major Penalties	Misconduct & GM Penalties	Goals Against Even Handed	Goals For Even Handed	Plus/Minus	Power Play Goals For	Penalty Killing Goals Against	Short Handed Goals For	Bad Pass Giveaway	FACE-OFFS W	L	%

VIDEO

USING THE VIDEO FOR EVALUATION AND GAME ANALYSIS

The VHS or Beta video machine is a common evaluation instrument used by today's hockey coach. Video is used extensively in game analysis for games played, prescouting, and training camp evaluation.

Scoring chances, defensive breakdowns, and team and individual errors can be analyzed. Segments of the video can be shown to the team the next day or even between periods if the video viewing equipment is available. The video assists the coaches in giving a thorough evaluation of the game played. When prescouting a team, a short video presentation can help prepare a team for the upcoming opponent. The opposition's breakouts, power play, penalty killing, forechecking, etc., can be highlighted in this presentation.

The video can also be used by the coach to assist with individual instruction for players. The player viewing himself on the video, with the coach showing and correcting errors, can assist in the teaching process. It is also important to show the player some good aspects of his game and to use the video as a positive teaching tool.

In training camp it is useful to video scrimmage games for replay, especially if the coach is undecided on the selection of some players. Similar to a team game analysis, the video can isolate segments of specific players' play.

The video has many uses when coaching hockey. To use the video correctly, it is important to have at least two people working in this area. The video machines, cameras, and television set for viewing, are all expenses which must be considered by a team before making a decision to use the video as a coaching tool. It should also be taken into consideration that the video can be overused in coaching. Long video viewing sessions on a regular basis will sometimes make players negative to its use. Highlighting clips of games which show both the positive and negative aspects of the previous game may be a more significant method of use. It is not necessary to have the players watch the video of every game, but it is a tool that the coaches can use extensively for analysis.

The video, like any coaching tool, is only as good or bad as the people using it. Use it wisely.

20. CONDITIONING

Conditioning for ice hockey should be a year round program to enable the player to reach his full potential. The physiological factors of strength, power, speed, agility, flexibility, reaction time, cardiovascular and muscular endurance should be tested for and improved as it relates to ice hockey.

THE TWELVE MONTH PLAN

To develop a conditioning programme for hockey, the year should be divided into four main periods.

- Preparation period (off season)
- Pre-season period
- Main period (competitive season)
- Passing period (post season)

APRIL	MAY	JUNE	JULY	AUG.	SEPT.	OCT.	NOV.	DEC.	JAN.	FEB.	MAR.
PASSING		PREPARATION			PRE-SEASON		MAIN PERIOD			PASSING	

1. Preparation Period (12 weeks)

The preparation period of training is extremely important for the player. During this period the hockey player must attempt to raise his total conditioning level as high as possible. In most cases the total conditioning level is not improved by any great percentages during the season and in some components of total fitness only a maintenance level is achieved during the competitive season.

The first step in the preparation period should be a fitness assessment profile to measure the athletes' strength, power, flexibility, muscular endurance, agility, fat percentage, and cardiovascular endurance (aerobic and anaerobic).

After the fitness assessment profile has been performed, the athletes should then go into an intensive training program to improve general fitness and especially weak areas.

2. Pre-Season (two to three weeks)

The pre season period usually extends from two to three weeks. It is a time to select players for the team and to have a number of exhibition and scrimmage games. Circuit training for general fitness is one of the best methods for conditioning during this period as it allows a large number of players to work out at the same time.

3. Main Period (competitive season)

During the competitive season it is important to improve, or at least maintain, the conditioning level achieved in the preparation period. The competitive season should consist of an anaerobic and aerobic cardiorespiratory endurance conditioning program, daily flexibility program, as well as a strength maintenance program.

As the season progresses it will become necessary to train more intensely for short periods of time to increase the fitness level which may have dropped due to the playing of a large number of games. To raise the fitness level it is necessary to train intensely for three ten-day microcycles. The microcycles should be performed at the end of September, December and two weeks before the end of the season. The microcycle training should be performed for ten straight days and should involve circuit training using a number of exercise stations.

Sept.	Oct.	Nov.	Dec.	Jan.	Feb.	March	April	May	June	July	August
Microcycle 1			Microcycle 2			Microcycle 3					

4. Passing or Transition Period (five weeks)

The passing period for ice hockey is a time when the hockey player recuperates from the long season, works on general fitness, and perhaps plays some different sports such as golf, baseball, tennis, swimming, etc.

During the first week to ten days of the passing period the player should have rest and relaxation combined with exercise in an enjoyable sport such as tennis, golf, swimming, etc. with no set exercise pattern. After the long hockey season it is important for the athlete to recuperate and take time out from a regimented exercise routine.

The next four weeks of the passing period should be spent on general fitness which would include some aerobic work consisting of running, cycling, or swimming distances of a minimum of two miles three times per week. Flexibility exercises should be done daily and other enjoyable sports should be played to maintain general fitness.

In summary the passing period is a time for recuperation and maintenance of general fitness. Although it is a time to rest from hockey and relax during this period, it is not a time to do no physical exercise as general fitness should be maintained.

PHYSIOLOGICAL FACTORS IMPORTANT IN ICE HOCKEY

The following factors are important for the total development of the ice hockey player: strength, speed, power, agility, movement time, flexibility, muscular endurance and cardiovascular endurance.

STRENGTH

Strength is extremely important in shooting, checking, and skating. Strength in the upper body and legs is essential and can be developed by using the principles of progressive resistance and overload. Overload refers to loading the muscle beyond the previous requirement. Progressive resistance refers to a resistance that becomes progressively greater. Strength can be developed by isotonic, isometric, and isokinetic methods.

Isotonics refer to exercising in which muscle tension overcomes the resistance and movement occurs. Examples of this are chin-ups and push-ups. Weight training in which 80 percent of a maximum weight is lifted four to eight times is the best as both the principles of overload and progressive resistance are put into play. Exercises with resistance such as shooting or skating, are the best for developing muscle strength in the actual movement.

Isometrics involve exercises where movement does not occur, although the muscles are under tension. Exercises such as pushing against an immovable object, like a wall or against a rope are examples of isometrics. Although isometrics develop strength, they are only effective if done for approximately 10 seconds, with maximum contractions done in stages through a complete range of motion.

Isokinetics refer to training where the muscle is loaded maximally throughout its full range of motion. Examples of these types of exercises are the Mini Gym, Apollo and some aspects of the Nautilus system. Isokinetics now appear to be the best method of strength development, although more research is needed as there are conflicting opinions - some experts favour free weights over machines.

Devices such as small weights placed on the skates and ankle weights are not effective strength developers because they do not use the principles of progressive resistance and overload.

Weight training exercises include bent arm pullover, straight arm pullover, wrist curl, curl, incline press, lat machine, power clean, half squat, knee extension, triceps press, forward raise.

STRENGTH TRAINING EXERCISES FOR ICE HOCKEY

GENERAL GUIDELINES

1. Always have a good warm-up.
2. If unfamiliar with training, be sure you are properly instructed on technique and work with a partner.
3. Perform all exercises with a smooth, even rhythm, through the full range of joint movement.
4. Work out every other day. Eight weeks is a minimum time period for any appreciable gains in strength.
5. Do not work the same major muscle groups two stations in a row. For example, exercise legs in one exercise set and arms in the next set.
6. Practise breath control by inhaling when lifting and exhaling when lowering.
7. Do three sets of each exercise with four to eight repetitions per set. A repetition is one range of movement with the weight.
8. Use weights that are 80 to 90 percent of maximum.
9. Rest 2 to 3 minutes between sets of exercises.
10. Progress through the weight training program week by week by adding repetitions until eight repetitions are reached. Then reduce the repetitions to four and add to the weight, and go through the progression again.
11. If muscular endurance is desired, the repetitions should be increased and the weight lessened.
12. **Important**: Do not perform maximum lifts during training. The starting weight is a load that one is able to use for the desired repetitions with the last two repetitions being somewhat difficult.

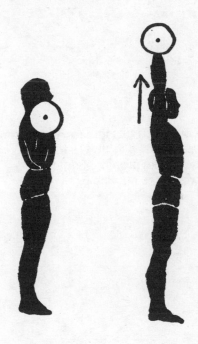

UPPER BODY

1. Military press: The feet are shoulder width apart, the barbell is raised to a bent arm position in front of the chest. The arms are slowly extended overhead.

2. Bent rowing: Bend from the waist down. The feet are apart with the arms extended downward. The hands are in the middle of the bar approximately eight inches apart. The head can be supported on a table with a towel used as a cushion. The bar is pulled up to the chest and then lowered.

3. Supine bench press: Lie back on a bench with the knees bent at right angles and the feet flat on the floor. The barbell is held flat on the chest. The arms slowly extend upward until fully extended. The weight is then lowered back to the chest.

4. Two arm curl: Use a reverse grip or a regular grip. Start with the feet astride and arms extended. Raise the bar to the chest and then lower to the starting position.

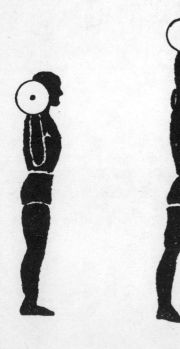

5. Tricep press: The feet are astride and the weight is lowered to the back of the shoulders. The grip is shoulder-width and the elbows are bent. The arms are extended with the weight thrust above the head. The weight is lowered back behind the shoulders.

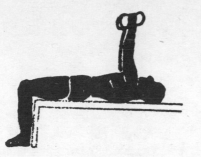

6. Lateral raise: While lying on a bench, the arms are downward and outward grasping ten-pound dumb-bells. The arms are extended and raised until the dumb-bells touch above the head.

7. Wrist roll: The feet are astride and a 20-to 30-pound weight is placed between the feet. Slowly wind up the rope until the weight is raised to the handle. Then, lower the weight slowly to the ground.

8. Forearm twist: A 20-pound weight is rotated left and right with the elbow bent at right angles.

TRUNK

1. Bent knee sit-ups: Lie on the back with the hands clasped around the back of the head and the knees bent. The sit-up is performed by raising the upper body until the elbows touch the knees.

2. Trunk extension and flexion: Lie on the stomach on a table with the trunk extended. The upper body is raised and lowered.

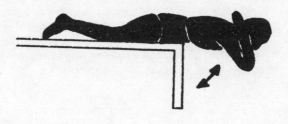

LEGS

1. One-half squat: The weight is placed on the shoulders with the feet apart. The heels are raised approximately one-and-a-half inches and a bench is placed behind the knees as a safety precaution. The knees are bent slowly to the half squat position.

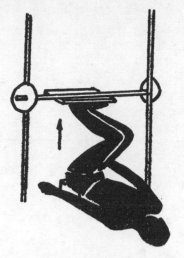

2. Leg thrust: Start in a lying position with the knees bent. Slowly extend the knees keeping the buttocks on the floor. Fully extend the knees and then lower to starting position. This exercise can also be performed in an upright position using the Universal Weight Machine.

3. Heel raise: Raise the toes two inches with blocks. The barbell is resting on the shoulders. Slowly rise up on the toes, hold and then return to the starting position.

NOTE: One workout per week during the season will maintain the strength gained during the off-season.

SPEED

Speed relates to applying a force to a mass, and strength and technique are key factors. The skating technique should be analyzed to determine if the correct mechanics involved in the start and skating stride are being used.

Strength is a key factor in speed and any exercise that develops strength in the legs, especially the extensor muscles, is advantageous.

Off-ice Training for Speed: Weight training exercises for the legs emphasizing the extension action of the legs are best for speed training, although all muscle groups should be exercised. Running distances of 40-100 meters at top speed are excellent off ice drills.

On-ice Training for Speed: Skating widths and lengths on the ice at full speed; also any other drills which involve skating from start to full speed.

POWER

Power is a combination of strength and speed, and the development of these two factors will improve power. Power is important in skating, shooting, and checking, and is a key factor in ice hockey.

Off-ice Training for Power: Weight training for strength will have an effect on power. It is believed that power can be directly developed by lifting a weight close to the maximum at the maximum rate. Exercises such as stair and hill running are also valuable as power developers for the legs.

On-ice Training for Power: Drills which involve skating or shooting against a resistance, such as pushing or pulling a resisting player up and down the ice or skating from the boards with large elastic bands attached to the waist, are good power development drills.

AGILITY

Agility is the ability to change directions quickly and is a key factor in ice hockey. Strength and reaction time are important contributing factors to agility. Agility can best be improved by practising a movement pattern correctly at increasingly faster speeds.

Off-ice Training for Agility: Drills that involve quick changes of direction improve agility. Moving back and forth on a coach's hand signals or running around obstacles such as chairs are examples of agility drills.

On-ice Training for Agility: Drills that involve skating and stickhandling around, under, and over pylons or other obstacles are good agility drills. All these drills should be done at top speed.

MOVEMENT TIME

Movement time may be defined as the time from the start of receiving a stimulus to the end of the movement. It is essential in most aspects of ice hockey, but is especially important for goalies. Movement time involves reaction and response time. Reaction time begins from receiving a stimulus and ends at the initiation of the response, while response time spans the initiation to the end of the response. Current research supports the fact that reaction time may be little affected by practice, but response time can be directly affected. Preparatory and distracting signals are factors involved in movement time. Movement time can be improved by continual practice of the correct movement pattern. These movement patterns can be practised on or off the ice using the exact movement patterns specific to the position. Examples of drills would be goaltender reaction drills with glove or stick hand, or forward shooting the puck quickly at a certain area of the net.

FLEXIBILITY

Flexibility exercises are important in ice hockey to ensure full range of motion in movement patterns and for the possible prevention of injuries. Flexibility exercises should be included in all warm ups for both practices and games. If ice time is limited, these exercises may be performed off the ice.

On-and Off-ice Training for Flexibility: The PNF or 3S method of flexibility is used now by many hockey teams. The method is based on the research conducted by Larry Holt at Dalhousie University and the information can be obtained from his book *Scientific Stretching for Sport*. The PNF or 3S method of flexibility training involves a series of isometric (muscle is under tension but does not move) contractions of the muscle to be stretched, followed by concentric (muscle moves and shortens) contractions of the opposite muscle group together with light pressure from the partner.

The steps are the following:
(a) Stretch the muscle to end point without pain.
(b) Partner then holds the limb(s) in a stretched position while isometric contraction for six seconds is performed.
(c) Stretch the muscle further with light pressure from your partner.
(d) Perform another isometric contraction with partner holding the limb(s).
(e) Repeat a total of three to four times.

This type of flexibility exercise should be done daily and requires a partner for all but one of the exercises.

Hamstring stretch: The person lies with one leg straight on the floor and the other straightened and raised as high as possible. The partner holds the leg on the floor and exerts pressure against the raised leg with his shoulder. The person attempts to lower the leg with an isometric contraction while the partner exerts the force in the opposite direction. Extend the leg further with light pressure from the partner and then repeat the isometric contraction. Repeat with the other leg.

Quadriceps stretch: The person lies on his stomach on the floor with one leg flexed and raised as high as possible. The partner extends pressure with one hand under the knee of the raised leg and the other on the back. The person attempts to pull the knee downward with pressure exerted by the partner in the opposite direction. The leg is then raised to a higher position with light pressure from the partner and another isometric contraction is repeated. Repeat with the other leg.

Groin stretch: The person sits with the legs as far apart as possible. The partner holds the legs at the ankles. The person then performs an isometric contraction against the pressure of the partner. The legs are then moved further apart with light pressure from the partner and another isometric contraction is performed.

Trunk stretch: The person sits on the floor with the legs straight and the trunk flexed as forward as possible. The partner exerts downward pressure on the shoulders. The person attempts to raise the trunk with an isometric contraction. The person then flexes further forward with light pressure from the partner. Repeat the isometric contraction.

Shoulder extension: The person is in a sitting position with back and legs straight. The arms are extended to the side at shoulder height and moved backward as far as possible. The partner grasps the wrists and exerts pressure backward as the person exerts force forward with the arms to execute the isometric contraction. The arms are moved further backward with pressure from the partner. Repeat the isometric contraction.

FLEXIBILITY PROGRAM - SLOW STRETCH

The program is to be done **daily** and does not require a partner. Exercises should be done slowly with the extreme position held for six seconds. Return to starting position. Repeat

Rotate the head: Rotate side to side, forward and back.

Arm rotation: With arms extended to the side, rotate both arms forward in large circles, finishing with small circles. Repeat by rotating backward in a similar manner.

Trunk rotation: With the hands on the hips, rotate the trunk to the left and then to the right.

Feet astride, floor touching: With the arms straight and the feet astride, touch the floor as far back as possible between the legs.

Hurdler's stretch: In a sitting position, extend one leg forward and the other leg back. Grasp the forward leg with both hands and attempt to bring the forehead to the knee. Repeat with the opposite leg forward.

Legs above the head: Lie back, cross the legs above the head and then touch the floor with the feet in front of the head.

Leg to forehead: In a sitting position, grasp one leg behind the knee with both hands. Bring the leg to the forehead, keeping the leg straight. Repeat with the other leg.

Bent knee sit-ups: The hands are clasped behind the head. The knees are bent with the feet flat on the ground. Start with the shoulders flat on the floor. Rise, touching the left elbow to the right knee and vice versa.

Chest raise: Lie on the stomach with the hands clasped behind the head and raise the upper body as far off the floor as possible.

Knee to chest: In a standing position, raise one knee to the chest and hold. Then repeat with the other leg.

MUSCULAR ENDURANCE

Muscular endurance is a muscle's ability to make repeated contractions over a long period of time.

Off-ice Training: Muscular endurance can be developed using weight training with a lighter load (50 percent maximum), with higher repetitions (20 or more) up to one's limits. Exercises such as push-ups, dips on the parallel bars, and chin-ups are also excellent upper body exercises used to develop muscular endurance.

On-ice Training: Any exercise which repeats muscle contractions over and over again on the ice (i.e., skating and shooting) develops muscular endurance. Dips can be performed using an open gate at the player's bench and push-ups can be performed during the warm up.

CARDIOVASCULAR ENDURANCE

Intermittent work is the nature of the game of ice hockey. A time analysis of a game of ice hockey is summarized below.

HOCKEY CARDIOVASCULAR DEMANDS

Time Components In Ice Hockey Play

	Boys Competitive League [1]			Inter-Collegiate [2]
Age group (yrs.)	10.7 (n=34)	12.2 (n=33)	14.4 (n=23)	21 (=10)
Game time (stop-time, mins.)	30	30	39	60
Total ice time (mins.) (percentage of game time)	12.7 (42)	12.5 (42)	16.2 (42)	24.50 (41)
No. of shifts (No/20 min. period)	8.0 (5.3)	8.5 (5.7)	10.5 (5.4)	17.4 (5.8)
Mean shift time (secs.)	102.6	88.5	93.7	85.4 (227 off-ice)
Mean inter-whistle time (sec.)	40.5	43.7	41.4	39.7
Whistle stop/shift (n, time-sec.)	2.5 (-)	2.0 (-)	2.3 (-)	2.3 (27.1)

The game times vary with the age group, but the percentage of time was the same (42%). The shift times varied, but average shift time was approximately one and one-half minutes with two whistles per shift and mean inter-whistle time of 40 seconds. The rest period between whistles is approximately 30 seconds and the number of shifts for intercollegiate was 17.4. For the intercollegiate hockey players the peak heart rate was 173 +/- 5.4 and resting heart rate between shifts was 120 +. Heart rates during a shift at play stoppages only reduced to 166 b/min. during play this time. Mean heart rates were 90 of max. as shown in Table 2.

	Boys Competitive League [1]			Inter-Collegiate [2]
Age Group (yrs.)	10.7 (n=19)	12.2 (n=28)	14.4 (n=22)	21 (=10)
Mean on-ice HR (b/min-1)	181+/- 2.4	187 +/- 2.5	194 +/- 1.8	173 +/- 5.4
Mean off-ice HR (b/min-1)	136 +/- 2.6	148 +/- 2.9	194 +/- 1.8	120 +

Values are means +/- SEM

THE ENERGY SYSTEMS

Cardiovascular endurance is directly related to the body's ability to supply adenosine triphosphate (ATP), a chemical which when broken down supplies the energy for muscle contraction.

ATP is supplied to the muscles by three methods: storage in the muscles (alactate or ATP-PC System); breakdown of glucose without oxygen (lactic acid system); and the breakdown of carbohydrates and fats in the presence of oxygen (oxygen system). The alactate system and the lactic acid system are without oxygen and are classified as anaerobic. The ATP-PC system resynthesizes ATP from the creatine phosphate stored in the muscle.

$$CP + ADP \leftarrow ATP + Creatine$$

---

[1] Cunningham and Paterson, unpublished data
[2] Green et. al., 1976

The supply of CP is limited and can last in all out-work from 10 to 15 seconds. This process is very important in ice hockey for supplying energy for the short burst sprint. Equally important is the fact that half the creatine phosphate can be restored between 21 and 22 seconds and 90 percent can be restored in 1 minute. This is extremely important for ice hockey as there is usually a stoppage of play every 30 seconds with two stoppages of play every shift. Training the anaerobic system can increase the levels of ATP and CP stored in the muscle and also can increase the activity of creatine kinase which facilitates the breakdown of creatine phosphate.

The lactic acid system is also a limited supplier of ATP. The by-product of this system is the build-up of lactic acid which causes fatigue when it reaches a high level.

$$\text{Glycogen} + Pi \text{ (inorganic phosphate)} + ADP \longrightarrow \text{lactate} + ATP$$

Training the lactic acid system increases the amount of PFK (phosphofructokinase), an enzyme which speeds up the rate and quantity of glycogen broken down. In addition, training allows the muscle to tolerate higher levels of lactate which eventually causes fatigue.

The oxygen system supplies an unlimited amount of ATP as long as the fuel can be supplied by carbohydrates and fats.

$$\text{Carbohydrates Fats} + O_2 + ADP + Pi \quad H_2O + CO_2 + ATP$$

Although ice hockey is considered primarily an anaerobic sport, the aerobic component is important over the two hour duration of the game. Also, each shift in ice hockey includes various tempos varying from all out effort to periods of stopping and gliding. It appears that by using the oxygen system at certain periods of the game the player minimizes the lactic acid system involvement. Training aerobically increases the myoglobin content (store for O_2) and increases the oxidation of fats and carbohydrates. All three energy systems are important for ice hockey and should be trained for maximum cardiovascular endurance.

TRAINING THE ENERGY SYSTEMS

Interval training is the best method for the systematic training of the energy systems. Although the traditional stops and starts in ice hockey are a form of interval training, there should be a definite system and progression for their use.

Principles of Interval Training

Interval training uses intermittent work interspersed with periods of rest to achieve the desired training improvement. In intermittent work the lactic acid accumulation is lower than when the work is done continuously. The ATP-PC is used more extensively and consequently the lactic acid system is not fully depleted. Interval training, according to Mathews, does the following:
1. Allows the ATP-PC system to be used over and over
2. Delays the onset of fatigue by not delving so deeply into the lactic acid system
3. Allows the system to become more tolerant to lactic acid
4. Works long enough at sufficient intensity to allow an improvement in the aerobic system

The manipulated variables used in interval training are the following:

(a) Rate and distance
(b) Repetitions and sets
(c) Duration of the relief interval
(d) Type of activity during relief interval
(e) Frequency of training

Terms:	Work interval	- Portion of interval training program involving high intensity work busts.
	Repetition	- One work interval
	Relief interval	- Time between work interval. Can be working, flexing or light jogging.
	Set	- Series of work and relief intervals.
	Training time	- Rate at which work is performed.

ON-ICE TRAINING FOR CARDIOVASCULAR ENDURANCE

Training the ATP-PC System (The following drill require that you divide your team into three groups.

1. Have each group skate 1 width of the rink or from the goal line to the centre line, in turn. They work for 5 seconds and rest 20 seconds. 5 repetitions = 1 set. Do 3 to 4 sets.

2. Have each group skate 2 widths of the rink or from the goal line to the centre line and back, in turn. They work for 5 seconds and rest 20 seconds. 5 repetitions = 1 set. Do 3 to 4 sets.

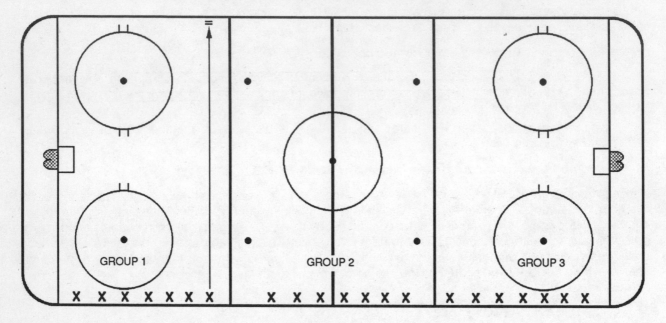

3. Have each group skate blueline to blueline, 4 times, in turn. They work for 12 to 15 seconds and rest for 45 seconds. 4 repetitions = 1 set; do 2 to 3 sets.

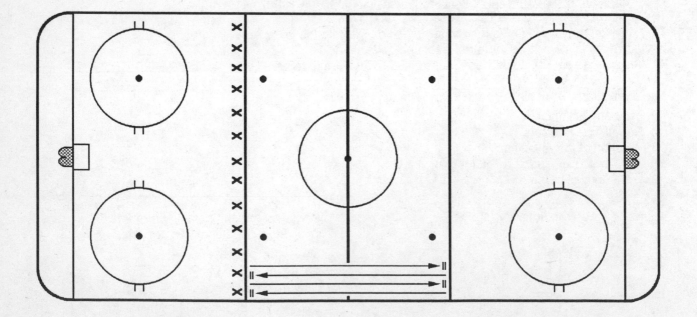

Training the Lactic Acid System (Drills 1 through 10 require the team be divided into three groups)

1. Have each group skate from the defensive face-off dot to the one at the far end, four times. They work for 30 seconds and rest for 2 minutes. 4 repetitions = 1 set; do 2 to 3 sets; allow 4 to 5 minutes between sets.

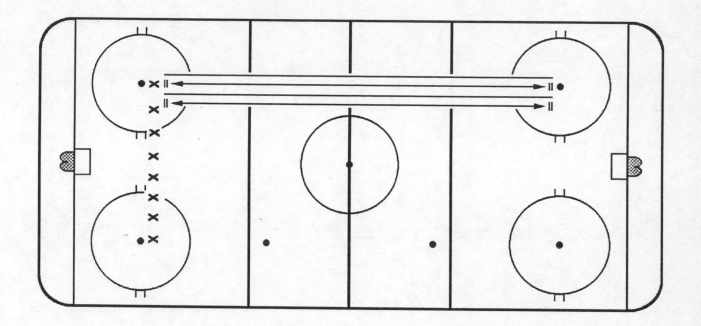

2. Have each group skate from goal line to goal line 4 times. They work for 40 to 45 seconds and rest for 2 minutes. 4 repetitions = 1 set; do 2 to 3 sets; allow 4 to 5 minutes between sets.

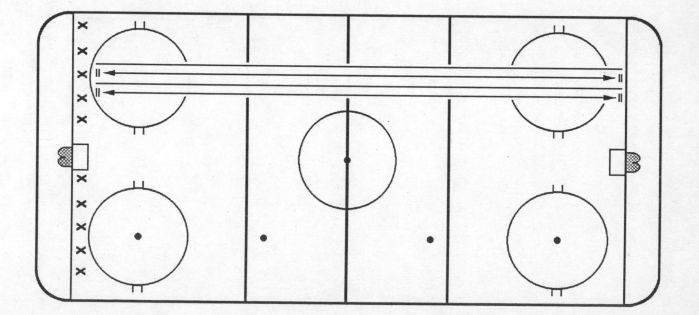

3. Have each group skate around the rink behind the nets, 1 & 1/2 laps and then go in the other direction 1 & 1/2 laps, in turn. They work 40 to 45 seconds and rest for 2 minutes. 4 repetitions = 1 set; do 2 to 3 sets; allow 4 to 5 minutes between sets.

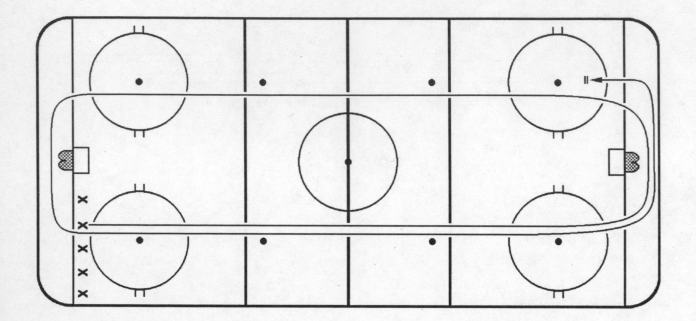

4. Have each group skate around the defensive zone face-off dots for 3 laps. They work 40 to 45 seconds and rest for 2 minutes. 4 repetitions = 1 set; do 2 to 3 sets.

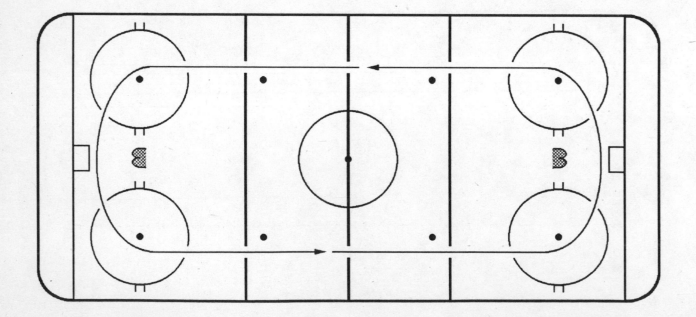

5. Have each group skate from near goal line to the far goal line and back, skate to the centre red line and back and skate to the near blueline and back, non-stop. They work for 40 to 45 seconds and rest for 2 minutes. 4 repetitions = 1 set; do 2 to 3 sets; allow 4 to 5 minutes between sets.

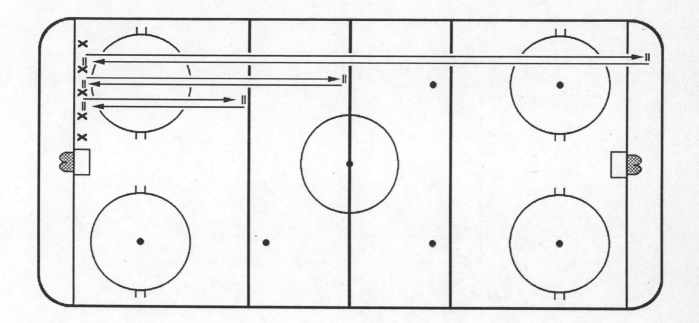

6. Have each group skate two laps around the rink. They work for 30 to 35 seconds and rest for 2 minutes. 4 repetitions = 1 set; do 2 to 3 sets; allow 4 to 5 minutes between sets.

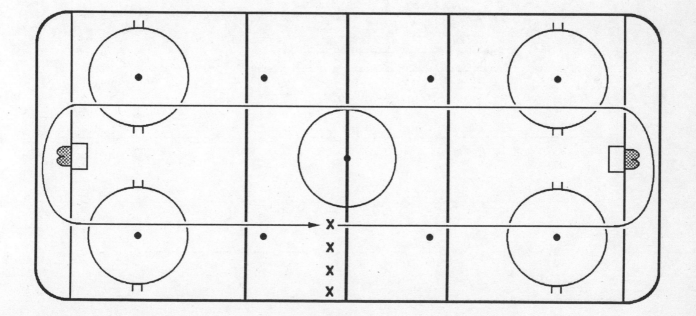

7. Defense: Skate forward to the centre red line, backward back to the blueline, then they turn and skate forward to the goal line. Do 3 times working on both backward turns.
Forwards: Skate forward across the rink and back 3 times, touching the boards with their sticks.
Goalies: Skate forward to the centre red line, drop to both knees (goal stick and catcher in the proper position). Then skate backward to the goal line and do a double leg slide to one side. Do 2 times.

They work for 30 to 35 seconds and rest for 2 minutes. 4 repetitions = 1 set; do 2 to 3 sets; allow for 4 to 5 minutes between sets.

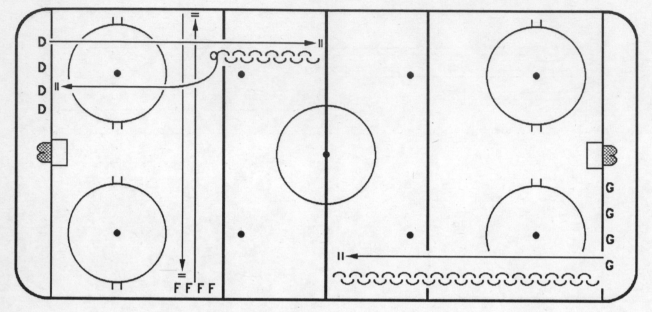

8. Have each group do stops and starts using the entire length of the ice, changing direction on the whistle. They work for 30 to 40 seconds and rest for two minutes. 4 repetitions = 1 set; do 2 to 3 sets; allow for 4 to 5 minutes rest between sets.

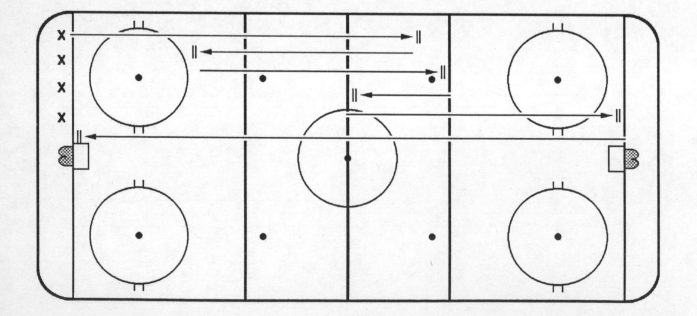

214

9. Have each group skate forward from the goal line to the centre red line, back to the near blueline, then to the far blueline, back to the centre red line, then to the far goal line and all the way back. They work for 40 to 50 seconds and rest for 2 minutes. 4 repetitions = 1 set; do 2 to 3 sets; allow for 4 to 5 minutes between sets.

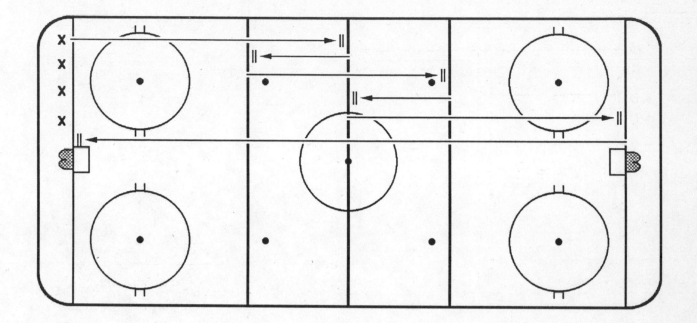

10. Have each group skate around the rink at 80 to 90 percent maximum speed for 30 to 40 seconds, skate slowly for 30 to 40 seconds, then repeat. 5 repetitions = 1 set; do 2 to 3 sets; allow 4 minutes rest between sets.

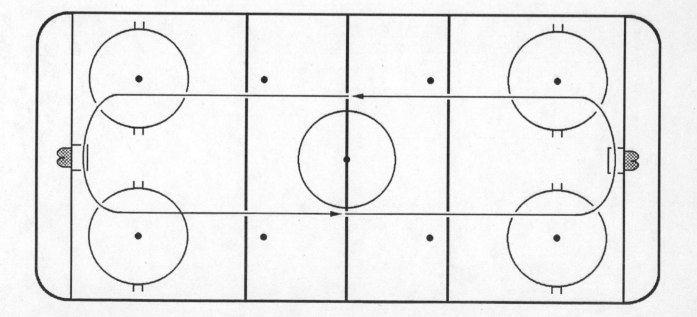

11. Play three-on-three or four-on-four scrimmage using the full ice. Players change while the puck is in play. When you change lines, the puck is passed back to the goalie. On off-sides, the puck is passed back to the goalie and the offending team must move outside the blueline. They work for 1 minute and rest for three minutes. Change on the whistle.

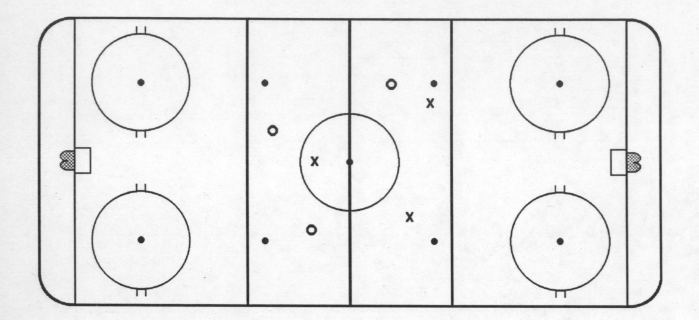

12. Divide the team into four groups and run relay races. Each player works for 40 seconds and rests for 2 minutes.

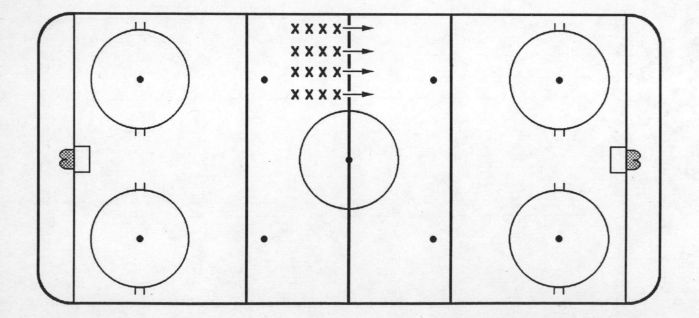

Training the Aerobic System

1. The entire team skates around the rink being sure to go behind each net. Skate for 3 minutes and then change direction and skate the other way for an additional 3 minutes.

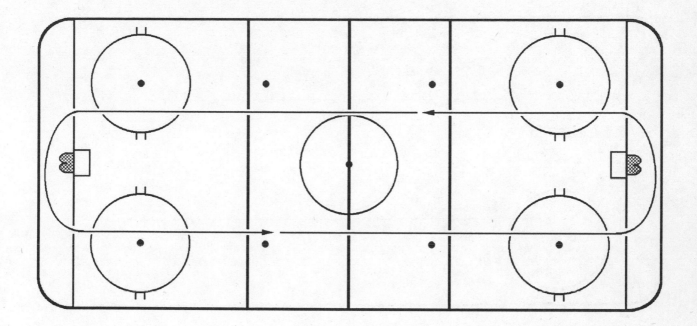

2. The team repeats drill 1 but this time skates in a "figure 8", crossing at the centre ice face-off dot.

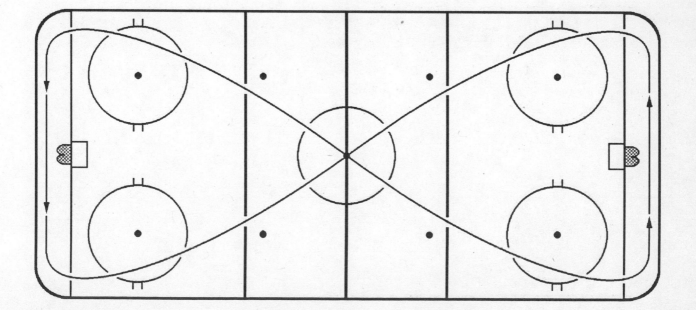

3. The Denver skate: Repeat drill 1 but move the nets towards the centre with each lap and then back after the first 3 minutes.

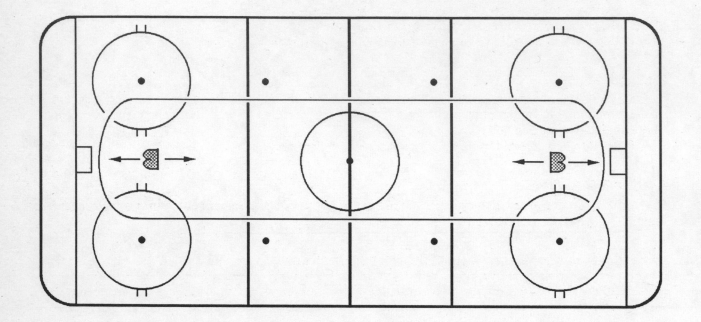

4. Have the team play two five-on-five scrimmages using half-ice. Each game is 10 minutes in length and you change lines after 5 minutes. They work for 5 minutes and rest for 5 minutes (not shown).

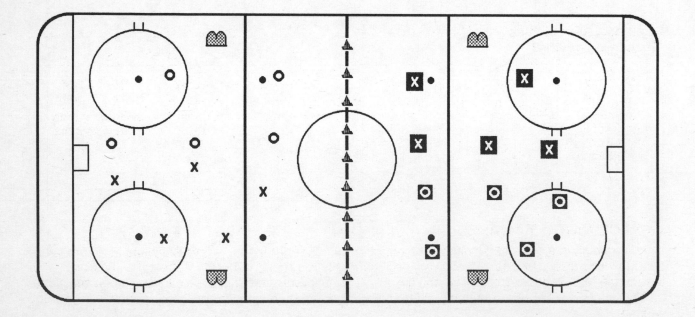

OFF-ICE TRAINING FOR CARDIOVASCULAR ENDURANCE

ANAEROBIC TRAINING

1. Short sprints

- Off-ice for 60 yards, approximately 10 seconds.
- Rest 30 seconds between repetitions (heart rate 140 beats/min).
- Five repetitions for one set.
- Rest longer after one set (heart rate down to 120 beats/min).
- Try to build to four sets of five repetitions for a total of 20 repetitions.

2. Longer sprints

- Off ice for 250 yards, approximately 40 seconds.
- Rest 2 minutes between repetitions.
- Four repetitions for one set.
- Try to build to two sets of four repetitions for a total of eight repetitions.

AEROBIC TRAINING

Run a minimum of two miles and attempt to reach six miles. Your goal should be to run at least to run at least 30 minutes per workout.

General Weekly Program - Weeks 1 to Week 8 (inclusive)

Monday	Tuesday	Wednesday	Thursday	Friday	Saturday
Strength Training	Anaerobic Short Sprints Long Sprints	Strength Training	Anaerobic Short Sprints Long Sprints	Strength Training	Aerobic Run a minimum of 2 miles
Aerobic run a minimum of 2 miles		Aerobic run a minimum of 2 miles		Aerobic run a minimum of 2 miles	

Note: During weeks 1 to 8 the program is based on strength training and the building of aerobic endurance. It is important for aerobic endurance that the running or skating distance is increased each week and that the goal should be to run six miles or skate for 45 minutes at the end of the eight-week session.

Running and/or Skating
Weeks 9 to Week 12

Monday	Tuesday	Wednesday	Thursday	Friday	Saturday
Strength Training Anaerobic Short Sprints Long sprints	Aerobic run five to six miles	Strength Training Anaerobic Short Sprints Long sprints	Aerobic run five to six miles	Strength Training Anaerobic Short sprints Long sprints	Anaerobic Short sprints Long sprints

OFF-ICE CIRCUIT TRAINING

Circuit training is a general conditioning method in which the athletes perform exercises at a number of different exercise stations. Circuit training generally develops muscular strength, muscular and cardiorespiratory endurance, power, and flexibility and allows a number of people to work out at the same time. Circuits can be set up in many different way and can be done with or without equipment such as weights.

Circuit training for ice hockey can be used in the following ways:

1. Directly prior to and/or during the training camp period
2. Throughout the season two to three times per week to maintain the fitness level
3. Two or three times during the season for an intensive ten day period to raise the fitness level
   During the off seasons as a general conditioning method

It should be noted that the best method of conditioning for the off-season should be specific training for strength (weight training), cardiovascular endurance (running short sprints and long distances), and flexibility training. Circuit training is general training but does not develop as high a level of strength as specific weight training and will have less effect on cardiorespiratory endurance than a sprint and endurance running program.

The following are examples of three different types of circuits for ice hockey. The first two are designed for an exercise area other than the arena, although a room large enough may be included in some arenas.

The third circuit can be used at the arena using available space, or on the ice if enough ice time is available.

Circuits No. 1 and No. 2 are intensive and can be used for three ten-day periods during the season to raise the fitness level or can be used three to five times per week during the off-season to improve the fitness level. Circuit No. 1 is the most demanding and requires equipment. Circuit No. 2, although still intensive, requires very little equipment. Circuit No. 3 can be used on-ice daily during the season as a warm-up general conditioning program, or once or twice per week by going through the circuit three times to maintain and improve the fitness level. This circuit requires a minimal amount of equipment.

Each of the three circuits has ten stations and with a standard hockey team of 20 players, two people work at each circuit for a total of 45 minutes for three complete circuits. An alternative method of using the circuit is to repeat the same exercise three times before changing to the next station. The exercise would still be 30 seconds with a 1 minute rest before starting the exercise once more.

NOTE: All weights listed in Circuit No. 1 are for junior hockey players aged 16 to 19 years.

Younger players should use only circuits No. 2 and No. 3.

CIRCUIT NO. 1

Purpose: To maintain and increase strength, power, and muscular and cardiorespiratory endurance power. This circuit is strenuous and can best be used three times a season for ten days to increase the strength levels.

Facility: Small gymnasium or a room of similar size with bleacher seats or stairs.

Equipment:

two barbells-30 kilos; four barbells-40 kilos; two barbells-10 kilos; two benches; four dumbbells- 7 kilos stopwatch; whistle

Two athletes work simultaneously at each station for 30 seconds, with one minute for changing stations and rest.

1. **Curls - Two barbells - 30 kilos**: Grasp the bar using an underhand grip with hands shoulder-width apart. With arms extended forward, raise the bar to the chest by bending your arm at the elbows and then lower the bar to the starting position. Repeat.
2. **Bench-leap**: Jump up onto a bench with both feet simultaneously. Jump back down and repeat.
3. **Bench press - two barbells - 40 kilos**: Lie on a bench and hold the bar above using a shoulder-width grip. Lower the bar so it touches the chest. Raise the bar back to the starting position. Repeat. Inhale at the start of the movement and exhale at the completion of the movement.
4. **Stair-running**: Run up a flight of stairs one step at a time, run back down and repeat.
5. **Reverse wrist curls - two barbells - 10 kilos**: In a seated position, rest your forearms along your thighs whichwhich are parallel to the floor. The arms and wrists should be extended past the knees. Hold the bar using an overhand grip and raise and lower the wrists as far as you can.
6. **Bench-hop**: Jump back and forth over a bench with both feet. Repeat.

7. **Bent over lateral raise** - four dumb-bells - 7 kilos: Bend over at the waist until the upper body is parallel to the floor. Hold a dumb-bell in each hand and raise them laterally until they are level with your upper body. Bend the elbows slightly. Lower and repeat.

8. **Sit-ups**: While lying on your back with knees bent and feet flat on the floor, clasp hands behind the head. Start with the shoulders flat on the ground and raise your upper body touching your left elbow to your right knee, etc. Repeat.

9. **Power, clean and press** - two barbells - 40 kilos: ending at the knees and keeping back straight, grasp the bar with an over or underhand grip. Extend your legs and lift the weight to the chest. The weight is then lifted up to the shoulders by bending the arms and the weight is then raised above the head by fully extending the arms. Lower the weight slowly to the floor and repeat.

10. **Stair-bounding**: Run up the stairs two at a time, run back down and repeat.

CIRCUIT NO. 2

Purpose: To maintain and develop strength, power and muscular and cardirepiratory endurance. This circuit can be used in a pre-season training program or during the season in three ten-day cycles to increse muscular strength and power.

Facility: A gymnasium or a large room with a high ceiling

Equiment: Two long ropes; two chinning bars; two benches; 4 - 7 kilo weights; two 10-kilobars; two wall ladders; stopwatch; whistle.

Two athletes work simultaneously at each station for 30 seconds. Allow one minute to rest and change stations.

1. **Rope climbing**: Climb the rope to the ceiling using the arms only.

2. **Bench-leap**: Jump up to the bench and then down with both feet at once. Repeat.

3. **Chin-ups**: Use the underhand grip. Completely extend the arms. Raise the chin above the bar. Do not swing the legs. Repeat.

4. **Squat jumps**: Start in a crouched position with both hands on the floor. Jump in the air completely extending the legs and arms. Repeat.

5. **Push-ups**: The back is straight. Push up, completely extending the arms. Lower the chest to the floor. Repeat.

6. **Bench-hop**: Jum over the bench with both feet. Jump back. Repeat.

7. **Ladder-climbs**: Climb the wall ladder using arms only. Repeat.

8. **Sit-ups**: Clasp hands behind the head. Bend knees with feet flat on the floor. Start with the shoulders flat on the floor. Rise, touching the left elbow to the right knee, etc. Repeat.

9. **Bent over lateral raise** - two dumbbells - 7 kilos: Bend at the waist until the upper body is parallel to the floor. Raise the dumbbells laterally until they are level with your upper body. Bend the elbows slightly. Lower and repeat.

10. **Reverse wrist curls** - one barbell - 10 kilos: Rest your arms along your thighs, which should be parallel to the floor. The hands and wrists should be extended past the knees. Use an overhand grip. Raise and lower the wrists as far as you can.

CIRCUIT NO. 3

Purpose: To increase and maintain muscular strength and cardiorespiratory endurance, power, and flexibility. This circuit requires no equipment and can be done off the ice in the space around the arena or on-ice if enough ice-time is available.

Facility: The ice arena or other space available in the arena.

Equipment: One wrist roll; two broom handles - 2 feet long; two ropes; two weights - 7 kilos; one stopwatch; whistle.

NOTE: In this circuit, one person does the exercise first for 30 seconds and then the partner does the exercise for 30 seconds. After both have done it, they move to the next station.

1. **Dips**: Open the gate to the benches. Raise and lower the body using the arms only.

2. **Sit-ups**: Clasp hands behind the head. Bend knees with feet flat on the floor. Rise, touching the left elbow to the right knee, etc. Repeat.

3. **Push-ups**: The back is straight. Push up, completely extending the arms. Lower the chest to the floor. Repeat.

4. **V-sit**: Lie flat on the ground. Raise the back and legs at the same time and touch the feet with the hands. Keep the arms and legs straight. Repeat.

5. **Arm circles**: With arms extended to the side, rotate both arms forward in large circles, finishing with small circles. Repeat by rotating backward in a similar fashion.

6. **Leg flexion**: Lie on the stomach. Partner gives resistance down on lower legs. Flex the legs at the knee and hips. Move slowly through the movement with resistance for ten seconds. Repeat.

7. **Leg extension**: Lie on the stomach with the legs flexed. Partner gives resistance. Extend the legs. Move slowly through the movement with resistance for 10 seconds. Repeat.

8. **Groin exercise**: Lie on the back. Legs apart and slightly bent. Partner stands with legs inside the knees and gives resistance. Press in for 10 seconds. Then with partner's legs on the other side, press out for 10 seconds.

9. **Wrist roll**: Roll the weight up by rolling the handle. Lower the weight in the reverse manner. Repeat.

10. **Hurdler's stretch**: In a sitting position, extend the right leg forward and left leg back. Grasp the right ankle with both hands and slowly bring the forehead to the knee. Repeat with the left leg forward. Repeat with both legs together. Do each segment of the exercise for 10 seconds.

ON-ICE CIRCUIT

Work two to each station; 30 seconds' work; 30 seconds' rest. Repeat.

Station 1: One minute to rest and change stations.

Station 2: Players start at the centreline and skate to the blueline and back to the centreline four times. Pick up the hockey stick and try to push back the other player.

Station 3: Play keep away inside the face-off circle.

Station 4: Continuous breakaways from the red line. One man chases the other man, shoots and changes each time.

Station 5: No sticks. Try to body check the man out of the face-off circle.

Station 6: One man skates forward with the puck between the bluelines and passes it to the other man skating backward. The man skating backward then skates forward with the puck and passes to the partner skating backward.

Station 7: No sticks. Fight for the puck along the boards.

Station 8: Continuous breakaways from the blueline. Pucks are picked up at the side of the net.

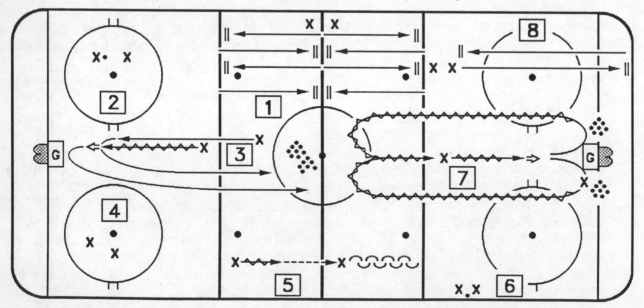

BIBLIOGRAPHY

1. Annarino, A. Developmental Conditioning for Physical Education and Athletics. St. Louis: C. V. Mosby Co., 1972

2. Astrand, P. O. and Podahl, K. Textbook or Work Physiology. New York: McGraw-Hill Book Co., 1977.

3. DeVries, H. A. "Flexibility, an Overlooked but Vital Factor in Sports Conditioning." Proceedings: International Symposium on the Art & Science of Coaching. Ontario, Canada: Fl. I. Productions, 1971.

4. Eriksson, B., Gollnick, P. and Saltin, B. "Muscle Metabolism and Enzyme Activities after Training in Boys 11-13 Year Old." Acta Physiol. Scand., 87: 485-497, 1973.

5. Falls, H. B., Wallis, E. L. and Logan, G. A. Foundations of Conditioning. New York: Academic press, 1970.

6. Fox, E., Mathews, D. K. and Bairstow, J. Interval Training for Lifetime Fitness. New York: Dial Press, 1974.

7. Fox, E. Sports Physiology. Philadelphia: W. B. Saunders Co., 1979.

8. Gardner, J. and Purdy, J. Computerized Running Training Programms. Los Aldos: Tafnews Press, 1970.

9. Green, H. J. "Glycogen Depletion patterns during Continuous and Intermittent Ice Skating." Med. Sci. Sports 10:3: 183-187, 1978.

10. Green, H. J. and Houston, M. E. "Effect of a Season of Ict Hockey on Energy Capacities and Associated Functions." Med. Sci. Sports 7: 299-303, 1975.

11. Green, H. "Metabolic Aspects of Intermittent Work with Specific Regard to Ice Hockey." Can. Jrnl. of App. Sport Sci. 4(4): 29-33.

12. Gollnick, p., Armstrong, R., Saltin, B., Saubert, C., Sembrowich, W. and Shepherd, R. "Effect of Training on Enzyme Activity and Fiber Composition of Human Skeletal Muscle." Jrnl. Appl. Physiolog. 34(1): 107-111, 1973.

13. Holt, L. Scientific Stretching for Sport. Ottawa: Coaching Association of Canada.

14. Jensen, C.R. and Fisher, G. A. Scientific Basis of Athletic Conditioning. Philadelphia: Lea and Febger, 1972.

15. Kiessling, K., Piehl, K. and Lundquist, C. "Effect of Physical Training on Ultrastructural Features in Human Skeletal Muscle." In Pernow, B. and Saltin, B. (Eds.) Muscle Metabolism During Exercise. New York: Planum Press, 1971, pp. 97 -101.

16. Proceedings, National Coaches Certification Program, Level 5. Ottawa: Canadian Amateur Hockey Association, 1975.

17. Proceedings, National Coaches Certification Program, Level 5. Ottawa: Canadian Amateur Hockey Association, 1975.

18. Proceedings, National Coaches Certification Program, Level 5. Ottawa: Canadian Amateur Hockey Association, 1975.

19. Proceedings, National Coaches Certification Program, Level 5. Ottawa: Canadian Amateur Hockey Association, 1975.

20. Proceedings, International Conference on the Coaching Aspects of Ice Hockey. Gothenburg, Sweden: 1981.

21. Patterson, D. H. "Respiratory and Cardiovascular Aspects of Intermittent Exercise with Regard to Ice Hockey." Can. Jrnl. of App. Sport Sci. 4(4) : 29-33.

22. Sorani, R., Circuit Training. Dubuque: Wm. C. Brown Co. Publishers, 1966.

23. Standte, H., Exner, G. and Pelte, D. "Effects of Short-Term, High Intensity (Spring) Training on Some Contractile and Metabolic Characteristics of Fast and Slow Muscle of the Rat." Pfugers Arch., 344: 159-168, 1973.

24. Stone, W. J. and Krull, W. A. Sport Conditioning and Weight Training. Boston: Allyn and Bacon, Inc., 1978.

25. Taylor, A. W. <u>The Scientific Aspects of Sports Training</u>. Springfield, Ill.: Charles C. Thomas, Publisher, 1975.

26. Thorstensson, A., Sjodin, B. and Karlsson, J. "Enzyme Activities and Muscle Strength after 'Sprint Training' in Man." <u>Acta. Physiol. Scand.</u> 94: 313-318, 1975.

27. Wilmore, J. H. <u>Athletic Training and Physical Fitness: Physiological Principles and Practices of the Conditioning Process</u>. Boston: Allyn and Bacon, Inc., 1977.

28. Wilson, G. and Hedberg, A. <u>Physiology of Ice Hockey: A Report</u>. Ottawa: Canadian Amateur Hockey Association, 1976.